D1263277

"It is rare that one book can pack so many resources and easy to digest information into a single volume! Families, school personnel, and professionals all need the extensive, and up-to-date tips, guides, and 'must-knows' provided here. It's obvious the author is both a seasoned researcher and practitioner—a winning combination."

—*Dr. Debra Moore, psychologist and co-author with Dr. Temple Grandin, of* The Loving Push: How Parents and Professionals Can Help Spectrum Kids Become Successful Adults

"This book is an essential resource for every educator that works with students with ASD! The easy-to-read format is complete with up to date research on evidence-based practices for this population, sample observation and assessment worksheets and case studies that allow the reader to apply the information presented."

—*Gena P. Barnhill, PhD., NCSP, BCBA-D, LBA, Director of Special Education Programs at Lynchburg College, Lynchburg, VA*

"Dr. Wilkinson has done it again. This updated and scholarly Second Edition reflects important recent changes regarding diagnosis and services for students with Autism Spectrum Disorder. With its numerous best-practice suggestions, it is a must-read for school psychologists, school social workers, and those who teach in general and special education."

—*Dr. Steven Landau, Professor of School Psychology in the Department of Psychology, Illinois State University by the same author*

Overcoming Anxiety and Depression on the Autism Spectrum
A Self-Help Guide Using CBT
Lee A. Wilkinson
ISBN 978 1 84905 927 5
eISBN 978 0 85700 710 0

of related interest

The Essential Manual for Asperger Syndrome (ASD) in the Classroom
What Every Teacher Needs to Know
Kathy Hoopmann
Illustrated by Rebecca Houkamau
ISBN 978 1 84905 553 6
eISBN 978 0 85700 984 5

Autism Spectrum Disorder and the Transition into Secondary School
A Handbook for Implementing Strategies in the Mainstream School Setting
Marianna Murin, Josselyn Hellriegel and Will Mandy
ISBN 978 1 78592 018 9
eISBN 978 1 78450 262 1

Autism from Diagnostic Pathway to Intervention
Checklists to Support Diagnosis, Analysis for Target-
Setting and Effective Intervention Strategies
Kate Ripley
ISBN 978 1 84905 578 9
eISBN 978 1 78450 024 5

Specific Learning Difficulties
What Teachers Need to Know
Diana Hudson
Illustrated by Jon English
ISBN 978 1 84905 590 1
eISBN 978 1 78450 046 7

A BEST PRACTICE GUIDE TO ASSESSMENT AND INTERVENTION FOR AUTISM SPECTRUM DISORDER IN SCHOOLS

SECOND EDITION

Lee A. Wilkinson

Jessica Kingsley *Publishers*
London and Philadelphia

This second edition published in 2017
by Jessica Kingsley Publishers
73 Collier Street
London N1 9BE, UK
and
400 Market Street, Suite 400
Philadelphia, PA 19106, USA

www.jkp.com

First edition published by Jessica Kingsley Publishers, 2010

Copyright © Lee A. Wilkinson 2010, 2017

Front cover image source: Shutterstock®. The cover image is for
illustrative purposes only, and any person featuring is a model.

All rights reserved. No part of this publication may be reproduced in any
material form (including photocopying, storing in any medium by electronic
means or transmitting) without the written permission of the copyright owner
except in accordance with the provisions of the law or under terms of a licence
issued in the UK by the Copyright Licensing Agency Ltd. www.cla.co.uk or in
overseas territories by the relevant reproduction rights organisation, for details
see www.ifrro.org. Applications for the copyright owner's written permission to
reproduce any part of this publication should be addressed to the publisher.

Warning: The doing of an unauthorised act in relation to a copyright work
may result in both a civil claim for damages and criminal prosecution.

Library of Congress Cataloging in Publication Data
A CIP catalog record for this book is available from the Library of Congress

British Library Cataloguing in Publication Data
A CIP catalogue record for this book is available from the British Library

ISBN 978 1 78592 704 1
eISBN 978 1 78450 250 8

Printed and bound in Great Britain

CONTENTS

PREFACE

Since the first edition of this book was published, the field of autism has expanded dramatically. New and significant developments have taken place in assessment and outcome research, practice guidelines, and treatment reviews. This revised and updated edition reflects the most recent progress in evidence-based assessment and intervention, and outlines the most current relevant and valued information necessary for the competent delivery of services for children and youth with autism spectrum disorder (ASD). The basic objective and perspective of the first edition remains unchanged. The primary aim is to provide school-based professionals with a balance of conceptual, practical, and empirical information designed to bridge the research-to-practice gap in identifying, assessing, and intervening with school-age children on the autism spectrum. Likewise, this edition continues to be guided by the fundamental premise that autistic traits exist along a spectrum of severity with respect to the core symptomatology, age of onset, and need for services.

The challenge to improve the services to children with ASD in our schools centers on the adoption of evidence-based practices in assessment and classroom intervention. An important theme woven throughout this book is the application of "best practice" guidelines in the assessment and treatment of school-age children and youth with ASD. A best practice may be defined as a technique, strategy, or methodology that, through experience and evidence-based research, has proven to reliably lead to a desired outcome. This requires an understanding of evidence-based research and the integrative process of embedding this knowledge into the school organization and delivery of services. Best practice guidelines are developed using the best available evidence in order to provide school-based professionals with evidence-informed recommendations that support practice and guide practitioner decisions regarding assessment and intervention in the school context. Best practices for school-based practitioners are also best practices for students and their families.

This revision continues to focus on best practice or state-of-the-art approaches to assessment and treatment for ASD. As with the first edition, this Guide provides current information and recommendations that are consistent with scientific research and empirically guided practice, rather than speculation and theory. While this edition retains the same basic structure as the previous one, the chapters have been revised to incorporate current research and developments in the field. This includes updated test information and the addition of new instruments. The list of evidence-based treatments and intervention strategies has also been adjusted to reflect the most recent rigorous scientific outcome reviews. Best practice in special education has been expanded to include evidence-based support strategies, procedures for working with families, and a discussion about special education law and legal issues. These revisions and additions make the text more a comprehensive and practical guide for the school-based professional.

PURPOSE

In order to adequately meet the needs of students with ASD, it is essential that school-based professionals understand the characteristics of this neurodevelopmental disorder, utilize appropriate assessment tools, provide evidence-based recommendations for intervention across the continuum of services, and offer consultation to educational staff and families. There has been a significant increase in the number of journal articles, book chapters, textbooks, and various publications outlining information regarding educational practices, supports, and procedures that are reportedly effective for students on the autism spectrum. Likewise, statutes, case laws, regulations, and policies provide a framework for educational planning and development of individualized educational programs for students identified with ASD. Even so, the existing literature can be confusing and at times conflicting. Moreover, recent national and state-wide surveys of school personnel knowledge, training, and practice in autism assessment and intervention suggest that they are in need of additional resources and training to meet the unique needs of students with ASD (Wilkinson, 2013; Williams *et al.*, 2011). As a result, there continues to be a need for an up-to-date resource that provides school-based practitioners and allied professionals with a best practice guide to screening, assessment, and intervention. This Guide is intended to meet the needs of school-based professionals such as school psychologists, counselors, speech/language pathologists, occupational therapists, counselors, social workers, administrators, and both general and special education teachers. Parents, advocates, and community-based professionals will also find this guide a valuable and informative resource. The text is designed to bridge the gap between research and the practical realities of practicing in today's schools. The overarching objective in preparing this edition was to provide a practical reference and resource, and guide for school-based professionals based on current research that could be used easily and efficiently by busy practitioners in their every day work. It serves as an essential guide and best practice reference for all school-based professionals who have the responsibility for the screening, assessment, and education of school-age students who may have a neurodevelopmental disorder such as ASD.

ORGANIZATION OF THE TEXT

Although no single text can provide a complete examination of the current and emerging research in ASD, this volume provides an up-to-date view of the status of the field that will guide practitioners in the selection, use, and interpretation of evidence-based assessment tools and intervention strategies for students with ASD. Each chapter features a consolidated and integrative description of best practice assessment and intervention/treatment approaches for children and youth with ASD. It brings the topics of assessment and intervention together in a single resource guide consistent with recent advances in evidence-based practice. This includes best practice procedures to help identify children based on the symptom criteria for the new Diagnostic and Statistical Manual of Mental Disorders, Fifth Edition (DSM-5; American Psychiatric Association, 2013) single diagnostic category of Autism Spectrum Disorder (ASD), which now encompasses the previous DSM-IV-TR (American Psychiatric Association, 2000) categorical subgroups of autistic disorder (autism), Asperger's disorder, and pervasive developmental disorder not otherwise specified (PDD-NOS).

The text consists of seven chapters corresponding to the growing emphasis on evidence-based practice and provides detailed, procedural guidelines for the screening and assessment of ASD, and the application of evidence-based interventions to the school setting. Chapter 1 presents an overview of the field and changes in conceptual and diagnostic perspectives of ASD. Chapter 2 features a review of selected screening tools and describes a multi-tier approach to screening and identifying children who may require a more comprehensive evaluation. Chapter 3 introduces the reader to the comprehensive development approach to assessment and describes the components of an evidence-based assessment battery for ASD. The assessment of co-occurring emotional and behavior problems is also discussed. Chapter 4 presents detailed case example reports to illustrate best practice in assessment. Chapter 5 describes current evidence-based treatments and interventions for ASD, and provides an example of how a scientifically-based intervention can be adapted to the classroom. Chapter 6 focuses on the delivery of special education services and placement options, individual education planning and support strategies, and procedures for working effectively with families. Chapter 7 concludes with a discussion of emerging trends and perspectives, and outlines areas for future research and practice. As with the first edition, "best practice" guidelines have been culled from the text and appear in boxes throughout the book to alert the reader to critical topics. A glossary of terms and appendices with useful supplementary information have also been retained.

ACKNOWLEDGMENTS FOR THE SECOND EDITION

I would like to thank everyone who over the past several years has provided me with suggestions for improving the first edition of this book. The preparation of this second edition would not have been possible without the support and encouragement of many people. I am grateful to my colleagues for their input and suggestions for this edition. I would like to thank the professionals at Jessica Kingsley Publishers for their invaluable assistance in bringing this book to fruition, most especially, Rachel Menzies, for her support of my work. I am especially grateful to my wife Amy, for her encouragement and help during the preparation of the manuscript. To my readers, I appreciate your interest in this edition and hope you find it to be a useful and informative guide. Once again, I would like to extend my appreciation to the children on the autism spectrum, their families, and the professionals with whom I have worked over the past two decades.

Lee A. Wilkinson, Ph.D.
West Palm Beach, FL
May, 2016

CHAPTER 1

INTRODUCTION AND OVERVIEW

More children and youth are being diagnosed with autism spectrum disorder (ASD) than ever before. Epidemiological research indicates a progressively rising prevalence trend for ASD over the past decade (Wing and Potter, 2009). Autism is much more prevalent than previously thought, especially when viewed as a spectrum condition with varying levels of symptom severity and need for support. Recent findings of the Centers for Disease Control and Prevention (CDC) Autism and Developmental Disabilities Monitoring Network ADDM (2014) indicate that one in every 68 school-age children (or 14.7 per 1,000 eight-year-olds) in multiple communities in the United States has been identified with ASD (Centers for Disease Control and Prevention [CDC], 2014). This estimate is roughly 30 percent higher than the estimate for 2008 (1 in 88), 60 percent higher than the estimate for 2006 (1 in 110), and 120 percent higher than the estimates for 2000 and 2002 (1 in 150). Approximately 80 percent of children identified with ASD either had eligibility for autism special education services at school or had an ASD diagnosis. The remaining 20 percent of children identified with ASD had documented symptoms of ASD in their records, but had not yet been classified as having ASD by a community provider. Autism is the fastest growing serious developmental disability in the United States and continues to be an important health concern (CDC, 2014).

A number of explanations for the dramatic increase in the incidence and prevalence of ASD have been advanced. It is widely accepted that at least a significant part of the reported increase in autism over the past decade is due to a combination of factors which include: (a) broadening of diagnostic criteria and concepts; (b) recognition that ASD frequently co-occurs with other conditions and includes a wide range of cognitive abilities; (c) increased awareness on the part of professionals and the public leading to more (and earlier) referrals for assessment; (e) increased sensitivity of diagnostic tools and better access to services; (d) decreasing age at diagnosis; (e) differences in the definition of autism and case-finding methods; (f) differences in the size of the population being studied, and (g) diagnostic substitution and reclassification of children with other disabilities (Fombonne, 2005; Polyak, Kubina, and Girirajan, 2015; Wilkinson, 2014a; Wing and Potter, 2009). Although a large proportion of the increase in the rate of ASD can be explained by these factors, researchers cannot rule out the possibility that there has been a true rise in the prevalence of ASD. Whatever the reasons, the current prevalence figures carry clear-cut implications for school professionals who share the challenge of identifying and providing interventions for an increasing number of children and youth with ASD (Wilkinson, 2014a).

ASD IN SCHOOLS

The increase in the occurrence of autism is also evident in the number of students with ASD receiving special educational services under the Individuals with Disabilities Education Act (IDEA, 2004). According to the U.S. Department of Education, Office of Special Education Programs, Data Analysis System (DANS), more than 5 million children ages 6 to 21 years received services through 13 disability categories in public school special education programs in 2012 (U.S. Department of Education, 2014). Although the overall population of students receiving services peaked in the 2004-05 school year and has declined since that time, the data indicate a divergence in the trajectories of the individual disability categories. For example, while the number of students identified with specific learning disability (SLD), emotional disturbance, and intellectual disability decreased relative to other disability categories, the number of students with autism increased dramatically between 2003 and 2012, increasing from 1.5 percent to 7.8 percent of all identified disabilities. Autism now ranks fourth among all IDEA disability categories for students age 6-21. Similarly, the percentages of the total student population ages 6 through 11, 12 through 17, and 18 through 21 served under the IDEA, Part B category of autism increased 165 percent, 285 percent, and 290 percent, respectively. Autism now accounts for nearly 1 percent of the overall student population in our schools. Despite the dramatic rise in the number of students receiving special education under the IDEA category of autism, it has been suggested that the increase may actually underestimate the numbers of students in need of support under this category (Brock, Jimerson, and Hansen, 2006; Fombonne, 2003; Newschaffer, Falb, and Gurney, 2005; Russell *et al.*, 2010; Safran, 2008). For example, more capable students with ASD may not be included in the IDEA count because they often demonstrate academic strengths and more subtle social liabilities, and thus may not be readily identified with ASD. Many may also be home-schooled, enrolled in private schools, be clinically diagnosed but not receiving services, have not come to the attention of a professional, or fail to meet the eligibility for the autism category in their respective school districts and states. Further, there is evidence to suggest that gender and cultural/ethnic differences in the presentation of ASD often go unrecognized in both the school and community, and that language-based and socioeconomic disparities in access to services may be barriers to identification (Travers *et al.*, 2014; Wilkinson, 2008a; Zuckerman *et al.*, 2013). As a result, it appears likely that there are a relatively large number of unidentified and underserved students with ASD in our schools.

THE CHALLENGE TO SCHOOL PROFESSIONALS

The unique needs and multifaceted nature of autism, including co-occurring (comorbid) disabilities, have significant implications for planning and intervention in the school context. Placement in general education settings continues to be a predominant service delivery option for students with disabilities, including ASD. Most students with ASD receive their education in general education classrooms with teachers who often have limited experience and training in working with children with special needs (Williams *et al.*, 2011). From the ages of 6 to 12, the child with ASD faces many challenges with transitions to new learning environments and contact with unfamiliar peers and adults. The core deficits of ASD (i.e., social reciprocity and interaction, communication, and repetitive behaviors) affect the educational process and may adversely impact a child's performance in the following areas: academics, social/emotional development, communication, adaptive skills, and the ability to use and maintain skills across home, school, and community settings. The social-communication domains of development become more divergent from typical expectations as the student progresses through school. Children with ASD frequently experience problems related to their social communication deficits such as poor regulation of attention, emotional distress, academic difficulties, and high rates of internalizing and externalizing problem behavior (Mazzone, Ruta, and Reale, 2012; Sikora *et al.*, 2012). As a result, they are at risk for academic underachievement, school drop-out, peer rejection, and co-occurring conditions such as anxiety and depression (Mazzone *et al.*, 2012; Ozsivadjian, Knott, and Magiati, 2012). Because autistic traits exist along a spectrum of severity with respect to the core symptomatology, even mild deficits in social and communicative competence can be associated with teacher-reported problems in socialization and a wide range of behavioral and academic difficulties (Skuse *et al.*, 2009). Thus, social skills deficits that fall below the threshold for a clinical diagnosis or autism eligibility for ASD can still result in functional impairment (Russell *et al.*, 2010). Therefore, school professionals must be prepared to recognize the presence of risk factors and early warning signs of ASD, engage in case finding, and be familiar with assessment tools and interventions in order to ensure that students are being identified and provided with the appropriate programs and services. Providing effective behavioral supports and interventions to the ever-increasing numbers of children with ASD continues to present a major challenge to the educational communities that serve them.

OVERVIEW OF AUTISM SPECTRUM DISORDER (ASD)

HISTORY OF CLINICAL CONCEPTUALIZATION

The earliest and most comprehensive description of what we now refer to as autism or ASD was documented by Leo Kanner (1943) who first introduced the term as a clinical syndrome to the scientific literature by describing eleven children with "early infantile autism." These children were characterized as relating better to objects than people and showing severe social and communication abnormalities as well as narrow and restricted interests. One year later, Hans Asperger separately published a work characterizing children with "autistic psychopathology" (Wing, 1981). These children were described as being verbally fluent but with peculiar language use and abnormal prosody. They were also socially isolated and demonstrated repetitive behaviors, a desire for sameness, interest in unusual topics, motor clumsiness, and a propensity toward rote memorization of facts. Clinical descriptions of ASD have changed considerably since this time. For example, the reconceptualization of autism into a separate class of neurobehaviorally-based disorders occurred with the publication of the DSM-III (American Psychiatric Association, 1980). Autistic disorder was introduced in the DSM-III-R (American Psychiatric Association, 1987) with new diagnostic criteria. ASD was recently considered as an umbrella term which included a group of five disorders described under the category of Pervasive Developmental Disorders (PDD) in the DSM-IV (American Psychiatric Association, 1994), which was updated with a text revision in 2000 (DSM-IV-TR; American Psychiatric Association, 2000). The five pervasive developmental disorders are: (1) autistic disorder (autism), (2) Asperger's disorder, (3) childhood disintegrative disorder, (4) Rett's disorder, and (5) pervasive developmental disorder not otherwise specified (PDD-NOS). According to the DSM-IV-TR, these associated neurobehavioral disorders are characterized by a varying degree of qualitative impairment in three key areas of development that result in a distinct abnormality in comparison to expected developmental or mental age. This includes impairments in (a) reciprocal social interactions; (b) verbal and nonverbal communication; and (c) restricted and repetitive behaviors or interests, which together are often referred to as the "autistic triad of impairments".

DSM-5

The most recent conceptualization of ASD is reflected in the Fifth Edition of the Diagnostic Statistical Manual of Mental Disorders (DSM-5; American Psychiatric Association, 2013). The DSM-5 includes a new diagnostic category of autism spectrum disorder (ASD), which collapses the previously mentioned distinct DSM-IV-TR subcategories, including autistic disorder, Asperger's disorder (syndrome), childhood disintegrative disorder, and pervasive developmental disorder not otherwise specified (PDD-NOS) into a single diagnosis. Further, the DSM-IV-TR three symptom domains (i.e., autistic triad) of social impairment, communication deficits and repetitive/restricted behaviors, interests, or activities have been replaced with two domains, (a) persistent deficits in social communication/interaction; and (b) restricted/repetitive patterns of behaviors, interests, or activities (RRB).

Under the DSM-IV-TR criteria, a person qualified for an ASD diagnosis by exhibiting at least six of twelve deficits in social interaction, communication or repetitive behaviors. In contrast, the DSM-5 requires a person to exhibit three deficits in social communication and at least two symptoms in the category of restricted range of activities/ repetitive behaviors. Changes also include greater flexibility in the criteria for age of onset and addition of symptoms not previously included in the DSM-IV-TR such as sensory issues and aversions. For example, the criteria now state that although ASD must be present from infancy or early childhood, it may not be identified until later in the individual's development. Likewise, unusual sensory responses (e.g., hyper- or hypo-reactivity to sensory input) are now included in the DSM-5 symptom criteria for restricted, repetitive patterns of behavior, interests, or activities (RRB). Individuals meeting criteria for ASD also receive a functional severity rating across a three-level scale (Level 1—requiring support, Level 2—requiring substantial support, and Level 3—requiring very substantial support) for both the social communication and restricted, repetitive behavior domains. Similarly, there are specifiers for the presence of accompanying intellectual disability and/or language impairment and associations with other known medical or genetic conditions (e.g., fragile X syndrome, Rett syndrome), environmental factors, other neurodevelopmental, mental, or behavioral disorders. The specifiers are not mutually exclusive; thus more than one specifier can be given (e.g., ASD with or without accompanying intellectual impairment or language impairment). Appendix A highlights the important changes from DSM-IV-TR-to DSM-5 for a diagnosis of ASD.

Another significant change in the criteria involves the diagnosis of co-occurring (comorbid) disorders. Unlike the DSM-IV-TR, the DSM-5 no longer prohibits the comorbid diagnosis of attention-deficit/hyperactivity disorder (ADHD). When the criteria are met for both disorders, both diagnoses are given. It should be noted that individuals with a well established DSM-IV-TR diagnosis of autistic disorder, Asperger's disorder, or pervasive developmental disorder not otherwise specified (PDD-NOS) will not lose his or her diagnosis and should be given the DSM-5 diagnosis of ASD. Lastly, the DSM-5 includes a new diagnostic category of Social (Pragmatic) Communication Disorder (SCD) that is designed to capture social communication impairments not accompanied by restrictive and repetitive behavior/interests (RRB). Because both components are required for diagnosis of ASD, social (pragmatic) communication disorder is diagnosed if no RRBs are present (American Psychiatric Association, 2013). Individuals who have marked deficits in social communication, but whose symptoms do not meet the criteria for ASD, may be evaluated for social (pragmatic) communication disorder.

CLINICAL VS. EDUCATIONAL DEFINITION

The definition of autism differs among the various diagnostic and classification schemes. Both IDEA and DSM-5 have had the greatest impact on the assessment and classification of children and youth with ASD. In 1990, the United States Congress amended the federal special education law (now called Individuals with Disabilities Education Improvement Act, or IDEA, 2004) to make autism a category of special education disability. Unlike the DSM-5, which is intended as a diagnostic and classification system for psychiatric disorders, IDEA is federal legislation enacted to ensure the appropriate education of children with special educational needs. The IDEA recognizes 13 different disability categories under which 3- through 21-year-olds may be eligible for services (see Appendix B). As defined by IDEA, the term "student with a disability" means a student: "with intellectual disability, hearing impairments (including deafness), speech or language impairments, visual impairments (including blindness), serious emotional disturbance, orthopedic impairments, autism, traumatic brain injury, other health impairments, or specific learning disabilities; and who, by reason thereof, needs special education and related services" (IDEA, 2004). According to IDEA regulations, autism is defined as follows:

> (1)(i) Autism means a developmental disability significantly affecting verbal and nonverbal communication and social interaction, generally evident before age three, that adversely affects a child's educational performance. Other characteristics often associated with autism are engagement in repetitive activities and stereotyped movements, resistance to environmental change or change in daily routines, and unusual responses to sensory experiences. (ii) Autism does not apply if a child's educational performance is adversely affected primarily because the child has an emotional disturbance, as defined by IDEA. (iii) A child who manifests the characteristics of autism after age three could be identified as having autism if the above criteria are satisfied. (Individuals with Disabilities Act of 2004, 34 CFR §300.8 (1)(i)-(iii))

IDEA shares a number of features with the DSM-5. Both are categorical systems (i.e., the individual meets or does not meet criteria) that focus on the description rather than the function of behavior, and have been used in legal decision making regarding special education placement and clinical treatment. Both definitions include impairments in social communication and restricted, repetitive patterns of behavior/ interests. The DSM-5 conceptualizes ASD as a clinically significant syndrome or pattern associated with disability or impairment in one or more important areas of functioning (American Psychiatric Association, 2013). The IDEA definition also requires that the core behaviors of autism impair or have a negative impact on the student's educational performance. Unlike the DSM-IV-TR which required onset of symptoms prior to age 3, the DSM-5 and IDEA do not preclude a diagnosis or classification at a later age. This is especially important because many individuals with ASD are not diagnosed in early childhood and can be identified for treatment and special education services at later ages.

Despite the similarities between the two systems, there are important distinctions between a clinical/medical diagnosis of ASD and a determination of eligibility for special education. School and mental health professionals should be aware that while the DSM-5 is considered the primary authority in the fields of psychiatric and psychological diagnoses, the IDEA definition is the controlling authority with regard to eligibility decisions for special education (Fogt, Miller, and Zirkel, 2003; Mandlawitz, 2002; Zirkel, 2014). While the DSM-5 criteria for ASD are professionally helpful, they are neither legally required nor sufficient for determining educational placement. Children with a clinical diagnosis of ASD do not automatically receive special education, nor are students who are eligible for special education under the IDEA category of autism required to have a clinical diagnosis of ASD. An evaluation assessing eligibility for special education does not replace a clinical diagnosis of ASD, nor does a clinical diagnosis of ASD determine eligibility for special education. School professionals should be certain that students meet the criteria for autism as outlined by IDEA and use the DSM-5 to the extent that the diagnostic criteria include the same core behaviors (e.g., impairment in social communication and interaction, and restricted, repetitive patterns of behavior/interests). It is important to remember that when it comes to special education, it is state and federal education codes and regulations (not DSM criteria) that determine eligibility decisions (Fogt *et al.*, 2003; Zirkel, 2014). Best practice in special education eligibility and program planning is discussed in Chapter 6.

THE GENDER GAP

Prevalence estimates of ASD are significantly higher among boys than among girls. According to the CDC (2014), boys are nearly five times more likely to be identified with ASD than girls. (1 in 42 boys were identified with ASD; 1 in 189 girls were identified with ASD.) In fact, research has found that even when symptoms are equally severe, boys are more likely to be identified with ASD than girls (Russell, Steer, and Golding, 2011). There is also evidence to indicate that among children up to age eight, girls are diagnosed later than boys (Shattuck *et al.*, 2009). This gender "gap" raises serious questions because many female students with ASD are being overlooked and will not receive the appropriate educational supports and services.

Although few studies have examined gender differences in the expression of autism, there are some tentative explanations for this disparity. Since females are socialized differently, ASD may not be manifested in the same way as typical male behavioral symptoms (Wilkinson, 2008a). For example, social communication and pragmatic deficits may not be readily apparent in girls because of a non-externalizing behavioral profile. Thus, girls who have difficulty making sustained eye contact and appear socially withdrawn may be perceived as "shy," "naive," or "sweet" rather than having the social impairment associated with an ASD (Wagner, 2006). Girls on the higher end of the spectrum also tend to have fewer special interests, better superficial social skills, language and communication skills, and less hyperactivity and aggression than boys. As a result, the behavior and educational needs of boys are much more difficult to ignore and are frequently seen by teachers and parents as being more urgent, further contributing to a referral bias and lessening the probability of a girl being identified as having the core symptoms of ASD. Likewise, over reliance on the male model with regard to diagnostic criteria might contribute to a gender "bias" and underdiagnosis of girls. Clinical instruments also tend to exclude symptoms and behaviors that may be more typical of females with ASD. In addition, the diagnosis of another disorder often diverts attention from autism-related symptomatology. In many cases, girls tend to receive unspecified diagnoses such as a learning disability, processing problem, or internalizing disorder (i.e., anxiety and depression). Unfortunately, the consequences of a missed or late diagnosis can result in girls facing social isolation, peer rejection, lowered grades, and a greater risk for mental health and behavioral distress such as anxiety and depression during adolescence and adulthood. Although a comprehensive review of this subject is beyond the scope of this Guide, best practice recommends that when a girl presents with a combination of social immaturity, restricted interests, limited eye gaze, repetitive behaviors, social isolation, and is viewed as "unusual" or "different" by parents, teachers and peers, the possibility of an ASD should be given consideration (Wagner, 2006). Likewise, girls who are diagnosed with ASD should be screened for internalizing problems such as anxiety and depression, and closely monitored for symptom occurrence.

CONCLUSION

We have only begun to appreciate the complex challenge of how to ensure that children with ASD are appropriately identified and provided with the opportunities and resources to learn, socialize, and become independent, responsible, and productive members of society. Unfortunately, caring for a child with autism places a serious burden on the health, social and financial well-being of individuals, families, and society. For example, the national cost of supporting children with autism, including direct non-medical costs, such as special education and early intervention services, and indirect costs, such as parental productivity loss, is estimated to be $61 billion to $66 billion a year in the U.S (Buescher, Cidav, Knapp, and Mandell, 2014; Lavelle *et al.*, 2014). Moreover, parenting a child with autism can place considerable stress on work, finances, personal health and psychological well-being, and marital relationships and responsibilities. Siblings, too, may be affected. Both the psychological and financial costs can be significantly reduced with early diagnosis and intervention/treatment. Therefore, it is critically important to identify those children in need of further assessment in order to reduce the time between symptom appearance and intervention.

The best practice guidelines outlined in this text address the issues related to screening, assessment, and intervention planning in a comprehensive and flexible manner that is consistent with evidence based-practice. In order to derive the most benefit from this Guide, it should be read in its entirety. Because of the overlap between chapters, there is some repetition in content. Also note that the terms autism spectrum disorder (ASD) and autism are used interchangeably throughout the text to reflect the scientific consensus that symptoms of the various autism subgroups represent a single continuum (or spectrum) of impairment that varies in level of severity and need for support (American Psychiatric Association, 2013). Readers are encouraged to consider the best practice screening and assessment paradigms described in Chapters 2 and 3 when selecting instruments. Similarly, the systematic reviews and information presented in Chapters 5 and 6 provide an overview of evidence-based interventions and effective special education practices. The reader is also advised to consult the index to locate best practice references in each chapter and to supplement the information available in this Guide with additional and newly published information, as appropriate. The next chapter focuses on best practice in the screening process and provides a review of validated instruments that can be used by school-based professionals to identify children in need of a comprehensive developmental assessment.

CHAPTER 2

BEST PRACTICE
IN SCREENING

Based on the information presented in the previous chapter, it is clear that the increased awareness and prevalence of autism, together with the benefits of early intervention, have created an urgent need for school professionals to identify children who may have an autism spectrum condition. Both the DSM-5 and IDEA focus on the importance of early identification, assessment, and intervention for children with ASD. Behavioral screening is an important first step in this process. Although ASD affects approximately 1 percent of the school-age population, it is not unusual for children with mild levels of impairment (e.g., without intellectual disability or noticeable language delay) to go unidentified until well after entering school (Brock, Jimerson, and Hansen, 2006). For example, a study examining the timing of identification among children with autism using a population-based sample from an ongoing surveillance effort across 13 sites in the United States found the gap between potential and actual age of identification (for those identified) to be in the range of 2.7 to 3.7 years. Combined with the fact that more than one quarter of cases were never identified as having ASD through age eight, these results illustrate the need for a more effective system of screening and identification for ASD in our schools (Shattuck *et al.*, 2009).

It is well established that early interventions for children with developmental disabilities are important for increasing cognitive, linguistic, social, and self-help skills (Dawson and Osterling, 1997; Rogers 1998). Early identification and diagnosis (a) enhances the opportunity for effective educational and behavioral interventions, (b) results in reduction of family stress by providing the families with specific techniques and guidance for decision making, and (c) improves access to medical care and community support (Cox *et al.*, 1999). A delay in identification postpones the timely implementation of intervention services and may contribute to parental distress in coping with ASD (Goddard, Lehr, and Lapadat, 2000; Goin-Kochel, Mackintosh, and Myers, 2006). Assisting parents to develop effective management techniques is likely to avoid or minimize the potential for secondary behavioral and emotional problems (Howlin, 1998; Howlin, 2005). Importantly, because children with ASD are likely to be educated in general education classrooms, delayed recognition of their problems can result in the implementation of ineffective or inappropriate teaching methods that fail to address the core social-communication deficits of ASD. Delays in diagnosis and identification also have wide implications for families. It is now accepted that autism is most likely among the most heritable of all childhood disorders and that for any family with a child with ASD, there is considerable risk that other children in the family may have social, language, or other neurodevelopmental problems (Bailey, Phillips, and Rutter, 1996; Holmboe *et al.*, 2014). Family histories of autism or autistic-like behavior or having an older sibling with autism are known risk factors. A delay in identification may result in siblings with the 'broader phenotype' being overlooked and as a result, these children may not receive the help needed to address their problems (Howlin and Asgharian, 1999). Thus, it is vital that school professionals devote increased attention to the screening and early identification of students who may have symptoms associated with ASD (Brock *et al.*, 2006; Wilkinson, 2014a).

BEST PRACTICE
Parents/caregivers should be considered as members of the professional team and included as full partners throughout the screening and evaluation processes.

CORE FEATURES OF ASD

The defining features of ASD are impairment in social interaction and communication, and restricted patterns of behavior. This includes difficulty communicating with others, processing and integrating information from the environment, establishing and maintaining reciprocal social relationships, taking another person's perspective, inferring the interests of others, and transitioning to new learning environments (Carter *et al.*, 2005). While all children with ASD experience these core deficits, we now recognize that autism-related traits are quantitatively distributed in the general population and that autism is best conceptualized as a spectrum disorder, rather than a categorical diagnosis (Constantino and Gruber, 2012; Constantino and Todd, 2003; Skuse *et al.*, 2009). Even mild degrees of social-communication impairment can significantly interfere with classroom performance and adaptation. Likewise, a combination of mild autistic symptomatology and other psychological liabilities (e.g., attention problems, mood problems, and aggression) can have an adverse effect on children's learning and behavior (Constantino and Gruber, 2012; Skuse *et al.*, 2009). It is also important to recognize that socialization deficits are a major cause of impairment in ASD regardless of the individual's level of cognitive or language ability (Carter *et al.*, 2005).

The core features of ASD may not diminish with development. Typically, children do not "outgrow" their limitations. Distress may actually increase as they approach adolescence and the social milieu becomes more complex and challenging. These difficulties may then persist into adulthood, where they continue to negatively impact adaptive functioning. Because children with mild or even moderate deficits in social and communicative competence are often overlooked, misdiagnosed with another psychiatric condition, or experience co-occurring disorders, it is critical that school professionals give greater priority to case finding and screening to ensure that children with symptoms of ASD are identified and have access to the appropriate intervention services (Brock *et al.*, 2006; Wilkinson, 2014b). The objective of this chapter is to provide school and allied professionals with a review of four validated ASD-specific screening instruments and to describe a multi-tier model for identifying children who are most likely to have ASD and thus, necessitate a comprehensive developmental assessment.

BEST PRACTICE
School professionals play a vital role by participating in case finding and screening activities to ensure that children with ASD are being identified and provided with the appropriate programs and services.

SCREENING, DIAGNOSIS, AND ASSESSMENT
Throughout this Guide, the term screening refers to the process of identifying school children most likely to have ASD and/or developmental delay. The terms diagnostic evaluation and diagnosis refer to the process of identifying a specific psychiatric disorder in clinical and medical settings, and the rendering of a diagnosis by a primary care provider, psychologist, or mental health professional which aligns with criteria in the DSM-5. Assessment is a term that describes the process of evaluating the child's level of functioning in multiple developmental areas by a team of school-based professionals to inform intervention planning and determine eligibility to receive special education and related services under IDEA.

BEHAVIORAL SCREENING

Screening is an important first step for securing the appropriate educational services for children with ASD. Developing screening tools to identify students with less severe symptoms of ASD tends to be especially difficult because the autism spectrum is comprised of a wide range of impairment without clear-cut boundaries (Wing and Potter, 2009). Until recently, there were few validated screening measures available to assist school professionals in the identification of students with the core symptoms of ASD (Campbell, 2005; Lord and Corsello, 2005). Because autism has traditionally been viewed as a "categorical" diagnosis, most rating scales were developed to categorically determine the presence or absence of ASD, rather than dimensionally assess the severity of ASD symptoms. Yet, research indicates that children with the same diagnostic classification are likely to be heterogeneous and that many childhood disorders, including ASD, fall along a continuum in the general population (Constantino and Gruber, 2012). Categorical classification fails to account for these quantitative differences between children with the same core symptoms.

During the past decade, however, significant advances in the development of screening instruments for autism have led to an improved ability to accurately identify children suspected of having ASD. There are now several reliable and valid screening tools and rating scales to quantify the severity of symptoms across the autism spectrum. These instruments may be used with children who present with risk factors (e.g., sibling or family history of autism) and/or when parents and teachers, or health care professionals observe or identify the presence of "red flags" (e.g., social, communication and behavioral concerns) of ASD.

BEST PRACTICE
Evaluation professionals should be familiar with the psychometric properties and utility of ASD screening and assessment instruments.

PSYCHOMETRIC PROPERTIES

Professionals should have an understanding of the basic psychometrics properties that underlie test use and development. For example, discriminant validity is an especially important psychometric characteristic to consider when evaluating the quality and usefulness of a screening instrument or more comprehensive measure. It refers to a test's accuracy in predicting group membership (e.g., ASD versus non-ASD). Discriminant validity can be expressed through metrics such as sensitivity and specificity, and positive predictive value (PPV) and negative predictive value (NPV). Sensitivity and specificity are measures of a test's ability to correctly identify someone as having a given disorder or not having the disorder. Sensitivity refers to the percentage of cases with a disorder that screens positive. A highly sensitive test means that there are few false negative results (individuals with a disorder who screen negative), and thus fewer cases of the disorder are missed. Specificity is the percentage of cases without a disorder that screens negative. A highly specific test means that there are few false positive results (e.g., individuals without a disorder who screen positive). False negatives decrease sensitivity, whereas false positives decrease specificity. An efficient screening tool should minimize false negatives, as these are individuals with a likely disorder who remain unidentified (National Research Council, 2001). Sensitivity and specificity levels of .80 or higher are generally recommended (Coonrod and Stone, 2005; Norris and Lecavalier, 2010).

Positive Predictive Value (PPV) and Negative Predictive Value (NPV) are also important validity statistics that describe how well a screening tool or test performs. The probability of having a given disorder, given the results of a test, is called the predictive value. PPV is interpreted as the percentage of all positive cases that truly have the disorder. PPV is a critical measure of the performance of a diagnostic or screening measure, as it reflects the probability that a positive test or screen identifies the disorder for which the individual is being evaluated or screened. NPV is the percentage of all cases screened negative that are truly without the disorder. The higher the PPV and NPV values, the more efficient the instrument at correctly identifying cases. It is important to recognize that PPV is influenced by the *sensitivity* and *specificity* of the test as well as the prevalence of the disorder in the sample under study. For example, an ASD-specific screening measure may be expected to have a higher PPV when utilized with a known group of high-risk children who exhibit signs or symptoms of developmental delay, social skills deficits, or language impairment. In fact, for any diagnostic test, when the prevalence of the disorder is low, the positive PPV will also be low, even using a test with high *sensitivity* and *specificity*.

BEST PRACTICE
Parent and teacher screening tools are ideal instruments to assist with the identification of ASD because they gather important information from people familiar with the student and are easy to administer and score.

SCREENING TOOLS FOR SCHOOL-AGE CHILDREN

Third-party screening questionnaires have been shown to discriminate well between children with and without ASD. Parent and teacher screening tools are especially ideal instruments for identifying children who are in need of a more comprehensive evaluation. They yield important information from individuals who know the child the best and are relatively easy to administer and score (Wiggins *et al.*, 2007; Wilkinson, 2014b). The following measures have demonstrated utility in screening for ASD in educational settings and can be used to determine which children are likely to require further assessment and/or who might benefit from additional support. They also afford the ability to measure autistic characteristics on a quantitative scale across a wide range of severity. All measures have strong psychometric qualities, are appropriate for school-age children, and time efficient (5 to 20 minutes to complete). Although training needs are minimal and require little or no professional instruction to complete, interpretation of the results requires familiarity with ASD and experience in administering, scoring, and interpreting psychological tests. Table 2.1 shows the ASD screening measures, together with information regarding format, administration time, discriminant validity, and applicable age ranges.

TABLE 2.1 SCREENING MEASURES FOR AUTISM SPECTRUM DISORDER

Measure	Age Range	Format	Sensitivity	Specificity	Time to Complete
ASRS	6:0 - 18:0	Questionnaire	.94	.92	5-15 Minutes
ASSQ	6:0 - 17:0	Questionnaire	.91	.86	10 Minutes
SCQ	4:0 - Adult	Questionnaire	.96	.80	10 Minutes
SRS-2	4:0 - 18:0	Questionnaire	.92	.92	10-20 Minutes

Note. ASRS – Autism Spectrum Rating Scales; ASSQ – Autism Spectrum Screening Questionnaire; SCQ – Social Communication Questionnaire; SRS-2 – Social Responsiveness Scale, Second Edition (School-Age Form).

BEST PRACTICE

ASD screening for school-age children should include tools such as the Autism Spectrum Rating Scales (ASRS), Autism Spectrum Screening Questionnaire (ASSQ), Social Communication Questionnaire (SCQ), and Social Responsiveness Scale, second edition (SRS-2).

AUTISM SPECTRUM RATING SCALES

The Autism Spectrum Rating Scales (ASRS; Goldstein and Naglieri, 2010) is a norm-referenced instrument designed to effectively identify symptoms, behaviors, and associated features of autism spectrum disorder (ASD) in children and adolescents aged 2 to 18. The ASRS has full-length and short forms for young children aged two to five years, and for older children and adolescents aged 6 to 18 years. The full-length ASRS (2–5 Years) consists of 70 items, and the full-length ASRS (6–18 Years) contains 71 items. Each item is scored on a Likert scale from 0 ("never") to 4 ("very frequently"). There are separate parent and teacher rating forms for both age groups. All scales are set to the T-score metric, with a normative mean of 50 and a standard deviation of 10. T-scores and percentiles are categorized as Low, Average (typical), Slightly Elevated, Elevated, and Very Elevated. The ASRS Scales include (a) Social/Communication, (b) Unusual Behaviors, and (c) Self-Regulation (6–18 Years). The Treatment Scales include (a) Peer Socialization; (b) Adult Socialization; (c) Social/Emotional Reciprocity; (d) Atypical Language; (e) Stereotypy; (f) Behavioral Rigidity; (g) Sensory Sensitivity; (h) Attention/Self-Regulation (2–5 Years); and (i) Attention (6–18 Years). The full-length form provides the most comprehensive assessment information, including the Total Score, ASRS Scales, and DSM Symptom Scales. The ASRS have been updated to align with the DSM-5 criteria for ASD (Goldstein and Naglieri, 2014). A DSM-IV-TR scoring option remains available to accommodate users who would like to continue to generate reports with the DSM-IV-TR Scale. The full length form is recommended for use when completing a comprehensive evaluation for ASD.

The ASRS Short Form (2–5 Years) and ASRS Short Form (6–18 Years) each contain a subset of 15 items from the full length form that that best differentiates children and youth diagnosed with ASD from those in the general population. Parents and teachers complete the same form which can be used as a screening measure to determine which children and youth are likely to require a more comprehensive assessment for an ASD. It is also suitable for monitoring response to treatment/intervention. Reliability data indicate high levels of internal consistency, good inter-rater agreement, and excellent test-retest reliability. Discriminative validity (classification accuracy) of both the full-length ASRS and ASRS Short Forms indicate that the scales were able to accurately predict group membership with a mean overall correct classification rate of 90.4 percent on the ASRS (2-5) and 90.1 percent on the ASRS (6-18). The full-length form can be completed in approximately 15 minutes, while the short-form can be completed in approximately 5 minutes.

AUTISM SPECTRUM SCREENING QUESTIONNAIRE

The Autism Spectrum Screening Questionnaire (ASSQ; Ehlers, Gillberg, and Wing, 1999) is a parent and teacher questionnaire comprised of 27 items designed to discriminate between more capable children with ASD and typically developing peers. The ASSQ has been widely used in clinical practice and is well validated in research, both with general population and clinical samples (Ehlers *et al.*, 1999; Mattila *et al.*, 2009; Posserud *et al.*, 2008; Posserud, Lundervold, and Gillberg, 2009). The questionnaire was designed for completion by informants in school and home settings. The ASSQ content addresses social interaction (11 items), verbal and nonverbal communication (6 items), restricted and repetitive behaviors (5 items), and motor problems (5 items). Social items include questions related to difficulties with friendship (e.g., "Wishes to be sociable, but fails to make relationships with peers"), prosocial behavior (e.g., "Lacks empathy"), and social communication (e.g., "Uses language freely but fails to make adjustment to fit social contexts or the needs of different listeners"). The respondent rates behavioral descriptions on a three-point scale, "not true" (0), "sometimes true" (1), and "certainly true" (2). Positively endorsed items are summed for a total score (range of 0–54). Various cut-offs and their corresponding sensitivity and specificity are reported to allow more flexible interpretation. For a non-clinical sample, the authors suggest a score of >13 when parents served as raters (sensitivity = .91, specificity = .77) and >11 for teachers (sensitivity = .90, specificity = .58). This threshold is recommended for use when it is essential to minimize the risk of missing mild autism cases (false negatives) (Ehlers *et al.* 1999; Posserud, Lundervold, and Gillberg, 2006). A more recent validation study indicated an optimal cut-off score of >17 on either parent or teacher questionnaire for discriminating between ASD and non-ASD cases in a general population sample (public schools) of seven- to nine-year-old children. Combining the results for both informants and using this cut-off score provided the most efficient screening results with a sensitivity value of .91 and a specificity value of .86 (Posserud *et al.*, 2009). Research indicates that the ASSQ possesses strong test-retest reliability, acceptable inter-rater reliability, and good internal consistency, and that it significantly differentiates high-functioning ASD from other childhood disorders (Ehlers *et al.*, 1999; Posserud *et al.*, 2009).

SOCIAL COMMUNICATION QUESTIONNAIRE
The Social Communication Questionnaire (SCQ; Rutter, Bailey, and Lord, 2003), previously known as the Autism Screening Questionnaire (ASQ), was initially designed as a companion screening measure for the Autism Diagnostic Interview-Revised (ADI-R; Rutter, Le Couteur and Lord, 2003). The SCQ is a parent/caregiver dimensional measure of ASD symptomatology appropriate for children of any chronological age older than four years. It can be completed by the

informant in less than 10 minutes. The SCQ is available in two forms, Lifetime and Current, each with 40 questions presented in a yes or no format. The items were chosen to match the ADI-R items that were found to have discriminative validity. Questions include items in the reciprocal social interaction domain (e.g., "Does she/he have any particular friends or best friend?"), the communication domain (e.g., "Can you have a to and fro 'conversation' with him/her that involves taking turns or building on what you have said?"), and the restricted, repetitive, and stereotyped patterns of behavior domain (e.g., "Has she/he ever seemed to be more interested in parts of a toy or an object [e.g., spinning the wheels of a car], rather than using the object as intended?"). Scores on the questionnaire provide an index of symptom severity and indicate the likelihood that a child has ASD. The SCQ has been found to have good discriminant validity and utility as an efficient screener for at-risk groups of school-age children. A threshold raw score of $\geq$15 is recommended to minimize the risk of false negatives and indicate the need for a comprehensive evaluation. This threshold score resulted in a sensitivity value of .96, a specificity value of .80, and a positive predictive value .93 in a large population of children with autism and other developmental disorders. Compared to other screening measures, the SCQ has received significant scrutiny and has consistently demonstrated its effectiveness in predicting ASD versus non-ASD status in multiple studies (Chandler *et al.*, 2007; Charman *et al.*, 2007; Corsello, *et al.*, 2007; Norris and Lecavalier, 2010).

SOCIAL RESPONSIVENESS SCALE (SECOND EDITION)

The second edition of the Social Responsiveness Scale (SRS-2; Constantino and Gruber, 2012) identifies the various dimensions of interpersonal behavior, communication, and repetitive/stereotypic behavior characteristic of ASD and quantifies symptom severity. The SRS-2 maintains continuity with the original instrument and extends the age range from 2.5 years through adulthood. There are four forms, each consisting of 65 items: Preschool Form (ages 2.5 to 4.5 years); School-Age Form (4 to 18 years); Adult Form (ages 19 and up); and Adult Self-Report Form (ages 19 and up). Nationally representative standardization samples were collected to support each form. The School-Age Form is unchanged in its item content from the first edition of the SRS (Constantino and Gruber, 2005) and can be completed in 15-20 minutes by informants (e.g., parents, teachers, day-care providers) who have observed the child's social interactions in naturalistic contexts. Each item is scored on a four-point scale: 1 ("not true"); 2 ("sometimes true); 3 (often true); and 4 ("almost always true"). Scores are obtained for five Treatment Subscales: Social Awareness (e.g., "Is aware of what others are thinking or feeling"), Social Cognition (e.g., Doesn't recognize when others are trying to take advantage of him or her"), Social Communication (e.g., "Avoids eye contact or has unusual eye contact"), Social Motivation (e.g., "Would rather be alone than with others"), and Restricted Interests and Repetitive Behavior (e.g., "Has an unusually narrow range of interests"). There are also two DSM-5 Compatible Subscales (Social Communication and Interaction and Restricted Interests and Repetitive Behavior) that allow comparison of symptoms to the new diagnostic criteria for ASD. Interpretation is based on a single score reflecting the sum of responses to all 65 SRS questions. Raw scores are converted to T-scores for gender and respondent. A total T-score of 76 or higher is considered severe and strongly associated with a clinical diagnosis of ASD. T-scores of 66 through 75 are interpreted as indicating Moderate deficiencies in reciprocal social behavior that are clinically significant and lead to substantial interference in everyday social interactions, while T-scores of 60 to 65 are in the Mild range and indicate deficiencies in reciprocal social behavior that are clinically significant and may lead to mild to moderate problems in social interaction. T-scores of 59 and below fall within typical limits and are not generally associated with clinically significant ASD. Findings across studies and groups consistently report sensitivity ranging from .78 to .91 with values clustering around .80. Specificity values range from .85 to .90 when contrasts involve a typically developing group. In a large scale clinical sample (School-Age Form), analyses indicated sensitivity and specificity values of .92 at a raw score of 62. This suggests that the SRS-2 is a robust instrument for discriminating between individuals with ASD and those unaffected by the condition. Large samples also provide evidence of good inter-rater reliability, high internal consistency, and convergent validity with the Autism Diagnostic Interview-Revised (ADI-R), Autism Diagnostic Observation Schedule (ADOS), and Social Communication Questionnaire (SCQ) (Charman *et al.*, 2007; Constantino *et al.*, 2003; Constantino and Gruber, 2012).

A TIERED SCREENING MODEL

The following three-tier (or three-step) model is recommended for screening students who demonstrate risk factors and/or warning signs of atypical development or where caregiver/parent concerns strongly suggest the presence of ASD symptoms (Wilkinson, 2014b).

BEST PRACTICE
All school professionals should be prepared to recognize the early warning signs or red flags of ASD across age and grade levels to ensure that children at-risk for ASD are being identified.

TIER ONE — CASE FINDING
The initial step is case finding. This involves recognizing the risk factors and/or warning signs of ASD. All school professionals should be aware of those students who display atypical social and/or communication behaviors that might be associated with ASD. Although no two

children are alike, at-risk students may demonstrate difficulties in the areas of social interaction, attention, impulse control and behavioral regulation. They may have difficulty interacting with peers, and display a narrow range of interests or intense preoccupation with specific objects. Delays in language milestones or pragmatic skills (social language), as well as the presence of repetitive behaviors, inflexibility, and difficulty transitioning have been associated with ASD. Pedantic or overly mature speech, stereotypic mannerisms, poor eye contact, and sensory sensitivity may also be observed in at-risk children. The failure to make friends, understand social rules and conventions, or display social reciprocity in interpersonal relationships are considered warning signs at all age and grade levels. The warning signs of ASD become more diverse as children get older when gaps in social skills become even more apparent. However, no child will exhibit all of these characteristics. The degree (i.e., mild to severe) to which any particular behavior is experienced will also vary from child to child. Case finding also requires that attention be given not only to teacher concerns about children's development, but to parental worry as well. Early identification depends on listening carefully to parents' concerns about their child's development and behavior. Family members are often the first to recognize that a student may have an ASD. Parent and/or teacher reports of social impairment, combined with communication and behavioral concerns, indicate the need for screening. Children who are identified with risk factors during this case finding phase should be referred for formal screening at Tier 2.

BEST PRACTICE
A standardized screening tool should be administered at any point when concerns about ASD are raised by a parent or teacher, or as a result of school observations or questions about developmentally appropriate social, communicative, and play behaviors.

TIER TWO — SCREENING

Once screened at Tier 2, individual scores can be used as an indication of the approximate severity of ASD symptomatology for students who present with elevated developmental risk factors and/or warning signs of ASD identified through case finding. Screening results are shared with parents and school-based team with a focus on intervention planning and ongoing observation. Discussion of broad intervention goals typically begins well before assessment for intervention planning or development of an intervention plan. Consequently, selection and implementation of initial interventions may occur while plans are being made to conduct a comprehensive evaluation. This includes positive behavioral support strategies that can be used with the entire class and other strategies that can be implemented individually with the student. Screening scores can also be used for progress monitoring and to measure change over time. This information can then inform the assessment process and future intervention decisions. It should be noted, however, that a "wait-and-see" approach without progress monitoring is not appropriate when there is a positive screen. Students with a positive screen should be referred for a more comprehensive assessment and intensive intervention planning as part of Tier 3. However, as with all screening tools, there will be some false negatives (e.g., children with ASD who are not identified as such). Thus, children who screen negative, but who appear to have a high level of risk and/or when parent and/or teacher concerns indicate developmental variations and behaviors consistent with ASD, should continue to be monitored, regardless of screening results.

BEST PRACTICE

Students who screen negative should be carefully monitored so as to minimize misclassification and ensure access to intervention services.

TIER THREE — COMPREHENSIVE DEVELOPMENTAL ASSESSMENT

Students who meet the threshold criteria in Tier 2 should be referred for a comprehensive developmental assessment and intensive intervention. Because they report good reliability and high levels of discriminative validity, results from the screening measures can be integrated into a comprehensive developmental assessment to assist in determining eligibility for special education services and guide intervention planning. Information from Tier 2 interventions can also be used to inform the assessment process. Assessment should include parent/caregiver interviews, developmental history, direct observation, and interaction with the referred student, combined with quantitative measures of social behavior, cognitive functioning, academic achievement, language and communication, adaptive behavior, sensory processing, and atypical behavior (Campbell, Ruble, and Hammond, 2014; Filipek *et al.*, 2000; National Research Council 2001). Assessment results are used to develop an individualized intervention plan which involves identifying goals, selecting interventions, and determining procedures for monitoring the student's progress. Progress is monitored and additional assessment and revisions to the intervention plan completed as needed. The essential components of a comprehensive developmental assessment are described in the next chapter.

LIMITATIONS

Although the ASSQ, ASRS, SCQ, and SRS-2 can be used confidently as efficient screening tools for identifying children across the broad autism spectrum, they are not without limitations. Some students who screen positive will not be identified with an ASD (false positive). On the other hand, some children who were not initially identified will go on to meet the diagnostic and/or classification criteria (false negative). Therefore, it is especially important to carefully monitor those students who screen negative so as to ensure access to intervention services if needed (Bryson, Rogers, and Fombonne, 2003; Wilkinson, 2014b). Gathering information from family and school resources during screening will also facilitate identification of possible cases. Autism specific tools are not currently recommended for the universal screening of typical school-age children (Johnson, Myers, and Council on Children With Disabilities, 2007). Focusing on referred children with identified risk-factors and/or developmental delays will increase predictive values and result in more efficient identification efforts (Coonrod and Stone, 2005; Lee *et al.*, 2007; Wilkinson, 2014b).

BEST PRACTICE

Gender differences should be taken into consideration when screening and evaluating children for ASD.

Gender differences should also be taken into consideration when screening. Research suggests that there may be sex differences in expression of the broader autism phenotype (Wilkinson, 2014b). Although few studies have examined effects of gender-specific differences on various screening measures, the ASRS, ASSQ, and SRS-2 have generally reported higher mean scores for boys than girls. Both the SRS-2 and ASSQ found higher scores for boys than girls on both the parent and teacher questionnaires, with the greatest difference in reports from teachers (Constantino and Gruber, 2012; Posserud, Lundervold, and Gillberg, 2009). These lower symptom scores for girls may reflect gender differences in autistic traits and expression of the phenotype. Recent research also suggests that certain single items may be more typical of girls than of boys with ASD and examining symptom gender differences at the individual item level might lead to a better understanding of gender differences in ASD (Kopp and Gillberg, 2011). Although this issue continues to be studied, practitioners should consider the importance of gender when scoring and interpreting both screening and evaluation instruments (Wilkinson, 2014b).

CONCLUSION

Epidemiological studies indicate a progressively rising prevalence trend for ASD over the past decade (CDC, 2014; Wing and Potter, 2009). Yet, compared with general population estimates, children with mild to moderate autistic characteristics remain an underidentified and underserved population in our schools. There is likely a substantial number of children with equivalent profiles to those with a clinical diagnosis of ASD who are not receiving services (Russell *et al.*, 2010; Safran, 2008; Skuse *et al.*, 2009). Research indicates that outcomes for children on the autism spectrum can be significantly enhanced with the delivery of intensive intervention services (National Research Council, 2001). However, intervention services can only be implemented if students are identified. Screening is the initial step in this process. School professionals should be prepared to recognize the presence of risk factors and/or early warning signs of ASD, and be familiar with screening tools to ensure that children at-risk for ASD are being identified (Wilkinson, 2014b). The next chapter examines the parameters of a developmental assessment and provides a review of tests and measures included in an assessment battery for ASD.

CHAPTER 3

BEST PRACTICE IN ASSESSMENT

The primary goals of conducting an assessment for ASD are to determine the presence and severity of ASD symptoms, develop interventions for educational planning, and collect data that will help with progress monitoring (Shriver, Allen, and Mathews, 1999). School professionals must also determine whether an ASD has been overlooked or misclassified, describe co-occurring (comorbid) disorders, or identify an alternative classification. This includes other neruodevelopmental disorders such as attention-deficit/hyperactivity disorder (ADHD), intellectual disability, developmental coordination disorder, language impairment, and specific learning disorder (disability), which frequently co-occur with ASD (American Psychiatric Association, 2013). Likewise, anxiety, depression, and disruptive behavior disorders are commonly co-occurring (comorbid) problems. This chapter describes a comprehensive developmental assessment approach and focuses on the tools and procedures for the assessment and identification of ASD included in recommendations of the American Academy of Neurology (Filipek *et al.*, 2000), the American Academy of Child and Adolescent Psychiatry (Volkmar *et al.*, 2014), and a consensus panel with representation from multiple professional societies (Filipek *et al.*, 1999, 2000).

BEST PRACTICE
The identification of autism should be made by a professional team using multiple sources of information, including, but not limited to, an interdisciplinary assessment of social behavior, language and communication, adaptive behavior, motor skills, sensory issues, and cognitive functioning.

COMPREHENSIVE DEVELOPMENTAL ASSESSMENT APPROACH

There are several important considerations that should inform the assessment process. First, a developmental perspective is critically important. While the core symptoms of ASD are present during early childhood, ASD is a lifelong condition that affects the individual's adaptive functioning from childhood through adulthood. Evaluating the child within a developmental assessment framework provides a yardstick for understanding the severity and quality of delays or atypicality (Klin *et al.*, 2005). Interviews and observation schedules, together with an assessment of social behavior, language and communication, adaptive behavior, motor skills, sensory issues, atypical behaviors, and cognitive functioning are recommended best practice procedures (Campbell, Ruble, and Hammond, 2014; National Research Council, 2001; Ozonoff, Goodlin-Jones, and Solomon, 2007). Because ASD affects multiple areas of functioning, an interdisciplinary team approach is essential for establishing a developmental and psychosocial profile of the child in order to guide intervention planning. A team of professionals including, but not limited to, a psychologist, general and special educators, a speech/language pathologist, occupational therapist, and in some cases a physician, should evaluate the child and collaborate to determine an appropriate classification or diagnosis. The following principles are intended to guide the assessment and evaluation process (Filipek *et al.*, 1999, 2000; Klin *et al.*, 2005; Volkmar *et al.*, 2014).

- Children who screen positive for ASD should be referred for a comprehensive assessment. Although the screening tools discussed in the previous chapter have utility in broadly identifying children who may have an autism spectrum condition, they are not recommended as stand alone diagnostic instruments or as a substitute for a more inclusive assessment. However, they may be used as components of a more comprehensive diagnostic battery.

- Assessment should involve careful attention to the signs and symptoms consistent with ASD as well as other co-occurring childhood disorders.

- When a student is suspected of having an ASD, a review of his or her developmental history in areas such as speech, communication, social and play skills is an important first step in the assessment process.

- A family medical history and review of psychosocial factors that may play a role in the child's development is a significant component of the assessment process.

- The integration of information from multiple sources will strengthen the reliability of the assessment results.

- Evaluation of academic achievement should be included in assessment and intervention planning to address learning and behavioral concerns in the child's overall school functioning.

- Assessment procedures should be designed to assist in the development of instructional objectives and intervention strategies based on the student's unique pattern of strengths and weaknesses.

- Because impairment in communication and social reciprocity are core features of ASD, a comprehensive developmental assessment should include both domains.

- Restricted and repetitive behavior (RRB) is also a core diagnostic feature of ASD and should be assessed.

The comprehensive developmental assessment approach requires the use of multiple measures including, but not limited to, verbal reports, direct observation, direct interaction and evaluation, and third-party reports (Filipek *et al.*, 1999; Shriver *et al.*, 1999). Although none of these assessment methods alone comprehensively focus on the DSM-5 or IDEA definitions of autism, together they provide reliable and valid procedures for making diagnostic and educational decisions within a developmental framework. Assessment is a continuous process, rather than a series of separate actions, and procedures may overlap and take place in tandem. Professionals and families collaborate and work together as partners to prioritize domains of functioning for assessment and intervention planning. While specific activities of the assessment process will vary and depend on the child's age, history, referral questions, and any previous evaluations and assessments, the following components should be included in a best practice assessment of ASD for school-age children (California Department of Developmental Services, 2002; Campbell *et al.*, 2014; Filipek *et al.*, 1999; Johnson *et al.*, 2007; Klin *et al.*, 2005; National Research Council, 2001; Ozonoff *et al.*, 2007; Payakachat *et al.*, 2012):

- Record review

- Developmental and medical history

- Medical screening and/or evaluation

- Parent/caregiver interview

- Direct child observation

- Parent/teacher ratings of social competence

- Cognitive/intellectual assessment

- Academic assessment

- Communication and language assessment

- Assessment of restricted and repetitive behavior (RRB)

- Adaptive behavior assessment.

BEST PRACTICE

Evidence-based assessment tools must not only demonstrate adequate psychometric properties, but also have relevance and utility to the delivery of services to students with ASD.

Evidence-based assessment requires using instruments with strong reliability and validity for the accurate identification of children's problems and disorders, for ongoing monitoring of children's response to interventions, and for evaluation of the outcomes of intervention (Mash and Hunsley, 2005; Ozonoff *et al.*, 2007). These procedures must also have demonstrated effectiveness in diagnosis, clinical formulation, intervention planning, and outcome assessment (Wilkinson, 2014a). Table 3.1 shows the recommended core measures included in a comprehensive developmental assessment for ASD. Although not exhaustive, these tools provide a reliable and valid assessment of the autistic dyad. Their selection was based on relevance to identification, differential diagnosis and classification, intervention planning, professional experience, or a combination of these in both the research and practice literature. School professionals are advised to select at least one measure from each area and become familiar with its administration, scoring, and properties. An ASD assessment worksheet is provided in Appendix C to help organize and structure the assessment battery. As a minimum qualification, individuals who administer, score, and interpret these instruments should have or be supervised by someone who has formal course work in psychological tests and measurements, understand the basic psychometrics that underlie test use and development, and have supervised experience in administering and interpreting psychological tests. All users of these instruments are expected to be familiar with the most current standards for educational and psychological testing and to adhere to the ethical principles and related standards of their particular profession when using the measures described in this chapter.

TABLE 3.1 MEASURES FOR ASSESSING THE CORE DOMAINS OF ASD

Measure	Format	Age Range	Time
Direct Observation			
ADOS-2	Direct Testing	12 months to adult	40 to 60 min
CARS-2	Observation	2 years to adult	5 to 10 min
Parent/Teacher Report			
ADI-R	Interview	2 years to adult	1.5 to 2.5 hrs
ASRS	Questionnaire	6 to 18 years	5 to 20 min
SCQ	Questionnaire	4 years to adult	10 to 15 min
SRS-2	Questionnaire	4 to 18 years	10 to 15 min
Academic Achievement			
KTEA-3	Direct Testing	4 years to adult	15 to 85 min
WIAT-III	Direct Testing	4 years to adult	45 to 104 min
WJ IV ACH	Direct Testing	2 years to adult	40 to 50 min
Cognitive/Intellectual			
DAS-II	Direct Testing	2.6 to 17 years	45 to 60 min
SB-5	Direct Testing	2 to 85 years	45 to 75 min
WISC-V	Direct Testing	6 to 16 years	48 to 65 min
Social Communication			
CASL	Direct Testing	3 to 21 years	30 to 45 min
CCC-2	Questionnaire	4 to 16 years	10 to 15 min
PLSI	Questionnaire	5 to 12 years	5 to 10 min
SLDT-E	Direct Testing	6 to 12 years	45 min
TOPL-2	Direct Testing	6 to 18 years	45 to 60 min
Restricted and Repetitive Behavior (RRB)			
RBS-R	Questionnaire	6 to 17 years	20 min
RBQ-2	Questionnaire	2 years to Adult	30 min

Adaptive Behavior			
ABAS-3	Questionnaire	Birth to Adult	15 to 20 min
DP-3	Interview	Birth to 12 years	20 to 40 min
VABS-II	Interview	Birth to 18 years	20 to 60 min

Note. ADOS-2 – Autism Disorder Observation Scale; CARS-2 – Childhood Autism Rating Scale; ADI-R – Autism Diagnostic Interview; ASRS – Autism Spectrum Rating Scales; SCQ – Social Communication Questionnaire; SRS-2 – Social Responsiveness Scale; KTEA-3 – Kaufman Test of Educational Achievement; WIAT-III – Wechsler Individual Achievement Test; WJ IV ACH – Woodcock-Johnson Tests of Achievement; DAS-II – Differential Ability Scales; SB-5 – Stanford-Binet Intelligence Scales; WISC-V-Wechsler Intelligence Scale for Children; CASL – Comprehensive Assessment of Spoken Language; CCC-2 – Children's Communication Checklist; PLSI – Pragmatic Language Skills Inventory; SLDT-E – Social Language Development Test-Elementary; TOPL-2 – Test of Pragmatic Language; RBS-R – Repetitive Behavior Scale; RBQ – Repetitive Behavior Questionnaire; ABAS-3 – Adaptive Behavior Assessment System; DP-3 – Developmental Profile; VABS-II – Vineland Adaptive Behavior Scales.

BEST PRACTICE

A comprehensive developmental assessment should include evaluation of multiple domains of functioning across multiple contexts/settings in order to differentiate ASD from other conditions and provide a complete student profile to facilitate intervention planning.

CORE ASSESSMENT DOMAINS

RECORD REVIEW

The first step in the assessment process is to review the child's early developmental history and current concerns with the parents or caregiver. The focus of the record review is to look at past behavior and help determine developmental trends. Sources of information may include previous medical, school, and psychological records. Data from other evaluations or intervention reports (e.g., behavioral, speech/language) are especially valuable sources of information.

For example, the parent and child might have had contact with community resources outside of the school setting (e.g., early intervention programs, agencies, private practitioners), which provides an opportunity for collecting additional background information. A review of records might also help to develop a more concise picture of existing concerns.

BEST PRACTICE

An important step in the core assessment process is to review the student's early developmental and medical history and current concerns with his or her parents. This should include a review of communication, social, and behavioral development.

DEVELOPMENTAL/MEDICAL HISTORY

A comprehensive developmental/medical history, generally in the form of a parent or caregiver interview, is an important foundation component of the assessment process. The parent or caregiver typically serves as the source for obtaining the child's developmental history and information regarding behaviors and milestones. This should include particular attention to the signs and symptoms of ASD including any concerns about regression; development of social, communication, and play skills; and presence of any repetitive behaviors or unusual interests. Inquiry should also be made as to any history of neurodevelopmental disorders such as autism, intellectual and learning disability, and/or psychiatric problems (e.g., depression) in the immediate and extended family. A careful review of medical history should also take into consideration any current or previously prescribed medications, their action and any reported side effects. It is important to understand that while parents have the greatest amount of information about their child, they tend to have the highest degree of adaptation (or scaffolding) to their child's communication and behavioral profile (Volkmar *et al.*, 2014). Likewise, the mild and atypical nature of symptoms of older school-age children with ASD can be complicated by challenges to the long-term memory of a parent, sibling, family member, or other caregiver.

BEST PRACTICE
All students assessed for ASD should receive a medical screening or examination to assist in determining the presence of any associated medical conditions or health risk factors. This includes a vision and hearing screening and referral for a formal evaluation if concerns are present.

MEDICAL SCREENING/EVALUATION
The purpose of a medical screening or examination is to identify co-occurring conditions that may require a thorough assessment and to ascertain whether there is an underlying etiology that explains the ASD symptoms. Accurately identifying co-occurring conditions assists in determining which interventions or treatments are appropriate for the child. Medical conditions associated with ASD include vision and hearing impairments, nutritional deficiencies, feeding/eating disorders, sleep disorders, seizures, and gastrointestinal (GI) conditions (Ryland *et al.*, 2012). Certain known genetic disorders are also associated with autism, including fragile X syndrome and tuberous sclerosis. Hearing and visual acuity should be routinely checked as part of the assessment process. The need for additional medical and/or laboratory tests may become evident, based upon the history and physical examination. In many cases, children under the age of ten may have had significant medical testing. This is particularly true in children with identified with intellectual impairment or learning disability for

which the presence of an ASD is being questioned. Similarly, cases where several years of normal development are followed by a marked developmental regression may suggest the need for further medical referral and evaluation (Volkmar *et al.*, 2014). With older children, the presence of a seizure disorder should also be questioned, particularly in students with lower cognitive functioning or who demonstrate a noticeable regression in their behavior (Minshow *et al.,* 2005).

BEST PRACTICE

The parent or caregiver interview plays an important role in evaluating a child's early developmental history and identifying behaviors associated with ASD.

PARENT/CAREGIVER INTERVIEW

Formal interview instruments play an important role in evaluating a child's developmental history and assessing behaviors associated with ASD (Lord *et al.*, 1997). Parents are experts on their particular child and, therefore, an essential source of information about their child regardless of the child's age (Goldstein *et al.*, 2009). Familiarity with standardized interview measures and appreciation of the complexities of developmental change are essential for assessment and evaluation purposes. At present, the Autism Diagnostic Interview, Revised (ADI-R; Rutter *et al.*, 2003) is the most reliable standardized measure that can be used to obtain an early developmental history of autistic behaviors. The ADI-R is considered the "gold standard" parent interview that identifies symptoms closely linked to the diagnostic criteria for autism described in the DSM-IV-TR (Lord and Corsello, 2005). It is typically administered by a trained clinician using a semistructured interview format. The interview contains 93 items and focuses on behaviors in three content areas or domains: Reciprocal Social Interactions e.g., emotional sharing, offering and seeking comfort, social smiling, and responding to other children); Language and Communication (e.g., stereotyped utterances, pronoun reversal, social usage of language); and Restricted, Repetitive, and Stereotyped Behaviors and Interests (e.g., unusual preoccupations, hand and finger mannerisms, unusual sensory interests). The long version of the ADI-R requires approximately two and a half to three hours for administering and scoring. A shorter version is available which includes only the items on the diagnostic algorithm, takes less time, (approximately 90 minutes), and may be used for clinical assessment. Although the ADI-R is able to identify the likelihood of autism, its validity is highly dependent on the interviewer's training and experience with this disorder. A major disadvantage of the ADI-R in a real-world setting is that it is labor intensive and requires more administration time than most school professionals are able to allocate. It also requires general experience in interviewing and a familiarity with autism in order to be effective.

The Social Communication Questionnaire (SCQ; Rutter *et al.*, 2003) discussed in the previous chapter may be considered as a viable alternative measure when time and training opportunities are limited (Charman and Gotham, 2013; Naglieri and Chambers, 2009). It contains the same questions included on the ADI-R algorithm, presented in a brief yes/no format that parents can complete on their own. The relevant content coverage of the SCQ, while briefer than the ADI-R, parallels the longer interview (Reciprocal Social Interaction, Qualitative Abnormalities in Communication, and Restricted, Repetitive, and Stereotyped Patterns of Behavior), making it appropriate for use with similar populations (Rutter *et al.*, 2003). The Lifetime form assesses the child's developmental history and can be used to support a diagnosis or classification of ASD, while the Current form might be useful in evaluating treatment and educational plans.

BEST PRACTICE

Direct behavioral observation of the student in both structured and natural settings should be included in the assessment process as this improves accuracy in the identification of ASD.

DIRECT OBSERVATION

A child who is being evaluated should be carefully observed in both structured and unstructured situations. Direct observation should take place throughout the assessment and intervention planning process. The specific format can be either formal or informal. Observational measures specifically designed for the assessment of ASD include the Autism Diagnostic Observation Schedule, Second Edition (ADOS-2; Lord *et al.*, 2012). The ADOS-2 is a revision of the original ADOS (Lord *et al.*, 1999) and like its predecessor is a semi-structured, standardized observational method used for assessing communication, reciprocal social interaction, play and the presence of restricted or repetitive behaviors or interests in individuals who have been referred because of a possible ASD. One of five different modules (Modules 1,2,3,4 or the Toddler Module) is chosen based upon the child's expressive language level and chronological age. Each module takes approximately 40-60 minutes to administer. The examiner creates a standardized social context and observes behaviors directly related to a diagnosis of ASD, including the quality of the child's engagement with the examiner, their patterns of communication, appropriateness of play, as well as the presence of stereotypic, repetitive, or atypical behaviors and interests. In Modules 1 to 4, behaviors are coded, interpreted and then compiled on algorithms that yield one of three classifications: Autism, Autism Spectrum, and Non-Spectrum. The Total ADOS-2 score is comprised of scores from two separate domains: Social Affect (SA), including communication and social interaction, and Restricted and Repetitive Behaviors (RRB). In the Toddler Module, algorithms yield "ranges of concern" rather than classification scores.

A new Comparison Score or severity metric for Modules 1 through 3 allows the examiner to compare a child's overall level of autism spectrum-related symptoms to that of children diagnosed with ASD who are the same age and have similar expressive language skills. Although the ADOS-2 affords an opportunity to directly observe behavior associated with ASD and is often referred to as the "gold standard" for assessing and diagnosing autism across ages, developmental levels, and language skills, it should always be used together with developmental history, parent/caregiver and teacher reports, other standardized testing, and naturalistic observation. Research has found that by combining the results of the "gold standard" ADOS-2 and ADI-R measures, 93 percent of more capable individuals with ASD research diagnoses met DSM-5 criteria (Mazefsky *et al.*, 2013). This highlights the importance of incorporating multiple evidence-based measures in the assessment process.

As with the ADI-R, the ADOS-2 is a sophisticated instrument that requires specialized training, background and experience in the assessment and treatment of autism, and practice to be utilized effectively. The ADOS-2 should be administered by an experienced professional with appropriate training who can use both quantitative and qualitative information to form a clinical impression from the standard activities. The perceived advantages and disadvantages of the ADOS have been examined via a national survey of practicing school and clinical psychologists (Akshoomoff, Corsello, and Schmidt, 2006). Advantages of the ADOS included its strength in capturing ASD-specific behaviors and the standardized structure provided for observation, while diagnostic discrimination and required resources were the most commonly identified disadvantages. Of those that indicated resources as a disadvantage, nearly all indicated time of administration as a disadvantage.

The Childhood Autism Rating Scale (CARS; Schopler, Reichler, and Renner, 1988) is one of the most widely used and empirically validated autism assessments. The second edition of the CARS

(CARS-2; Schopler *et al.*, 2010) is a practitioner-completed behavior rating used to identify and distinguish children with ASD from those with other developmental disorders, as well as to determine symptom severity. The CARS-2 consists of two 15-item rating scales based on the frequency of the behavior, intensity, atypicality, and duration of the behavior in question and a parent questionnaire. The Standard Version Rating Booklet (CARS-2-ST) is equivalent to the original CARS and is used with children younger than 6 years of age and those with communication difficulties or below-average cognitive ability. The High-Functioning Version Rating Booklet (CARS-2-HF) is an alternative for assessing verbally fluent children and youth, 6 years of age and older, with average or above-average intellectual ability which makes it more responsive to those with more subtle social impairments and behavioral problems. The Questionnaire for Parents or Caregivers (CARS-2-QPC) is an unscored questionnaire designed to assist in gathering parent/caregiver information about behaviors related to autism. Information from the QPC can be integrated with other evaluation data when making final CARS-2 ratings. To complete the ratings on the CARS-2 scales, the school-based professional must have convergent information from multiple sources such as direct observation, parent and teacher interviews, prior assessments of cognitive functioning and adaptive behavior, and information from the QPC (Schopler *et al.*, 2010). Parents and teachers should not be asked to complete the CARS-2-ST/HF forms. Only well-informed professionals should complete the ratings. The psychometric properties of the CARS-2 indicate a high degree of internal consistency and good inter-rater reliability. Preliminary research findings suggest that a high proportion of individuals who meet the clinical cut-off for autism on both the CARS-2-ST and CARS-2-HF meet the criteria for autism based on both the DSM-IV-TR and DSM-5 (Dawkins, Meyer, and Van Bourgondien, 2014). The ratings from the CARS-2 should be considered as only one part of a multimodal, multidisciplinary decision-making process in the identification of children with ASD.

Techniques to supplement these instruments may be used to obtain additional information regarding the core domains. Informal measures such as the ASD Observation Checklist shown in Appendix D can be used as part of the assessment process when observing, interviewing the parent/teacher, and/or directly interacting with the student. It provides a framework for observing and recording behaviors in each of the core developmental areas. When using informal observation measures, it is very important to have an understanding of the way children respond at various ages and developmental levels, both children with ASD and their typical peers.

BEST PRACTICE
Parent and teacher ratings are one of the most important sources of information about deficits in the core ASD domain of social communication and social interaction across home and school contexts.

PARENT/TEACHERS RATINGS
Questionnaires specially designed to measure ASD-related behaviors, reported by parents and teachers, provide the professional with a method of assessing symptom presentation and severity. Because social impairment is a defining core feature of ASD, the determination of social functioning is fundamental to the assessment and evaluation of the student. It is important to recognize, however, that children with ASD vary widely in their social comprehension and interaction. Social impairments are also common in many other childhood disorders and therefore, must be compared with the pervasive impairment found in ASD. The best practice assessment of social functioning requires data collection from multiple sources. Data can be collected

through observation during assessment (e.g., formal testing, interviews, play observations) and via direct observation of the child in naturalistic settings such as school or home. Questionnaires completed by parents and teachers are one of the most vital sources of information about the child's social responsiveness and social-communication skills. For example, the Autism Spectrum Rating Scales (ASRS; Goldstein and Naglieri, 2010) and the Social Responsiveness Scale (SRS-2; Constantino and Gruber, 2012) described in the previous chapter are well researched and validated instruments that are user-friendly and efficient. There is strong evidence that both the ASRS and SRS-2 can accurately distinguish ASD from general population groups as rated by teachers and parents. The ASRS full length form samples a wide range of behaviors associated with ASD and when used in combination with other assessment information can help inform diagnostic and classification decisions, guide treatment and intervention planning, and monitor effectiveness of a specific treatment or intervention (Goldstein and Naglieri, 2010). It is recommended for use when a thorough evaluation of behavior associated with ASD is needed. Likewise, the SRS-2 has shown utility as a measure of social responsiveness across home and school contexts and may be incorporated into the core assessment battery as well. A significant strength of the SRS-2 is its facility in quantitatively measuring autistic traits and symptoms across the complete range of severity (mild to severe). This is especially important when identifying the more subtle characteristics of autism and more capable children and youth with ASD (i.e., without intellectual disability). The SRS-2 forms are also useful for quantifying response to intervention/treatment over time. Both the ASRS and SRS-2 should be used within the context of a comprehensive evaluation, including developmental history and assessment of intellectual, language, and adaptive behavior functioning.

Practitioners considering other popular third party rating scales such as the Gilliam Autism Rating Scale, Second Edition (GARS-2; Gilliam, 2006), should exercise caution due to its significant weaknesses, including poor sensitivity (i.e., underidentification of children with ASD) and questionable test structure (Campbell *et al.*, 2014; Norris and Lecavalier, 2010; Pandolfi, Magyar, and Dill, 2010; Volker *et al.*, 2016). The GARS-2 is not recommended for inclusion in a core assessment battery and should not be used for classification or eligibility determination. Although a third edition (GARS-3; Gilliam, 2014) has been published, no critical, peer-reviewed studies of its technical adequacy were found at the time of writing. Of course, no single rating scale or assessment tool should be used to identify a student with ASD as they provide only one piece of convergent information needed to complete a comprehensive developmental assessment.

BEST PRACTICE
Formal assessment should include standardized evaluation tools with established reliability and validity to determine present levels of performance and identify priority educational needs.

DIRECT TESTING ISSUES
The direct assessment of cognitive/intellectual ability, language skills, and academic achievement of children with ASD can present a challenge for practitioners due to social difficulties, language issues, frequent off-task behavior, high distractibility, sensory problems, and variable level of motivation (Ozonoff *et al.*, 2007). Several principles should be applied during the testing process. First, the evaluation should incorporate the appropriate reinforcement procedures. For example, typical reinforcement strategies (e.g., praise) may not be effective with children with ASD who are often less motivated by social reinforcement to complete testing activities. Tangible reinforcement such as access to a preferred activity or toy may be more effective and reinforcing than social praise. Second, many children with ASD have both attention and sensory processing issues, and will require

a testing area that is quiet and free from distractions. More frequent breaks may be also required, and there may be a need for multiple, shorter testing sessions. Third, practitioners should be aware of the child or adolescent's language and social-communication competency, and consider using both verbal and nonverbal tasks throughout the assessment process (Campbell *et al.*, 2014). Lastly, the psychometric characteristics described in the previous chapter should be considered when selecting a test or instrument.

BEST PRACTICE
The measurement of cognitive ability is critical for making a determination of ASD and for intervention planning purposes. Evaluation of cognitive functioning in both verbal and nonverbal domains is necessary to develop a profile of strengths and weaknesses.

COGNITIVE/INTELLECTUAL FUNCTIONING

A critical domain of the core assessment is intellectual or cognitive functioning. Establishing the level of cognitive ability is important for both classification and intervention planning purposes. For example, the level of intellectual functioning is associated with the severity of autistic symptoms, skill acquisition and learning ability, and level of adaptive functioning, and is one of the best predictors of long-term outcome (Harris and Handleman, 2000; Howlin, 2005; Stevens *et al.*, 2000). Because the IQs of children with ASD have the same properties as those obtained by other children age 5 years and older, they are reasonable predictors of future educational performance (Klinger, O'Kelley, and Mussey, 2009; Sattler and Hoge, 2006). Thus, an appropriate measure of IQ is considered to be an essential component of the core assessment battery.

BEST PRACTICE
Although intelligence test profiles can be helpful in understanding cognitive strengths and weaknesses, they should never be used to determine or confirm the presence of ASD.

The primary goal of conducting an intellectual evaluation includes establishing a profile of the child's cognitive strengths and weaknesses in order to facilitate educational planning and to help determine the presence of any cognitive limitations that might warrant eligibility for other special educational programming. Many individuals with ASD have an intellectual impairment or below average cognitive functioning. Prevalence data from the CDC (2014) found that 31 percent of children with ASD were classified as having IQ scores in the intellectual disability range (IQ ≤70), 23 percent in the borderline range (IQ = 71–85), and 46 percent in the average or above average range (IQ >85). Assessment of cognitive strengths and weaknesses is particularly important because of the characteristically uneven profile of skills demonstrated by children with ASD. Even those with average or above average cognitive ability demonstrate a variable pattern of abilities. For example, the gap between intellectual and adaptive skills is often large and significant (American Psychiatric Association, 2013). Practitioners should also be aware of validity issues when testing younger children, lower-functioning, and nonverbal children. It is important that the individual test chosen (a) be appropriate for both the chronological and the mental age of the child; (b) provides a full range of standard scores; and (c) measures both verbal and nonverbal skills (Filipek *et al.*, 1999). Of course, the use of any single score to describe the intellectual abilities of a child with ASD is clearly inappropriate. Although research suggests that discrepant cognitive abilities tend to be more common in children on the autism spectrum, this finding is not universal for children with ASD. It also needs to be emphasized that there are no specific cognitive profiles that can reliably differentiate children with ASD from children with other disorders (Klinger *et al.*, 2009; Sattler and Hoge, 2006; Volkmar *et al.*, 2014). While intelligence test profiles can be helpful in understanding the cognitive strengths and weaknesses of a child with autism, they should never be used to confirm or determine a diagnosis or eligibility for ASD (Campbell *et al.*, 2014; Klinger *et al.*, 2009; Ozonoff *et al.*, 2007; Ryland *et al.*, 2014). A comprehensive developmental assessment should be completed before reaching a clinical or educational conclusion about a given child. In addition, the cognitive measures described in this section are not appropriate for children who have little or no useful speech or whose structural language is severely impaired. Nonverbal instruments should be used with children who have severely limited vocabulary and language skills (e.g., ability to communicate with only single words). For example, the Leiter International Performance Scale-Third Edition (Leiter-3; Roid *et al.*, 2013) may be appropriate with this group of children as it evaluates nonverbal cognitive, attentional and neuropsychological abilities of typical as well as atypical children and youth.

Although there is no single best cognitive measure for children with ASD, the Wechsler Intelligence Scales are often considered the "gold standard" in the evaluation of intellectual functioning across age groups. The Wechsler Intelligence Scale for Children-Fifth Edition (WISC-V; Wechsler, 2014) is the latest version of the most frequently used intelligence measure for school-age children and youth. The WISC-V takes 48–65 minutes to administer and generates a Full Scale IQ (formerly known as an intelligence quotient or IQ score) which represents a child's general intellectual ability. It also provides five primary index scores: Verbal Comprehension Index (VCI), Visual Spatial Index (VSI), Fluid Reasoning Index (FRI), Working Memory Index (WMI), and Processing Speed Index (PSI) that represent a child's abilities in more discrete cognitive domains. The WISC-V overlaps in age with the Wechsler Preschool and Primary Scale of Intelligence-Fourth Edition (WPPSI-IV; Wechsler, 2012) (age 6 years) and the Wechsler Adult Intelligence Scale-Fourth Edition (WAIS-IV;

Wechsler, 2008) (age 16 years) to allow practitioners the opportunity to select the more appropriate instrument depending on the referral question and child characteristics.

The Stanford-Binet Intelligence Scales-Fifth Edition (SB-5; Roid, 2003) is a well known and popular instrument for measuring intelligence in individuals from 2 to 85 years of age. The SB-5 contains separate sections for Verbal IQ (based on five verbal subtests) and Nonverbal IQ (based on five nonverbal subtests). The Full Scale IQ provides a global summary of the current general level of intellectual functioning and is composed of both the Nonverbal IQ (general ability to reason, solve problems, visualize, and recall information presented in pictorial, figural, and symbolic form) and the Verbal IQ (ability to reason, solve problems, visualize, and recall important information presented in words and sentences either printed or spoken). Factor scores can be calculated for Fluid Reasoning, Knowledge, Quantitative Reasoning, Visual-Spatial Processing, and Working Memory, which are useful for identifying strengths and weaknesses in children with ASD.

The Differential Abilities Scales (DAS-II; Elliott, 2007) is also an option for evaluating the cognitive ability in children with ASD. The DAS-II assesses both intellectual and academic skills and can be administered to children across a wide chronological and mental age range (2.5 through 17 years), making it appropriate for repeat administrations and to monitor progress. Especially helpful for the ASD population is the option of out-of-range testing (e.g., administration of tests usually given to children of a different age). Norms for school-age children are available for the preschool battery, permitting use of the test with older children with significant intellectual limitations. The DAS-II also provides a Special Nonverbal Composite (SNC) score which summarizes the nonverbal domains and is particularly useful when testing children with ASD who are verbal but may have a mild to moderate language impairment.

Other cognitive measures that can be used with children with ASD include the Woodcock-Johnson IV Tests of Cognitive Abilities (WJ IV Cog: Schrank, McGrew, Mather, and Woodcock, 2014), the

Kaufman Assessment Battery for Children, Second Edition (KABC-2: Kaufman and Kaufman, 2004a), the Reynolds Intellectual Assessment Scale, Second Edition (RIAS-2: Reynolds and Kamphaus, 2015a), and the Cognitive Assessment System, Second Edition (CAS2: Naglieri, Das, and Goldstein 2014).

Many school-age children are already placed in special education programs and may have had a recent psychoeducational evaluation. When records of standardized testing indicate stable cognitive abilities over time or when a more extensive battery is not needed, instruments such as the Kaufman Brief Intelligence Test, Second Edition (K-BIT-2; Kaufman and Kaufman, 2004b), the Reynolds Intellectual Screening Test, Second Edition (RIST-2; Reynolds and Kampaus, 2015b), and the Wechsler Abbreviated Scales of Intelligence, Second Edition (WASI-II; Wechsler, 2011) may provide sufficient data for assessment purposes. They may also be utilized to determine whether an in-depth intellectual assessment is needed or to reassess after a comprehensive evaluation has been completed.

BEST PRACTICE
Assessment of academic achievement is important for the purposes of educational decision making and intervention planning. Areas of strength and weakness can often go unrecognized.

ACADEMIC ACHIEVEMENT
Specific learning disorder (disability) commonly co-occurs with ASD (American Psychiatric Association, 2013). Thus, an assessment of academic achievement is necessary for the purposes of educational decision making and planning. An evaluation of academic functioning will often reveal a profile of strengths and weaknesses. For example, it is not unusual for students with ASD to have precocious reading skills (sometimes called hyperlexia) and ability to decode words at a

higher level than others of the same age and functional ability while at the same time having poor comprehension and difficulties with abstract language. For other students, calculation skills may be well developed, whereas mathematical concepts are delayed.

For school-age children, the most frequently used general achievement tests include the Woodcock-Johnson IV Tests of Achievement (WJ IV ACH; Schrank, Mather, and McGrew, 2014), Wechsler Individual Achievement Test, Third Edition (WIAT-III; Wechsler, 2009), and Kaufman Test of Educational Achievement, Third Edition (KTEA-3; Kaufman and Kaufman, 2014). The WJ IV ACH is a comprehensive achievement battery comprised of 20 tests designed to measure four broad academic domains: reading, written language, mathematics, and academic knowledge. Eleven of the most frequently used achievement tests are included in the Standard Battery, which has three parallel forms. There is a single form of the Extended Battery containing nine additional measures which allows for a more in-depth diagnostic assessment of specific strengths and weaknesses. The selective testing feature of the WJ IV ACH offers examiners the option to only administer the specific tests relevant to any referral questions. The WIAT-III includes 16 subtests that combine to form seven composites: Oral Language, Total Reading, Basic Reading, Reading Comprehension and Fluency, Written Expression, Mathematics, Math Fluency, and a Total Achievement Score. The evaluator can choose to administer individual subtests, a selection of subtests, or all subtests, depending on the grade level or the presenting difficulties of the student. The KTEA-3 is also an individually administered general achievement battery that provides an analysis of a student's academic strengths and weaknesses in reading, mathematics, written language, and oral language, and allows the examiner to administer a single subtest or any combination of subtests to assess achievement in one or more domains.

BEST PRACTICE

A thorough speech-language-communication evaluation should be conducted for all students referred for a comprehensive assessment. Because social communication deficits are among the core features of ASD, particular attention should be given to the pragmatic functions of language.

SOCIAL COMMUNICATION AND LANGUAGE

The assessment of communication skills is critical component of a comprehensive ASD assessment. The level of expressive language, together with IQ, is a good predictor of long-term outcome, so it is an especially important domain to measure in terms of intervention planning (Paul, 2005; Stone and Yoder, 2001; Twachtman-Cullen, 1998). A variety of traditional instruments, such as the Peabody Picture Vocabulary Test, Fourth Edition (PPVT-4; Dunn and Dunn, 2007), Expressive One-Word Picture Vocabulary Test, Fourth Edition (EOWPVT-4; Martin and Brownell, 2010), Test for Auditory Comprehension of Language, Fourth Edition (TACL-4; Carrow-Woolfolk, 2014), and Clinical Evaluation of Language Fundamentals, Fifth Edition (CELF-5; Wiig, Semel, and Secord, 2013) can be used to measure the receptive and expressive language skills of school-age children with ASD. Although these standardized measures provide important information about specific parameters of speech and language, they provide only limited information about pragmatic (social) language skills which are typically difficult to identify in more capable children with ASD. Pragmatics is broadly defined as the ability to understand and use language in social-communicative contexts. This includes: (a) using language for different purposes; (b) changing language according to the needs of a listener or situation; (c) understanding non-literal language; and (d) following rules for conversations (Paul and Wilson, 2009; Wilkinson, 2011). Because social communication deficits are among the core challenges of

ASD, a best practice assessment should include an evaluation of pragmatic competence and not be limited to the formal, structural aspects of language (i.e., articulation and receptive/expressive language functioning). Particular attention should be given to the social communicative functions of language (e.g., turn-taking, understanding of inferences and figurative expressions) as well as to the nonverbal skills needed to communicate and regulate interaction (e.g., eye contact, gesture, facial expression, and body language). A variety of assessment strategies should be used, including direct assessment, naturalistic observation and interviewing significant others, including parents and educators, who are valuable sources of information (Paul, 2005; Paul and Wilson, 2009; Twachtman-Cullen and Twachtman-Bassett, 2014).

Assessments to identify pragmatic language deficits tend to be less well developed than tests of language fundamentals. There are fewer standard measures available to assess these skills in children with ASD. Valid norms for pragmatic development and objective criteria for pragmatic performance are also limited (Reichow *et al.*, 2008; Young *et al.*, 2005). Among the standardized instruments that focus on the social communicative functions of language are the Comprehensive Assessment of Spoken Language (CASL; Carrow-Woolfolk, 1999), Test of Pragmatic Language, Second Edition (TOPL-2; Phelps-Terasaki and Phelps-Gunn, 2007), Social Language Development Test-Elementary (SLDT-E; Bowers, Huisingh, and LoGiudice, 2008), Children's Communication Checklist, Second Edition (CCC-2; Bishop, 2006) and Pragmatic Language Skills Inventory (PLSI; Gilliam and Miller, 2006).

The CASL is an individually and orally administered language assessment battery for individuals ages 3 through 21. It contains fifteen stand-alone subtests tests that can be administered and scored individually or given together to obtain a global language composite score. Research suggests that the Pragmatic Judgment and Inferences subtests of the CASL can be used to document difficulties in the social use of language in children and adolescents with ASD (Reichow *et al.*, 2008). The TOPL-2 is a standardized, norm-referenced test designed to effectively assess pragmatic language ability in students 8 to 18 years and provides an in-depth, comprehensive analysis of social communication in context. It evaluates students' social communication skills, telling how well they listen, choose appropriate content, express feelings, make requests, and handle other aspects of pragmatic language. The TOPL has been found to be helpful in documenting pragmatic language deficits in children with ASD relative to typical peers (Young *et al.*, 2005). The SLDT-E is also useful in identifying 6- to 12-year-old children with pragmatic language deficits who are in need of intervention and language therapy. The test is designed to assesses the language required to appropriately infer and express what another person is thinking or feeling within a social context, to make multiple interpretations, take mutual perspectives, and negotiate with and support their peers. Statistical data and reports suggest that the test differentiates students with language disorders or ASD from typically developing students (Bowers, *et al.*, 2008; Twachtman-Cullen and Twachtman-Bassett, 2014). An adolescent version of the SLDT is also available for students age 12 to 17 years (SLDT-A; Bowers, Huisingh, and LoGiudice, 2010).

In addition to direct testing, questionnaires or ratings of pragmatic behavior by someone who knows the child well can be used to assess social language skills in children with ASD. The CCC-2 is a standardized measure designed to assess communication skills in the areas of pragmatics, syntax, morphology, semantics, and speech of children ages 4 to 16. A Caregiver Response Form is completed by an adult who has regular contact with the child, usually a parent, teacher, therapist, or other professional. The CCC-2 identifies children with pragmatic language impairment by comparing performance in different language domains (e.g., pragmatics vs. syntax and morphology). It has been found to demonstrate a high level of sensitivity in identifying pragmatic language impairment in higher-functioning individuals with ASD who have structural language and nonverbal cognitive scores within typical limits (Volden and Phillips, 2010).

The PLSI is also a norm-referenced rating scale designed to assess children's pragmatic language abilities by obtaining judgments from parents or other adults who have regular contact with the child. It has 45 items and can be completed by an adult (e.g., parent, teacher, teacher assistant) who knows the child well and is familiar with that child's language skills. The PLSI has three subscales: (a) Personal Interaction Skills; (b) Social Interaction Skills; and (c) Classroom Interaction Skills and produces a Pragmatic Language Index (PLI) score. The test demonstrates high levels of internal consistency, excellent inter-rater agreement, good test-retest reliability, and correlates highly with Test of Pragmatic Language (TOPL). Because the CCC-2 and PLSI are third party checklists, they have the advantage of sampling a broad range of pragmatic skills in the child's natural environment which formal standardized pragmatic test instruments often fail to measure. Consistent with best practice guidelines, the scores from instruments described in this section should not be used in isolation to make decisions regarding classification and intervention planning. Results from other measures, direct observations, and parent interviews are necessary for effectively identifying impairment in social (pragmatic) language skills (Paul and Wilson, 2009; Twachtman-Cullen and Twachtman-Bassett, 2014).

BEST PRACTICE
Restricted and repetitive behavior (RRB) is a core feature of ASD. Professionals should give increased attention to the assessment and presence of these behaviors, and their impact on student functioning.

RESTRICTED AND REPETITIVE BEHAVIOR (RRB)

The DSM-5 criteria for ASD include restricted and repetitive behavior (RRB) as a core diagnostic feature, together with the domain of social communication and social interaction deficits. Similarly, the IDEA definition of autism makes reference to engagement in repetitive activities and stereotyped movements, and resistance to environmental change. RRBs include: (a) stereotyped or repetitive speech, motor movements, or use of objects; (b) excessive adherence to routines, ritualized patterns of verbal or nonverbal behavior, or excessive resistance to change; (c) highly restricted, fixated interests that are abnormal in intensity or focus; and (d) hyper- or hypo-reactivity to sensory input or unusual interest in sensory aspects of the environment (American Psychiatric Association, 2013). Factor analytic studies of RRBs have identified two sub-groups; one comprising repetitive sensory and motor behaviors (RSMB), such as repetitive hand or finger movements and rocking, and the other consisting of behaviors such as narrow interests, rigid routines, and rituals routines, which are collectively referred to as insistence on sameness (IS) (Bishop *et al.*, 2013; Bishop, Richler, and Lord, 2006; Richler *et al.*, 2010).

Research indicates that repetitive behaviors may be among the earliest-emerging signs of autism (Wolff *et al.*, 2014). There is also evidence to suggest that different types of RRB may be predictive of co-occurring psychiatric disorders. For example, children with ASD who demonstrate high levels of ritualistic and sameness behavior have been found to show more severe symptoms of anxiety and depression (Stratis and Lecavalier, 2013). Parents of individuals with ASD also report that RRBs are one of the most challenging features of ASD due to their significant interference with daily life. They can significantly impede learning and socialization by decreasing the likelihood of positive interactions with peers and adults. Given the importance of RRBs as a core feature of ASD, clinicians and practitioners should give increased attention to the assessment and presence of these behaviors, and their impact on the adaptability and psychological well-being of children and youth with ASD (Stratis and Lecavalier, 2013).

Interviews and questionnaires are the most frequently used methods of measuring RRBs. For example, the previously described ADI-R can be used to identify the restrictive behaviors such as compulsions/verbal rituals, unusual preoccupations, circumscribed interests, resistance to minor changes in the environment, unusual attachment to objects, and stereotyped body movements. The Social Communication Questionnaire (SCQ) parallels the ADI-R RRB domain and includes items related to specific types of repetitive behaviors. Additionally, the ASRS and SRS-2 incorporate scales and treatment clusters assessing stereotypical behaviors, sensory sensitivity, and highly restricted interests characteristic of ASD. Direct observation measures also provide an opportunity to assess RRBs. For example, the ADOS-2 algorithm includes both Social Affect (SA) and Restrictive and Repetitive Behaviors (RRB) domains. Similarly, the CARS-2 includes observational ratings for items in the categories of Adaptation to Change/Restricted Interests and Taste, Smell, and Touch Response and Use.

Several specialized parent/caregiver questionnaires have been designed that focus solely on restricted and repetitive behaviors and provide a more complete understanding of the impact of RRB factors on adaptive functioning. Of these questionnaires, the most commonly used are the Repetitive Behavior Scale-Revised (RBS-R; Bodfish *et al.*, 2000) and the Repetitive Behavior Questionnaire-2 (RBQ-2; Leekam *et al.*, 2007). Both cover a wide range of repetitive behaviors and were designed as a quantitative index of RRB, rather than relying exclusively on broad-based ASD measures to assess RRBs. The RBS-R is a parent report of repetitive behaviors in children, adolescents, and adults with ASD. It consists of 43 items and includes the following subscales: Stereotyped Behavior, Self-Injurious Behavior, Compulsive Behavior, Ritualistic Behavior, Sameness Behavior, and Restricted Behavior. For each subscale, the number of items endorsed is computed as well as the severity score for the subscale. On the last question, respondents are asked to consider all of the behaviors described in the questionnaire, and provide a global severity rating. The RBS-R has been reported to have adequate psychometric properties, and acceptable reliability and validity for each subscale (Bodfish *et al.*, 2000; Boyd *et al.*, 2010; Esbensen *et al.*, 2009; Gabriels *et al.*, 2005; Lam and Aman, 2007).

The Repetitive Behavior Questionnaire-2 (RBQ-2; Leekam *et al.*, 2007) is also parent-completed 20-item questionnaire suitable for children (with or without autism) of all ages. It includes items directly derived from a standardized clinical interview tool, the Diagnostic Interview for Social and Communication Disorders (DISCO; Wing *et al.*, 2002). Item responses fall into four groups which correspond to four specific areas: Repetitive Motor Movements, Rigidity/Adherence to Routine, Preoccupation with Restricted Interests, and Unusual Sensory Interests. Questionnaire scores can be added to provide a Total Repetitive Behaviors Score. As with previous research on RRBs, two clusters can be identified: RSMB, which corresponds to repetitive motor movements and unusual sensory interests, and IS, which corresponds to adherence to routine and restricted interests. The reliability and validity of the RBQ-2 has been supported in children and adolescents (Lidstone *et al.*, 2014).

BEST PRACTICE
Adaptive functioning should be assessed for all students, as this domain is pivotal in the identification of ASD. Discrepancies between cognitive ability and adaptive behavior can help identify objectives and strategies for intervention and treatment.

ADAPTIVE BEHAVIOR

Assessment of adaptive behavior functioning is considered one of the most critical components of a comprehensive evaluation for children with ASD as it captures information on the child's functional adjustment in everyday situations and improves classification accuracy (Caterino, 2014; Klin *et al.*, 2005; Tomanik *et al.*, 2007). Many children with ASD, while scoring in the average and above range on IQ tests, are functionally impaired because they are unable to translate their cognitive abilities into efficient adaptive behavior. Research has found both childhood and adolescent adaptive behavior to be strong, independent predictors of a wide variety of adult outcomes (e.g., employment, life satisfaction) beyond that of either symptom severity or intellectual/language functioning (Klinger *et al.*, 2015). Because adaptive behavior skills are highly linked to success in adulthood for children and youth with ASD, a formal adaptive behavior measure should be routinely included in a comprehensive ASD assessment protocol. Likewise, an assessment of adaptive behavior should always accompany intellectual testing, because identification of co-occurring intellectual disability cannot be made unless adaptive functioning (i.e., social interaction and communication) is below that expected for general developmental level.

The most widely used adaptive measure with children suspected of ASD is the Vineland Adaptive Behavior Scales-II (VABS-II; Sparrow, Balla, and Cicchetti, 2005). The VABS-II is organized within a three domain structure: Communication, Daily Living, and Socialization. An Adaptive Behavior Composite score summarizes functioning in these domain areas. A Motor Skills Domain (< 6 years) and an optional Maladaptive Behavior Index which elicits internalizing, externalizing and other behavioral problems that may interfere with an individual's adaptive behavior are also available. The VABS-II can be administered by either a semi-structured interview or by parent/caregiver and teacher rating forms. It includes supplementary normative data for individuals with autism and demonstrates good psychometric properties, including internal consistency, inter-rater reliability and content validity (Carter *et al.*, 1998; Sparrow *et al.*, 2005). Practitioners may also find the VABS-II useful for progress monitoring and to assess the effects of various treatments or interventions on levels of adaptive functioning.

The Developmental Profile-Third Edition (DP-3; Alpern, Boll, and Shearer, 2007) can be used as an efficient measure of development and adaptive behavior in several critical domains. Designed to evaluate children from birth through age 12 years, 11 months, the DP-3 provides a General Development score, as well as scale scores in the following domains: (a) Physical; (b) Adaptive Behavior; (c) Social-Emotional; (d) Cognitive; and (e) Communication. While a parent interview is the preferred method of administration, the DP-3 provides an alternative Parent/Caregiver Checklist that can be completed by the child's parent or other caregiver who is knowledgeable about the child's functioning.

The Adaptive Behavior Assessment System-Third Edition (ABAS-3; Harrison and Oakland, 2015) may also be an appropriate option when time is a constraint, as it can be administered via questionnaire-checklist procedures, rather than an interview, in approximately 15 to 20 minutes. The ABAS-3 assesses 11 essential skills areas in three major adaptive domains (Conceptual, Social, and Practical) and produces a General Adaptive Composite (GAC). The measure includes five rating forms designed to be completed by parents, family members, teachers, daycare staff, supervisors, counselors, or others who are familiar with the daily activities of the individual being evaluated. The ABAS-3 can be used to assist in disability classification, identify an individual's strengths and limitations, and to document and monitor the individual's performance over time. It is also compatible with DSM-5 and IDEA.

BEST PRACTICE
Depending on the referral question(s), goals of assessment, and family/teacher priorities, a comprehensive developmental assessment may include other domains that affect adaptive functioning.

ADDITIONAL DOMAINS OF ASSESSMENT

Children and youth on the autism spectrum frequently demonstrate additional challenges beyond those associated with the core domains of ASD. These accompanying problems may interfere with school performance and adversely affect adaptability. Thus, other areas of concern should be included in the assessment battery depending on the presenting problem, history, and core evaluation results. These may include:

- Sensory processing

- Executive function, memory, and attention

- Motor skills

- Behavioral/emotional problems

- Family system.

A list of assessment tools for additional domains is displayed in Table 3.2.

TABLE 3.2 ASSESSMENT MEASURES
FOR ADDITIONAL DOMAINS

Measure	Format	Age Range	Time
Behavioral/Emotional Problems			
ASEBA	Rating Scale	6 to 18 years	10 to 20 min
BASC-3	Rating Scale	2 to 21 years	10 to 20 min
CDI-2	Self-Report	7 to 17 years	15 to 20 min
RCMAS-2	Self-Report	6 to 19 years	10 to 15 min
Executive Function, Memory, and Attention			
BRIEF-2	Questionnaire	5 to 18 years	5 to 10 min
Conners 3	Rating Scale	6 to 18 years	10 to 20 min
D-KEFS	Direct Resting	8 to 89 years	90 min
WRAML-2	Direct Testing	5 to 90 years	<60 min
NEPSY-II	Direct Testing	3 to 16 years	60 min
Family System			
PSI-4	Questionnaire	1 month to 12 years	10 to 20 min
Motor Skills			
Beery VMI	Direct Testing	2 years to adult	10 to 15 min
BOT-2	Direct Testing	4 to 21 years	45 to 60 min
Sensory Processing			
SPM	Questionnaire	5 to 12 years	15-20 min
SP-2	Questionnaire	3 to 14 years	5-20 min

Note. ASEBA – Achenbach System of Empirically Based Assessment; BASC-3 – Behavior Assessment System for Children; CDI-2 – Children's Depression Inventory; RCMAS-2 – Revised Children's Manifest Anxiety Scale; BRIEF2 – Behavior Rating Inventory of Executive Function; Conners-3 – Conners Third Edition; NEPSI-II – Developmental Neuropsychological Assessment; PSI4 – Parenting Stress Index; D-KEFS – Delis-Kaplan Executive Function System; Beery VMI – Developmental Test of Visual Motor Integration; BOT-2-Bruininks – Oseretsky Test of Motor Proficiency; SMP – Sensory Processing Measure; SP-2 – Sensory Profile.

BEST PRACTICE
Sensory challenges can have an adverse effect on the student's functioning and ability to benefit from intervention and may be a focus of attention.

SENSORY PROCESSING

Atypical or unusual sensory responses are relatively common in children with ASD. Although they are not universal or exclusive to this neurodevelopmental disorder, a large percentage of children with ASD (78 to 90%) have sensory processing problems (Baranek, 2002; Crane, Goddard, and Pring, 2009; O'Neill and Jones, 1997). Sensory issues are now included in the DSM-5 symptom criteria for restricted, repetitive patterns of behavior, interests, or activities (RRB), and include hyper-or hypo-reactivity to sensory input or unusual interest in sensory aspects of the environment, such as apparent indifference to pain/heat/cold, adverse response to specific sounds or textures, excessive smelling or touching of objects (American Psychiatric Association, 2013). When present, these problems can interfere with adaptability in many areas of life (communication, daily living, socialization, occupational). For example, sensory processing problems have been found to be associated with eating problems and physical aggression in children with ASD (Mazurek, Kanne, and Wodka, 2013; Nadon et al., 2011). Because they are often overlooked in many ASD assessment procedures, attention to sensory problems should be an important component of an evaluation when they appear to be a prominent and concerning feature of the individual's behavioral profile (Dunn, 2001; Harrison and Hare, 2004).

Although broad-based ASD measures include sensory issues, questionnaires are available that focus solely on the sensory processing domain. For example, the Sensory Profile, Second Edition (SP-2; Dunn, 2014) and the Sensory Processing Measure (SPM; Parham et al., 2007) are both parent/caregiver questionnaires that can be used to assess sensory processing and behaviors across various childhood environments. The SP-2 is a widely administered family of questionnaires which measure children's responses to certain sensory processing, modulation, and behavioral/emotional events in the context of home, school, and community-based activities. Each form provides a combination of Sensory System (Auditory, Visual, Touch, Movement, Body Position, Oral), Behavior (Conduct, Social-Emotional, Attention), and Sensory Pattern (Seeking, Avoiding, Sensitivity, Registration) scores. A short version (Short Sensory Profile-2) is available for screening and can be completed in 5 to 10 minutes. The Sensory Profile School Companion-2, a school-based measure, is also available to evaluate a child's sensory processing skills and their affect on classroom behavior. It can be used in conjunction with other SP-2 measures to provide a comprehensive evaluation of sensory behavior across home and school settings (Crane *et al.*, 2009; Dunn 2001; Kern *et al.*, 2007).

The Sensory Processing Measure (SPM; Parham *et al.*, 2007) is a norm-referenced assessment that produces scores for two higher level integrative functions (praxis and social participation) and five sensory systems (Visual, Auditory, Tactile, Proprioceptive and Vestibular Functioning). Processing vulnerabilities within each system include under- and over-responsiveness, sensory-seeking behavior, and perceptual problems. Three forms comprise the SPM (Home Form, Main Classroom Form, and School Environments Form), which provide a comprehensive picture of children's sensory processing difficulties at home and school. Each requiring 15 to 20 minutes, the Home and Main Classroom Forms yield eight parallel standard scores: Social Participation; Vision; Hearing; Touch; Body Awareness (proprioception); Balance and Motion (vestibular function); Planning and Ideas (praxis); and Total Sensory Systems. An Environment Difference score allows direct comparison of the child's sensory functioning at home and at school. Both the SP-2 and SPM have been used with children with ASD and have utility in program planning and developing accommodations for unusual sensory responses.

BEST PRACTICE

Deficits in executive function, memory, and attention can adversely affect the student's learning and classroom performance and may warrant assessment.

EXECUTIVE FUNCTION

Research suggests that children with ASD often have difficulties with executive functioning (Hill, 2004; Ozonoff, South, and Provencal, 2005; Pennington and Ozonoff, 1996; Ozonoff, 1997). Executive function is a broad term that includes many of the skills required to prepare for and execute complex behavior, such as planning, inhibition, organization, working memory, self-monitoring, cognitive flexibility, and set-shifting. They play an important role in the acquisition of knowledge and social skills; the better children are at focusing and refocusing their attention, holding information in mind and manipulating it (i.e., working memory), resisting distraction, and adapting flexibly to change, the more positive the social, adaptive, and academic outcomes. Understanding executive functioning in children, specifically those children with ASD, is important to improving their educational and psychological well-being, and will lead to more informed intervention practices.

Two of the more widely used broad measures of executive functioning are the Developmental Neuropsychological Assessment, Second Edition (NEPSY-II; Korkman, Kirk, and Kemp, 2007) and the Delis-Kaplan Executive Function System (D-KEFS; Delis, Kaplan, and Kramer, 2001). Both may be used to directly measure a student's inhibition skills, motor planning, problem solving and planning, mental flexibility, and working memory, among other skills. The NEPSY-II measures the neuropsychological abilities of children ages 3 to 16 years in six domains: 1) Attention and Executive Functioning; 2) Language; 3) Memory and Learning; 4) Sensorimotor; 5) Social Perception; and 6) Visuospatial Processing. It offers 32 subtests that the examiner can tailor to the specific examinee. In addition to tests of memory and executive functioning, the NEPSY-II also includes tests on Theory of Mind (which assesses the ability to recognize the feelings and thoughts of others) and Affect Recognition (which measures the ability to recognize feelings expressed on faces) both of which should be useful for assessing children with ASD (Caterino, 2014).

The Delis-Kaplan Executive Function System (D-KEFS; Delis, Kaplan, and Kramer, 2001) was designed exclusively for the assessment of critical executive functions such as flexibility of thinking, inhibition, problem solving, planning, impulse control, concept formation, abstract thinking, and creativity in both verbal and spatial modalities. The D-KEFS is composed of nine stand-alone tests that can be administered individually or along with other D-KEFS tests, depending on the assessment needs of the specific examinee and/or the time constraints on the examiner. In school settings, the D-KEFS can be used to complement the assessment of abilities measured by traditional tests of intellectual ability and academic achievement with the evaluation of higher-level cognitive abilities. The D-KEFS has been utilized with a number of different clinical populations, including ASD (Kleinhans, Akshoomoff, and Courchesne, 2003; Kleinhans, Akshoomoff, and Delis, 2005).

Questionnaires completed by parents, teachers, and students are another important source of information regarding this domain. For example, the Behavior Rating Inventory of Executive Function, Second Edition (BRIEF-2; Gioia *et al.*, 2015) is a parent- or teacher-rated questionnaire for children ages 5 to 18 that can be used to assess executive functioning in children with ASD. The BRIEF-2 is comprised of the following clinical scales which represent specific areas of executive functioning: Inhibit, Shift, Emotional Control, Initiate, Working

Memory, Plan/Organize, Organization of Materials, Task-Monitor, and Self-Monitor. Summary indexes include Behavior Regulation (BRI), Emotion Regulation (ERI), Cognitive Regulation (CRI), and a Global Executive Composite (GEC). The BRIEF-2 also includes a self-report measure for older children and adolescents 11 to 18 years of age. Because executive functions are important to school success, the inclusion of the BRIEF-2 as an additional measure enables the practitioner to assess impaired multi-task performance, document the impact of executive function deficits on real-world functioning, and to plan educational accommodations (Clark, Prior, and Kinsella, 2002). There is research to suggest that the BRIEF profile of children with ASD is one of elevated scores across all subscales, particularly the Shift subscale which measures cognitive flexibility and transitioning (Gioia *et al.*, 2002).

MEMORY

Memory is arguably the most important function of cognition and a critical aspect of learning and academic success. The Wide Range Assessment of Memory and Learning, Second Edition (WRAML-2; Sheslow and Adams, 2003) is a direct, comprehensive measure of memory function that can be useful in evaluating learning and school-related problems of children with ASD. It evaluates both immediate and delayed memory ability together with the acquisition of new learning. The WRAML-2 includes a Core Battery and supplemental subtests that provide index scores for General Memory, Verbal Memory, Visual Memory, Working Memory, and Attention and Concentration. A brief four subtest Memory Screening Form that correlates highly with the full test is also available. The Core Battery takes less than an hour to administer. A Screening Battery, consisting of four subtests from the Core Battery, provides an overview of memory functioning and can be completed in 10 to 15 minutes.

Another test of verbal memory is the California Verbal Learning Test – Children's Version (CVLT–C; Delis *et al.*, 1994). The CVLT–C is designed for children from 5 to 16 years of age, and measures multi-trial learning and long-term recall abilities for verbal information. It applies the process approach to capture information about rate of learning, short- and long-term retention and retrieval, recall errors, interference effects, ability to utilize cues to improve recall, and learning strategy. The CVLT–C can be used to help identify deficient learning strategies and develop appropriate remedial programs. The Standard Form can be administered in 20 minutes, plus a 20 minute delay.

ATTENTION

School-age children with ASD frequently demonstrate symptoms associated with attention-deficit/hyperactivity disorder (ADHD) (Ghaziuddin, 2002; Goldstein, Johnson, and Minshew, 2001; Murray, 2010). Research indicates that ADHD is a common initial diagnosis for many children with ASD. For example, studies conducted in the US and Europe indicate that children with ASD in clinical settings present with comorbid symptoms of ADHD with rates ranging between 37 percent and 85 percent (Rao and Landa, 2014). These symptoms may include inattention, impulsivity, hyperactivity and other features such as low frustration tolerance, poor self-monitoring, temper and anger management problems, and mood changes in the classroom (Loveland and Tunali-Kotoski, 2005; Rao and Landa, 2014; Sikora et al., 2012; Towbin, 2005). More severe externalizing, internalizing and social problems, as well as more impaired adaptive functioning and autistic traits have been reported in children with both ASD and ADHD than children identified with only ASD (Rao and Landa, 2014). Therefore, it is essential that practitioners recognize the high co-occurrence rates of these two disorders as well as the potential increased risk for social and adaptive impairment associated with comorbidity of ASD and ADHD. School-based professionals should also be aware that the DSM-5 has removed the previous DSM-IV-TR hierarchical rule prohibiting the concurrent diagnosis of ASD and ADHD. An assessment of ADHD characteristics may be included when inattention and/or impulsivity are indicated as presenting problems.

Measures such as the Conners Third Edition (Conners, 2008) can be used to assess attention-deficit/hyperactivity disorder (ADHD) and its most commonly associated problems and disorders (i.e., oppositional defiant disorder and conduct disorder) in children and youth ages 6 to 18 years. The Conners 3 features multiple content scales that measure ADHD-related concerns such as inattention and hyperactivity as well as related problems in executive functioning, learning, aggression, and peer/family relations. Ratings scales include Parent (Conners 3-P), Teacher (Conners 3-T), and Student Self-Report (Conners 3-SR) forms. Short forms are also available for screening students who require further assessment as well as for monitoring the success of intervention programs. In addition, the Conners 3 includes two auxiliary scales: the Conners 3 ADHD Index (Conners 3AI) and the Conners 3 Global Index (Conners 3GI). Assessment Reports, Progress Reports, and Comparative Reports are also provided to help gather and record information, summarize results, and facilitate discussion. The Conners 3 has also been updated to provide a new scoring option for the DSM-5 Symptom Scales and is considered a technically sound instrument that when used in combination with other psychometric measures, interviews, and clinical observations can serve as a valuable tool for ADHD assessment (Kao and Thomas, 2010).

BEST PRACTICE
Given the importance of visual-motor processing and motor skills in learning and classroom performance, this area may be included as a component of a comprehensive assessment battery.

MOTOR SKILLS

Although motor problems are not a core symptom of ASD, many children with ASD demonstrate delays in fine and gross motor coordination and visual-motor integration even when intellectual/cognitive ability is taken into consideration. Moreover, these problems occur across the entire spectrum and appear independent of gender (Fournier *et al.*, 2010). When present, motor problems may interfere with performance in many developmental and functional domains across home and school contexts. For example, a recent study found 91 percent of children with ASD were considered developmentally delayed in terms of their gross motor skill performance and in need of early supportive interventions (Liu *et al.*, 2014). It should also be noted that developmental coordination disorder, a neurodevelopmental disorder characterized by deficits in the acquisition and execution of coordinated motor skills, commonly co-occurs with ASD (American Psychiatric Association, 2013). Developing an intervention plan and/or accommodations to address gross and fine-motor deficits may have a positive effect on children's cognitive functioning, language development, social communicative skills, and contribute positively to daily life skills. Consequently, the significance of motor proficiency for children with ASD should not be overlooked in assessment practice.

The Beery–Buktenica Developmental Test of Visual-Motor Integration, Sixth Edition (Beery VMI; Beery, Buktenica, and Beery, 2010) is one of the most widely used assessments to evaluate how efficiently individuals can integrate their visual and motor abilities. The examinee is asked to copy a series of 24 geometric forms, arranged in developmental sequence, from less to more complex in the Test Booklet. A Short Form, consisting of 15 drawings, is often used with two- to eight-year-old children. Both formats can be administered either individually or to a group in 10 to 15 minutes. The Beery VMI also provides supplemental Visual Perception and Motor Coordination tests which make it possible to compare an individual's test results with his or her distinct visual perceptual and the motor control skills (one or both of the supplemental tests may be used.). Practitioners will find the age norm information useful in helping parents better understand their child's current developmental level. Visual, motor, and visual-motor teaching activities and other material for use with school-age children are also available.

A comprehensive measure of gross and fine motor skills may be completed with the Bruininks-Oseretsky Test of Motor Proficiency, Second Edition (BOT-2; Bruininks and Bruininks, 2005). The BOT-2 consists of eight subtests, four in the gross-motor area (Bilateral Coordination, Balance, Running Speed, and Agility, Strength) and four in the fine-motor area (Fine-Motor Precision, Fine-Motor Integration, Manual Dexterity, and Upper-Extremity Coordination). Four composite scores are available, including Fine-Manual Control, Manual Coordination, Body Coordination, Strength/Agility, and Fine-Motor Coordination. A Short Form consisting of one to two items from each of the eight areas is also available and can be administered in 15 to 20 minutes. The BOT-2 has been empirically validated for individuals diagnosed with autism, developmental coordination disorder, and mild/moderate intellectual disabilities (Deitz, Kartin, and Kopp, 2007).

BEST PRACTICE

Children and youth with ASD often present with co-occurring emotional and behavioral problems that require further assessment and specific intervention.

BEHAVIORAL/EMOTIONAL PROBLEMS

Research indicates that anxiety, depression, and disruptive behavior disorders commonly co-occur with ASD, all which contribute to overall impairment (American Psychiatric Association, 2013; Doepke *et al.*, 2014; Ghaziuddin, 2002). For example, an evaluation of psychiatric comorbidity in young adults with ASD revealed that 70 percent had experienced at least one episode of major depression and 50 percent reported recurrent major depression (Mazzone, Ruta, and Reale, 2012). Anxiety disorders are also a common comorbid problem for children and youth with ASD (Kim *et al.*, 2000). Although prevalence rates vary from 11 percent to 84 percent most studies indicate that approximately one-half of children with ASD meet criteria for at least one anxiety disorder. Moreover, rates of anxiety are reportedly higher than those in children with language disorders, conduct disorder, or in clinically anxious typically developing children (Ozsivadjian *et al.*, 2012). Research also suggests that unusual and intense fears are frequent triggers/stressors for anxiety in children with ASD and can interfere significantly with functioning (Mayes *et al.*, 2013). In addition, girls with ASD appear to be at greater risk for internalizing problems such as anxiety and depression than boys on the autism spectrum (Solomon *et al.*, 2012). Practitioners should be aware of these co-occurring conditions when evaluating a child with confirmed or suspected ASD (Campbell *et al.*, 2014). The accurate identification and understanding of comorbid emotional/behavioral conditions in children with ASD is essential in developing more comprehensive and effective interventions (Doepke *et al.*, 2014).

Assessment of co-occurring behavior/emotional problems is challenging, because there are no validated autism-specific tools specifically designed for this purpose (Deprey and Ozonoff, 2009). However, self-report measures such as the Children's Depression Inventory, Second Edition (CDI-2: Kovacs, 2010) and the Revised Manifest Anxiety Scale, Second Edition (RCMAS-2; Reynolds and Richmond, 2008) can be used to assess symptoms of anxiety and depression in school-age children and youth with ASD. The CDI-2 is a comprehensive multi-rater assessment which quantifies depressive symptomatology using reports from children/adolescents (full-length and short); teachers, and parents (or alternative caregivers). The Self-Report Form is 28-item assessment that yields a Total Score, two scale scores (Emotional Problems and Functional Problems), and four subscale scores (Negative Mood, Negative Self-Esteem, Ineffectiveness, and Interpersonal Problems). The CDI-2 Parent and Teacher Forms consist of items that correspond to the Self-Report version. A Self-Report Short Form is also available and can be used as an efficient screening measure. When results are combined with other sources of information, the CDI-2 can assist in the early identification of depressive symptoms, the diagnosis of depression and related disorders, and the monitoring of treatment effectiveness.

The Revised Manifest Anxiety Scale, Second Edition (RCMAS-2; Reynolds and Richmond, 2008) is a 49-item self-report instrument designed to assess the level and nature of anxiety in children from 6 to 19 years old. Four scores include a Total Anxiety score and scores for three anxiety-related scales: Physiological Anxiety, Worry, and Social Anxiety. The RCMAS-2 also includes validity scales which measure Defensiveness and Inconsistent Responding. There is also a content-based cluster that asks specifically about performance anxiety so that practitioners can focus on this particular topic in follow-up evaluation and activities. The Short Form can be completed in approximately five minutes and is appropriate when there are time constraints or when only a brief measure of total anxiety is needed for screening. The RCMAS-2 can be used to provide information related to various problems, including stress, test anxiety, school avoidance, and peer and family conflicts.

Although these self-report measures have utility for use with more capable children on the autism spectrum, it is important to recognize that both the CDI-2 and RCMAS-2 do not have a normative database for ASD and lack robust empirical investigation with this group of children. It should also be noted that difficulties in sustaining a reciprocal conversation, reporting events, perspective taking, and limited insight may present challenges to accurate self-reporting (Doepke *et al.*, 2014).

Behavior rating scales can also provide important information about emotional/behavioral problems in children with ASD. The Achenbach System of Empirically Based Assessment (ASEBA) is a widely used broad-based behavior rating system for identifying co-occurring internalizing and externalizing problems across home and school contexts. The ASEBA school-age assessment forms (Achenbach and Rescorla, 2001) include the Child Behavior Checklist (CBCL/6-18) which obtains reports from parents, close relatives,

and/or guardians regarding children's competencies, the Teacher Report Form (TRF/6-18), designed to obtain teachers' reports of children's academic performance, adaptive functioning, and behavioral/emotional problems, and the Youth Self-Report Form (YSR/11-18), for respondents ages 11-18. Ratings from the CBCL, TRF, and YSR are scored in the areas of Aggressive Behavior; Anxious/Depressed; Withdrawn/Depressed; Attention Problems; Rule-Breaking Behavior; Social Problems; Somatic Complaints; and Thought Problems. The ASEBA school-age forms also include six scales related to six DSM-5 diagnostic categories: Anxiety Problems; Depressive Problems; Attention Deficit/Hyperactivity Problems; Somatic Problems; Oppositional Defiant Problems; and Conduct Problems. An Autism Spectrum Problems scale is available for ages one-and-a-half to five. Previous studies have suggested that elevated scores on the Social Problems and Thought Problems scales may be associated with ASD (Bolte, Dickhut, and Poustka, 1999; Duarte *et al.*, 2003).

Another broad-based measure for assessing co-occurring problems in children with ASD is the Behavior Assessment System for Children-Third Edition (BASC-3; Reynolds and Kamphaus, 2015c). The BASC-3 is a comprehensive set of rating scales and forms, including the Teacher Rating Scales (TRS), Parent Rating Scales (PRS), Self-Report of Personality (SRP), Student Observation System (SOS), and Structured Developmental History (SDH). The TRS/ PRS clinical scales include: Aggression; Anxiety; Attention Problems; Atypicality; Conduct Problems; Depression; Hyperactivity; Learning

Problems; Somatization; and Withdrawal. Composite scales include: Externalizing Problems, Internalizing Problems, School Problems, Adaptive Skills, and Behavioral Symptoms Index. The BASC-3 also features a Developmental Social Disorders Scale and an Autism Probability Index. It should be noted that although the BASC-3 provides broad-based information on the child's problem adaptive behavior at home and in the community, the VABS-II and ABAS-3 are recommended for a more comprehensive assessment in the core domain of adaptive behavior.

BEST PRACTICE
The identification of parenting stress and parent–child relationship problems can alert the assessment team to the need for additional family support or counseling.

FAMILY SYSTEM
Many parents of children with ASD experience a higher overall incidence of stress in comparison to parents of neurotypical children and consequently are more susceptible to negative health and social outcomes. Parents are often overwhelmed by the challenges of caring for a child with ASD and are more likely to experience depression, anxiety, and isolation which adversely affect family functioning and marital relationships (Estes *et al.*, 2009). For example, research has shown that parents of children with autism exhibit a characteristic stress profile which includes a high level of stress and anxiety related to the child's uneven intellectual profiles, deficits in social relatedness, disruptive behaviors and long-term care concerns (Barnhill, 2014; Koegel *et al.*, 1992; Osborne *et al.*, 2008). Mothers are especially vulnerable to high levels of distress and fatigue which may negatively affect their mental health (Feinberg *et al.*, 2014; Giallo *et al.*, 2013; Hoffman *et al.*, 2009). Because autism impairs social relatedness and adaptive functioning,

parental stress can decrease helpful psychological processes and directly influence the parent or caregiver's ability to support the child with a disability (Estes *et al.*, 2009). Targeting problem behaviors may help reduce parenting stress and, thus, increase the effectiveness of interventions. The identification of parenting stress and parent–child relationship problems can also alert the assessment team to the need for additional support or counseling (Weiss *et al.*, 2012).

An instrument with established psychometric properties that has been used with the ASD population is the Parenting Stress Index, Fourth Edition (PSI-4; Abidin, 2012). The PSI-4 is a 120-item inventory that focuses on three major areas of stress in the parent–child relationship: (a) child characteristics; (b) parent characteristics; and (c) stress stemming from situational or demographic conditions. Two domains, Child and Parent, combine to form the Total Stress scale. Within the Child Domain, six subscales (Distractibility/ Hyperactivity, Adaptability, Reinforces Parent, Demandingness, Mood, and Acceptability) evaluate sources of stress based on the parent's report of child characteristics. Within the Parent Domain, seven subscales (Competence, Isolation, Attachment, Health, Role Restriction, Depression, and Spouse/Parenting Partner Relationship) measure sources of stress related to parent characteristics. In addition, a Life Stress scale provides information about the amount of parent stress caused by factors outside the parent–child relationship. A PSI-Short Form (PSI-4SF) consisting of 36 items from the full inventory is available and provides a Total Stress Scale which can be completed in 10 minutes. The PSI-4 is an effective measure for evaluating the parenting system and identifying issues that may lead to problems in the child's or parent's behavior. This information may be used for designing a treatment plan, for setting priorities for intervention, and/or for follow-up evaluation.

BEST PRACTICE

Professional judgment and experience is essential for the accurate identification of ASD, regardless of the strengths and limitations of an evidence-based instrument.

CONCLUSION

This chapter described the comprehensive developmental approach to assessment and the components of both a core assessment battery and additional domains for children suspected of ASD. These tests and measures have been shown to be relevant to the evaluation, identification, diagnosis, intervention planning, and outcome measurement of ASD in scientifically-based investigations. Despite the validity of the assessment tools described here, a diagnosis or classification of ASD should never depend solely on a single measure or combination of measures. These measures cannot "answer" a difficult diagnostic question or solve a complex case. Experienced professional judgment is essential for accurate diagnosis and identification, regardless of how carefully a practitioner weighs the strengths and limitations of an evidence-based instrument (Charman and Gotham, 2013). Choosing instruments for a specific need (e.g., adaptive behavior) also provides important standardization and structure to support professional judgment and intervention planning. Few studies have directly compared the various instruments, so there is no definitive guide to selecting among the different assessment tools. Moreover, due to evolving changes in the definition of autism and development of new measures, instruments used in the assessment process must be reviewed and evaluated frequently. The next chapter presents case examples to illustrate application of the comprehensive developmental approach to assessment for ASD.

CHAPTER 4

CASE EXAMPLES

The case examples in this chapter illustrate the comprehensive developmental approach to assessment. The results of a hypothetical evaluation are presented for two students, as they might be presented in a psychoeducational report and interpretive narrative.

CASE EXAMPLE 1: DANIEL

Daniel was a seven-year-old second grade student with a history of behavioral problems both at school and home. His educational history included long-standing difficulties in the areas of social interaction, attention and impulse control, and aggression. Although an engaging child with a precocious vocabulary, Daniel had a "blunt" communicative style and was not sensitive to many nonverbal social cues. As a result, he frequently misread the communication of others. Daniel was also described as highly argumentative, resistant, immature and not well-accepted by other children. Although capable in many academic areas, he demonstrated significant difficulty in the areas of appropriateness of response, task persistence, attending and topic maintenance. Few children want to play, sit or work with Daniel owing to his frequent intrusive and disruptive behavior. He was also considered "bossy" with other students and had significant nonacademic challenging behaviors such as interrupting, distracting others, and constantly talking about topics of special interest such as super heroes. Daniel seemed to have his own agenda and rules which he expected other students to follow. Among Daniel's strengths were his well-developed visualization skills and memory for facts and details. He also had a strong desire for structure, rules and order.

REASON FOR REFERRAL

Daniel was referred for an individual psychoeducational evaluation to assess strengths and weaknesses in the areas of intellectual functioning, academic achievement, and social/emotional development. He was initially referred to the school's support team to assist with developing interventions to address problems with inattention, social relatedness, task completion, and disruptive behavior in the classroom. Following positive screening results on the Autism Spectrum Rating Scales (ASRS), Daniel was referred for a comprehensive evaluation to determine the presence and severity of ASD and develop an intervention plan.

ASSESSMENT METHODS

Parent Interview

Stanford-Binet Intelligence Scales, Fifth Edition (SB-5)

Behavior Rating Inventory of Executive Function, Second Edition (BRIEF-2)

Woodcock-Johnson Tests of Achievement, Fourth Edition (WJ IV ACH)

Beery-Buktenica Developmental Test of Visual-Motor Integration, Sixth Edition (Beery VMI)

Autism Spectrum Rating Scales (ASRS)

Repetitive Behavior Scale, Revised (RBS-R)

ASD Observation Checklist

Pragmatic Language Skills Inventory (PLSI)

Vineland Adaptive Behavior Scales, Second Edition (Vineland-II)

Behavior Assessment System for Children, Third Edition (BASC-3)

Revised Manifest Anxiety Scale, Second Edition (RMAS-2)

BACKGROUND INFORMATION/ DEVELOPMENTAL HISTORY

Background information obtained from an interview with Daniel's mother indicates that Daniel was enrolled in a private preschool at three years of age. Presenting problems at that time included difficulty following directions, transitioning, and maintaining on-task behavior. Daniel was also reported to have problems relating and playing cooperatively with other children. He was observed to talk repetitively about certain topics and seldom participated in group activities. At home, he was described as argumentative and often had temper tantrums when required to follow household rules. Developmental milestones were achieved within normal expectations, including crawling at 6 months, walking at 11 months, and speaking his first words at 12 months. Daniel's mother reports that the family history is positive for attention and learning problems. Although Daniel's challenging behavior has been in evidence since early childhood, his parents became even more concerned upon entrance to kindergarten where he was described as disruptive and oppositional. Although improvement has been noted, Daniel continues to experience significant social and behavioral challenges in his current classroom. Both vision and hearing exams were completed during the past year, with both reported to be within normal limits. An annual physical examination indicated no specific health related issues or concerns.

TEST OBSERVATIONS

Daniel was easily engaged in the testing activities. His affect was continually elevated throughout the session. Although able to follow directions adequately, Daniel experienced difficulty maintaining reciprocity in conversation. He was verbally interactive and responsive, but often provided tangential and inappropriate responses. Eye contact was initially intermittent, but reasonably good when directly engaged by the examiner. Although Daniel demonstrated some inattentiveness, rapport and attention were considered adequate for testing purposes. The results of the current assessment should be considered a valid and reliable estimate of Daniel's current intellectual, academic, and social/behavioral functioning.

COGNITIVE FUNCTIONING

Daniel was administered the Stanford-Binet Intelligence Scales, Fifth Edition (SB-5) to assess his cognitive abilities. The SB-5 provides composite scores for Verbal IQ, Nonverbal IQ, and Full Scale IQ, and five cognitive factors: Fluid Reasoning, Knowledge, Quantitative Reasoning, Visual-Spatial Processing, and Working Memory. These factors reflect different areas of cognitive competencies and are comprised of both verbal and nonverbal skills. On the SB-5, Daniel earned a Full Scale IQ score of 116, which places him at the 86th percentile compared to same-age peers. Daniel's verbal reasoning abilities were measured in the high average range (VIQ=112) and above those of 79 percent of his peer group. The VIQ measures verbal knowledge and understanding obtained from the school and home learning environment and reflects the ability to apply verbal skills to new situations. Verbal abilities across factors were generally consistent with the exception of Working Memory, which produced a below average equivalent score for his age. Daniel's general ability to reason, solve problems, visualize, and recall information presented in pictorial, figural, and symbolic form was also measured in the high average range (NV IQ=119) and at the 90th percentile. Particular strength was noted with items involving Fluid Reasoning and Visual Spatial Processing. Somewhat lower performance was observed with Working Memory tasks. Daniel's relatively weak verbal and nonverbal working memory competencies may reflect problems in his memory processes and difficulty maintaining concentration and impulse control. A weakness in working memory may make the processing of complex information more time consuming for Daniel and result in more frequent errors on a variety of learning tasks.

EXECUTIVE FUNCTION

The Behavior Rating Inventory of Executive Function, Second Edition (BRIEF-2) was completed by Daniel's mother and classroom teacher to further assess Daniel's ability to initiate, plan, organize, and sustain problem-solving working memory. Analysis of his profile indicates clinically significant elevations on the Behavioral Regulation (BRI), Emotional Regulation (ERI), Cognitive (CRI) and Global Executive Composite (GEC) Indexes across home and school settings. Daniel's profile reflects marked difficulty with metacognitive problem-solving, organizing and planning strategies, systematic problem-solving, emotional regulation, self-monitoring, cognitive flexibility, and holding information in working memory. The overall test results of the BRIEF-2 indicate a significant global executive dysfunction despite his level of cognitive ability. The most salient area of impairment includes behaviors associated with transitions, problem-solving flexibility, the ability to alternate attention and change of focus. Daniel's problems with self-monitoring indicate that he has difficulty reading and evaluating the effects of his behaviors on others, and that he may have difficulty evaluating his behaviors and their possible consequences. Significant problems in basic executive inhibitory control and cognitive flexibility in both home and school contexts suggest that Daniel may exhibit the cognitive rigidity and adherence to routine and sameness often observed in children with ASD.

ACADEMIC ACHIEVEMENT

Academic achievement, as compared to that of other students of the same age, was assessed with the Woodcock-Johnson IV Tests of Achievement.

(WJ IV ACH). Daniel's overall academic achievement, as measured by the WJ IV Broad Achievement standard score, was in the high average range. Among the WJ IV ACH achievement measures, his standard scores were high average for the Broad Reading, Basic Reading Skills, Broad Mathematics and Math Calculation Skills clusters. A review of Daniel's achievement test profile indicates exceptional word identification skills and ability to read with fluency. In contrast, average performance was noted with reading comprehension tasks. Daniel does not appear to demonstrate a deficit in academic skill development relative to age and grade level expectations.

VISUAL-MOTOR SKILLS
The Beery-Buktenica Developmental Test of Visual-Motor Integration, Sixth Edition (Beery VMI) was utilized to assess Daniel's ability to integrate visual and motor skills. His standard score of 103 and corresponding percentile rank of 58 are consistent with age appropriate performance in this developmental area. Although characterized by impulsivity and disorganization, Daniel's overall VMI performance does not suggest functional impairment or a delay in visual-motor skills.

ASD MEASURES
The Autism Spectrum Rating Scales (ASRS), full-length form, was completed by Daniel's parent and teacher to assess features and characteristics associated with an autism spectrum disorder (ASD). The ASRS covers a wide range of autism-related behaviors such as difficulty with communication skills, deficits in attention, and problems in engaging both peers and adults in social interaction. The ASRS also incorporates symptom criteria from the Diagnostic and Statistical Manual, Fifth Edition (DSM-5). An examination of Daniel's parent and teacher-reported ASRS scores indicates very elevated ratings on the Peer Socialization (PS), Adult Socialization (AS), Atypical Language (AL), Behavioral Rigidity (BR), and Attention Treatment (AT) Scales.

Scores at this level suggest a limited interest and capacity to successfully engage in activities that develop and maintain relationships with other children and adults. Ratings on the Behavioral Rigidity (BR) scale may also reflect Daniel's difficulty tolerating changes in his environment, routines, activities, or behaviors. Similarly, very elevated ratings on Attention Treatment Scale appear consistent with Daniel's inability to appropriately sustain and focus attention. Very elevated scores were also noted on the Unusual Behaviors (UB) and Self-Regulation (SR) ASRS scales across settings. The Unusual Behaviors (UB) Scale may reflect Daniel's difficulty managing changes in routine, engagement of stereotypical behaviors/restricted interests, and overreaction to sensory experiences. An elevation on the Self-Regulation (SR) scale also suggests deficits in attention and/or motor impulse control. Daniel's Total Score and DSM-5 scores are in the very elevated range for both parent and teacher respondents. Item level responses are positive for problems with perspective taking, social communication, peer socialization, social/emotional reciprocity, and repetitive behaviors. Taken together, Daniel's Total Score and DSM scale scores indicate the presence of moderate to severe symptoms directly related to the DSM-5 diagnostic criteria and many of the associated features and characteristics of autism spectrum disorder (ASD).

REPETITIVE AND RESTRICTED BEHAVIOR (RRB)

Daniel's parent completed the Repetitive Behavior Scale-Revised (RBS-R) to provide further information on the presence and impact of repetitive and restricted behavior and interests (RRBs). Ratings were highest on the Ritualistic Behavior, Sameness Behavior, Restricted Interest, and Compulsive Behaviors subscales. Daniel was observed to frequently engage in repetitive questioning and insist on certain topics of conversation; arrange certain objects in a particular pattern or place; insist on the same routine and have difficulty with transitions; become upset if interrupted in what he is doing; and have an intense preoccupation with one subject or activity. The lowest ratings on the RBS-R subscales were found for Stereotyped Behavior (e.g., repetitive motor movements) and Self-Injurious Behavior. Daniel's Global Rating Score indicates moderate to severe problems in the RRB domain which occur frequently and significantly interfere with everyday functioning.

DIRECT OBSERVATION

Daniel was observed in multiple settings throughout the school day, including his classroom and playground. The ASD Observation Checklist (Appendix D) was used to guide the observation process. Daniel demonstrated several behaviors associated with impairment in social interaction, including significant difficulty maintaining and sustaining reciprocity with his peers. He was often inappropriately intrusive and appeared to have little sense of other children's boundaries. Although there was no evidence of speech abnormalities or echolalia, Daniel had difficulty using tone and volume appropriately, and frequently engaged in excessive conversation about specific topics without regard for other children's interest. He was also observed to make inappropriate comments to both peers and adults. Although no repetitive or stereotyped motor movements were observed, Daniel presented with a somewhat awkward gait and demonstrated mild difficulties with graphomotor tasks. He also appeared to be highly disorganized and had difficulty with activities involving multiple steps. Challenging behavior was readily observed when required to terminate a preferred activity and transition between learning centers, most notably anger, tantruming, and refusal.

PRAGMATIC LANGUAGE

The Pragmatic Language Skills Inventory (PLSI) was completed by Daniel's classroom teacher to provide information relative to Daniel's social communication skills. Endorsements in the areas of Classroom Interaction, Social Interaction, and Personal Interaction indicate relatively poor interaction skills compared to average students of the same age. Qualitative analysis of his response form indicates difficulty "understanding the meaning of simple similes, metaphors, and idioms," "maintaining a topic or keeping a topic going," "recognizing when the teacher is cuing a routine," "knowing when to talk and when to listen," "taking turns in conversation," and "understanding what causes people not to like him or her." Daniel's overall Pragmatic Language Inventory (PLI) score falls within the below average range and indicates significant limitations in pragmatic language skills.

ADAPTIVE BEHAVIOR

The Vineland Adaptive Behavior Scales, Second Edition (Vineland-II) was completed by an interview with Daniel's mother to assess Daniel's ability to master personal and social demands in the home setting. The Vineland-II assesses adaptive behavior in three domains: Communication, Daily Living Skills, and Socialization. It also provides a composite score that summarizes a student's performance across all domains. A review of Daniel's profile indicates relative strength in the Communication skills domain. Greatest weakness was observed in the Socialization domain, where Daniel's adaptive level was considered moderately low in both the Interpersonal and Coping skills subdomains. A comparison of Daniel's Communication and Socialization standard scores indicates a significant and meaningful difference between scores, with this difference occurring in only one percent of the normative population. Daniel's Adaptive Behavior Composite score of 83 classifies his general adaptive functioning as moderately low compared to children of the same age. Daniel's repertoire of adaptive skills is significantly discrepant relative to his measured cognitive functioning.

BEHAVIORAL/EMOTIONAL FUNCTIONING

Daniel's teacher completed the Behavior Assessment System for Children, Third Edition (BASC-3) Teacher Rating Scale (TRS) to provide information regarding Daniel's adaptive and problem behaviors in the classroom. Her ratings indicate clinically significant concerns in the composite domains of Externalizing Problems, School Problems, Behavioral Symptoms, and Adaptive Skills. At-risk concerns were also endorsed in the area of Internalizing problems. Daniel's Clinical Scales indicate that his verbal aggression and inappropriate behavior, poor academic engagement, difficulty interacting with peers, and inattentiveness are especially concerning and problematic. Daniel's teacher reported that Daniel frequently argues when he does not get his own way, is easily upset and angered, and has many conflicts with his classmates. Daniel's low scores on the Adaptive Scales represent significant problems in adjusting to change, communication effectiveness, social interaction, and organizational skills.

The BASC-3 Parent Rating Scale (PRS) was completed by Daniel's mother to provide a measure of Daniel's adaptive and problem behaviors in community and home settings. Similar to Daniel's teacher, she endorsed concerns with Daniel's aggressive behavior, atypicality, and attention. Anxiety-based behaviors were also endorsed. Daniel's Adaptive Scales reflect ongoing concerns with his inappropriate behavior, limited flexibility, poor social skills, and functional communication problems. Daniel's mother reported that Daniel frequently complains about not having friends and has difficulty controlling and maintaining his behavior and mood. He also doesn't adjust well to changes in routine, and often seems unaware of others. The BASC-3 items endorsed by Daniel's teacher and parent resulted in an at-risk Autism Probability Index score. Children who present with elevated scores on this index likely exhibit a variety of behaviors that are unusual and experience problems with developing and maintaining social relationships. Daniel's BASC-3 TRS and PRS scores indicate significant behavior and adaptive problems across both school and home settings. Children with similar scores have impaired social and communication skills, poor behavioral and academic adjustment, and have an increased risk for more substantial behavior problems and poor outcomes.

The Revised Manifest Anxiety Scale, Second Edition (RMAS-2) was completed in an interview format with Daniel in order to assess co-occurring internalizing problems. A review of Daniel's RCMAS-2 profile indicates significant elevations across the Physiological Anxiety (PHY), Worry (WOR) and Social Anxiety (SOC) Scales. Daniel endorsed a high level of worry and concerns in social and performance situations. High scores on this scale suggest a child who internalizes much of his anxiety experience. Endorsements on the Social Anxiety scale indicate a concern about self vis-à-vis other people and anxiety relative to effectiveness and ability to concentrate and perform academic tasks. Daniel endorsed items such as "I get nervous around people," "I worry that others do not like me," and "I feel that others do not like the way I do things." Daniel's Total Anxiety score indicates a moderate level of anxiety and impairment in his ability to cope with maturational and environmental stressors.

SUMMARY AND RECOMMENDATIONS

Daniel was referred for an individual psychoeducational evaluation to assess strengths and weaknesses in the areas of intellectual functioning, academic achievement, and social-emotional development. The results of the current assessment indicate that he is functioning in the high average range of general intellectual ability. Daniel earned a Full Scale IQ (FSIQ) score of 116 on the Stanford Binet Intelligence Scales, Fifth Edition (SB-5). He demonstrated relative strength with cognitive measures involving fluid reasoning and visual-spatial processing. Marked weakness was evident with cognitive tasks involving both verbal and nonverbal working memory ability. The results of the Woodcock-Johnson IV Tests of Achievement (WJ IV ACH) indicate that when compared to others at his age level, Daniel's performance is high average in Broad Reading, Basic Reading Skills, Broad Mathematics and Math Calculation Skills. His current levels of academic performance indicate a notable precociousness in word identification skills and reading fluency. In contrast, reading comprehension was measured at a somewhat lower level. Daniel does not appear to demonstrate a deficit in academic performance relative to age and grade-level peers.

Broad-based behavior rating scales are consistent across home and school settings indicating a range of psychological liabilities, including problems in social skills development, functional communication, attention, adaptability, and overall behavior. Daniel also has significant difficulty managing the executive function domains of working memory, planning and organization, and the ability to inhibit and self-monitor his behavior. Further, Daniel's relatively low overall adaptive behavior indicates that he has not been able to translate his cognitive ability into effective social skills. Observation and ratings on autism-specific measures indicate moderate-to-severe impairment in reciprocal social behavior and responsiveness both at home and school. Daniel demonstrates deficits in social interaction and communication and a consistent pattern of qualitative difficulties initiating and sustaining connected relationships with peers and adults appropriate for his developmental level. He also has difficulty with tolerating changes in his environment, displays unusual and repetitive patterns of behavior and interests, uses language in an atypical manner, and has problems with inattention and impulse control. Daniel's impairment and atypicalities presented in the communication, socialization, and behavioral domains across settings are characteristic features of ASD, and adversely impact his educational performance with respect to social-emotional development and learning. Co-occurring externalizing and internalizing problems also negatively affect Daniel's social adjustment and classroom productivity.

In terms of intervention planning, Daniel will require a focus on social skills, interactive appropriateness, and communication effectiveness. His educational needs are best met in a classroom that provides a structured setting and support, a multimodal approach to instruction, and a focus on communication and social effectiveness. Daniel's problems in social relatedness may be addressed through the use of social stories, social skills instruction in the classroom, and activities designed to enhance peer interaction and cooperation. Strategies should focus on relating and communicating with peers and adults (initiating, maintaining, turn-taking) both at home and at school. Daniel may be assigned a "peer buddy" identified for a specific time/activity, and social skills taught and practiced in a daily classroom context. Classroom instruction should include an emphasis on visually structured strategies and activities such as a work system, written instructions, schedules, and other visual supports. Those who work with Daniel should also be aware of common stressors which may include unstructured situations, such as transitions and changes in routine. It may be advisable to utilize "priming" as a method of preparing Daniel for an activity that he is expected to complete by allowing him to preview the activity before it is presented. Cognitive-behavioral programs such as "Exploring Feelings" may be utilized to address concerns related to anxiety and internalizing behavior issues. Daniel is also in need of an individual behavior support plan to address his challenging behavior. This should include a functional behavior assessment (FBA) to guide intervention planning. Similarly, positive behavior support (PBS) strategies should be used to teach socially acceptable alternative/replacement skills and behaviors in the classroom. A comprehensive speech/language evaluation should also be completed to obtain further qualitative and quantitative information regarding Daniel's social communication status. Daniel's current levels of problems appear to be persistent and pervasive enough to warrant consideration for a special education planning. The assessment team should integrate the results of the current evaluation, together with multiple sources of information, to determine the appropriate intervention goals, special education eligibility, and classroom placement to meet Daniel's educational needs.

CASE EXAMPLE 2: KAYLA

Kayla was a nine-year-old fourth grade student who had difficulties relating and communicating with peers and adults, transitioning problems, poor task completion, and occasional oddities in behavior. Although she did not display behavioral challenges such as temper tantrums or "meltdowns," Kayla would often ignore her teacher's requests and refuse to participate in classroom activities. She was not interested in seeking out other girls and preferred the company of adults. Although a capable student, Kayla had few friends in school and at home. She was considered "different" by her peers and often seemed to be in her own world. In class, she was a quiet and reserved student who usually stayed on the periphery of the group and preferred solitary activities such as creating small, imaginary worlds with blocks and figures, and playing games involving puppies or kittens for extended periods of time. At home, Kayla was viewed as a "sweet" and agreeable child who was compliant and well liked by her adult relatives. Yet Kayla's parents also expressed concern about their daughter's periods of aloofness, inattentiveness, and lack of initiative and social responsiveness.

REASON FOR REFERRAL

Kayla was referred for an individual psychoeducational evaluation to assess strengths and weaknesses in the areas of intellectual functioning, academic achievement, and behavioral adjustment. Referral information indicates a long standing history of social and behavioral challenges in the classroom and at home. Following positive screening results on the Social Communication Questionnaire (SCQ), Kayla was referred for a comprehensive evaluation to assist in determining the appropriate educational program and services.

ASSESSMENT METHODS

Parent Interview/Record Review

Wechsler Intelligence Scale for Children, Fifth Edition (WISC-V)

Developmental Neuropsychological Assessment, Second Edition (NEPSY-II)

Wechsler Individual Achievement Test, Third Edition (WIAT-III)

Beery-Buktenica Developmental Test of Visual-Motor Integration, Sixth Edition (Beery VMI)

Children's Communication Checklist, Second Edition (CCC-2)

Social Responsiveness Scale, Second Edition (SRS-2)

Childhood Autism Rating Scale, Second Edition, High Functioning Version (CARS-2 HF)

Questionnaire for Parents or Caregivers (CARS-2-QPC)

Repetitive Behavior Questionnaire-2 (RBQ-2)

Adaptive Behavior Assessment System, Third Edition (ABAS-3)

Children's Depression Inventory, Second Edition, Self-Report (CDI-2-SR)

ASEBA Child Behavior Checklist (CBCL) and Teacher's Report Form (TRF)

Parenting Stress Index, Fourth Edition, Short Form (PSI-4-SF)

PARENT INTERVIEW/RECORD REVIEW

Background information obtained from the parent interview and school records indicates that Kayla received a preschool evaluation at age 3 years 10 months. Concerns at that time included problems in the areas of social skills, transitioning, and atypical sensory experiences.

A review of Kayla's social and developmental history indicates health problems, including sleep difficulties, stomach problems, allergies, and frequent colds. Early motor and speech/language developmental milestones were considered to have been met within broad normal limits. Kayla walked alone at 12 months, spoke her first word at 11 months, and used phrases by 36 months. According to her mother, Kayla demonstrated sensory defensiveness in response to loud sounds, rough textures, and sticky foods. She was considered very "shy" in social situations, made limited use of eye contact, and seemed to have little interest in interacting with her peers. Kayla's family history is positive for depression and mental health concerns.

Reports from Kayla's preschool teacher described Kayla as a very quiet and immature child who did not actively participate in classroom activities, but rather seemed to prefer solitary play. She was also observed to "fixate or obsess on one thing" for extended periods of time and talked only when spoken to by other children and adults. Some oppositional behavior was reported when required to follow teacher directions and participate in play groups. Cognitive ability was considered normative, with a Full Scale IQ of 105 obtained on the Wechsler Preschool and Primary Scale of Intelligence, Third Edition (WPPSI-III). Expressive and receptive vocabulary skills were commensurate with measured intellectual ability. Pre-academic skills indicated relative strength in visual memory and readiness skills. Although a relative weakness in social skills and language processing was indicated, Kayla was considered to have the cognitive and academic readiness skills needed to function satisfactorily in a general education classroom. As a result, she was not considered eligible to receive special educational services. At the time of referral, sensory screenings indicated that both vision and hearing were within normal limits.

TEST OBSERVATIONS

Kayla was cooperative and attentive throughout the testing session. Although initially reticent, interaction and spontaneity increased as she became more comfortable with the testing environment. Kayla completed all tasks presented, but initiated few interactions and made eye contact only when directly engaged by the examiner. There were no stereotypic or restricted patterns of behavior observed during the testing session. Difficulties were noted with expressive language, with responses limited to short phrases and brief responses. Occasional problems were noted in the areas of word finding, vocabulary, and pragmatics. Prompting and encouragement were required to maximize test results. The results of the current assessment should be viewed within the context of Kayla's behavioral presentation.

COGNITIVE FUNCTIONING

Kayla was administered the Wechsler Intelligence Scale for Children, Fifth Edition (WISC-V) to assess her general cognitive ability. The WISC-V includes five primary index scores that represent intellectual functioning in specified cognitive areas—Verbal Comprehension Index (VCI), Visual Spatial Index (VSI), Fluid Reasoning Index (FRI), Working Memory Index (WMI), and Processing Speed Index (PSI). The Full Scale IQ (FSIQ) score summarizes ability across cognitive functions and provides a representation of general intellectual ability. Kayla's FSIQ was measured in the average range (FSIQ = 108) and at the 70th percentile compared with same-age peers. Although Kayla's overall verbal reasoning abilities were considered average, her performance on the Verbal Comprehension Index (VCI) reflects a varied set of abilities. She demonstrated average performance with vocabulary items, but a significant weakness on comprehension tasks requiring the ability to provide solutions to everyday problems and explain the underlying reasons for social rules or convention. Kayla's Visual Spatial Index (VSI) indicates average skills with tasks requiring visual-spatial reasoning, integration and synthesis of part-whole relationships, and attentiveness to visual detail. Relative strength was noted on fluid reasoning tasks (FRI) involving quantitative reasoning, classification and spatial ability, and knowledge of part-to-whole relationships. Kayla's fluid abilities were particularly strong when compared with her performance on tasks involving language-based skills. Performance on the Processing Speed Index (PSI) was average but variable. She demonstrated greater efficiency with tasks demanding attention to detail, compared with those requiring fine-motor skills, short-term memory, and psychomotor speed and accuracy. Kayla's Working Memory Index (WMI) performance was relatively low compared with her performance on fluid reasoning tasks. She performed better than only 34 percent of her peer group in this area. A weakness in working memory suggests that Kayla may experience difficulties holding information in short-term memory, manipulating it, and producing a response at a level comparable with same-age peers.

EXECUTIVE FUNCTION

Subtests of the Developmental Neuropsychological Assessment, Second Edition (NEPSY-II) were administered to further assess Kayla's executive functioning skills. Kayla's below expected-level scores on the subtests comprising the Attention and Executive Function content domain suggest that she has poor selective and sustained attention, limited working memory and motor persistence, planning and organization, impaired initiation and productivity, and weak cognitive flexibility. The Social Perception subtests of the NEPSY-II (Affect Recognition and Theory of Mind) were also administered to assess Kayla's ability to recognize facial affect and to understand others' perspectives. Kayla's test performance fell below the expected level and may reflect difficultly understanding the thoughts and feelings of others, problems interpreting nonverbal communication, and poor ability to use contextual information to make inferences about others and their behavior.

ACADEMIC ACHIEVEMENT

The Wechsler Individual Achievement Test, Third Edition (WIAT-III) was administered to assess Kayla's oral language, reading, writing, and mathematics skills. Her Total Achievement Score was measured in the average range and at the 73rd percentile compared with same-age peers. There was minimal variability among the Oral Language, Total Reading, Basic Reading, Reading Comprehension and Fluency, Written Expression, Mathematics, and Math Fluency composites. Kayla's weakest scores, although within the average range, were in Oral Language, including listening comprehension, expressive vocabulary, and short-term memory. Kayla's achievement test results are generally consistent with grade- and age-level expectations.

VISUAL-MOTOR SKILLS

The Beery-Buktenica Developmental Test of Visual-Motor Integration, Sixth Edition (Beery VMI) was utilized to assess Kayla's ability to integrate visual-motor skills. Her standard score of 90 and corresponding percentile rank of 25 suggest a relative weakness in this developmental area. Administration of the Visual Perception and Motor Coordination supplemental subtests revealed significant difficulty with fine-motor expression and control.

PRAGMATIC LANGUAGE

The Children's Communication Checklist, Second Edition (CCC-2) was completed by Kayla's mother and teacher to provide information relative to Kayla's overall communication competence and everyday pragmatic functionality. Kayla's General Communication Composite (GCC) score was measured at the 25th percentile and indicates a relative weakness in overall communication ability when compared with her general intellectual functioning. Although subtests measuring structural language competence (i.e. Speech, Syntax, Semantics, and Coherence) were average, Kayla demonstrated significant weakness with pragmatic language items (i.e. Initiation, Nonverbal Communication,

Scripted Language, Social Relations, and Interests). Endorsements were noted for "appears anxious in the company of other children," "is left out of activities by other children," "ignores conversational overtures from others," and "does not recognize when other people are upset or angry." Kayla's CCC-2 results indicate disproportionate problems in pragmatic language skills and suggest a communicative profile of autism spectrum disorder (ASD).

ASD MEASURES

The Social Responsiveness Scale, Second Edition (SRS-2) was completed by Kayla's mother and teacher to assess Kayla's levels of social awareness, social information processing, reciprocal social communication, social anxiety/avoidance, and restricted interests and repetitive behavior. Kayla's total score across settings was in the moderate to severe range and suggests deficiencies in reciprocal social behavior that are clinically significant. Scores in this category are characteristic of children with ASD and suggest substantial interference in everyday social interactions in most settings. A review of parent and teacher reports indicates significant elevations on both the Social Communication and Interaction (SCI) and Restricted Interests and Repetitive Behavior (RRB) DSM-5-compatible subscales. Kayla appears to struggle with social interactions due to her low motivation, poor social awareness, and restricted interests.

The Childhood Autism Rating Scale, Second Edition, High Functioning Version (CARS-2-HF) was also utilized to assess the continuum of behavioral symptoms related to autism and to assist in educational planning. The CARS-2-HF was completed from direct observation, previous psychological and teacher reports, social and developmental histories, speech/language assessments, review of school records, and parent interview. The CARS-2 Questionnaire for Parents or Caregivers (QPC) was also used to inform the CARS-2 ratings. A review of Kayla's profile indicates a mild to moderate level of impairment in the categories of Social-Emotional Understanding;

Relating to People; Listening Response; Taste, Smell, and Touch Response and Use; Fear or Anxiety; and Adaptation to Change/ Restricted Interests. She appears to be easily distressed by attempts to interrupt or change topic or activity and displays special interests or preferences for specific activities or topics. Kayla also exhibits a high level of unusual visual and auditory responses across settings and sensory issues that create stress in everyday environments. Likewise, she may also appear more fearful or anxious when compared with the typical child of the same age in a similar situation. Additionally, Kayla's ability to describe and understand emotional states appears somewhat limited. She is likely to ignore or misunderstand the expression or perspective of others. Information from the QPC also confirms early developmental difficulties related to social interaction and communication skills, repetitive behaviors, and unusual sensory interests. Kayla's Total Raw score and corresponding T-score indicate mild to moderate symptoms of ASD and an average level of autism-related behaviors compared with children identified with ASD.

RESTRICTED AND REPETITIVE BEHAVIOR (RRB)

Kayla's mother completed the Repetitive Behavior Questionnaire, Second Edition (RBQ-2) to provide a more inclusive understanding of repetitive and restrictive behaviors (RRBs) that might affect Kayla's adaptive functioning. Scores were highest on the Preoccupation with Restricted Patterns of Interest, Rigidity/Adherence to Routine, and Unusual Sensory Interest Scales. Items in the "marked or notable behavior" response range included: insists that aspects of daily routine must remain the same; has a fascination with specific objects; plays the same music, game or video, or reads the same book repeatedly; has special objects she likes to carry around; and has a special interest in the smell of people/objects and the feel of different surfaces. Items involving Repetitive Motor Movements received the lowest ratings. Kayla's Total Repetitive Behaviors score was significantly elevated and indicates a moderate impairment in everyday functioning.

ADAPTIVE BEHAVIOR

The Adaptive Behavior Assessment System, Third Edition (ABAS-3) was completed by Kayla's mother to assess Kayla's adaptive behavior functioning in everyday situations. The General Adaptive Composite score (GAC) summarizes performance across all skill areas. Kayla obtained a GAC score of 80, placing her current overall level of adaptive behavior at the 9th percentile and in the below-average range. She received significantly low scores in the Functional Academics, Communication, Self-Care, and Social Skill areas. These items focus on practical, everyday activities required to function, meet environmental demands, care for oneself, and interact with others effectively and independently. Kayla's difficulties with communication skills including speech, vocabulary, listening, conversation and nonverbal communication were rated as a significant area of weakness within her everyday adaptive functioning. Similarly, her ability to interact socially, initiate and maintain friendships, express and recognize emotions, and assist others when needed was considered well below average. Kayla's adaptive behavior can be described as significantly lower than is typical for her age and cognitive level.

BEHAVIORAL/EMOTIONAL FUNCTIONING

The Children's Depression Inventory, Second Edition, Self-Report (CDI-2-SR) was utilized to quantify a range of depressive symptoms in Kayla's everyday functioning. Her scores on the Interpersonal Problems, Ineffectiveness, and Negative Mood subscales were significantly elevated and may reflect Kayla's difficulties in interactions with other people, social avoidance, and social isolation. She may also be experiencing negative mood, sadness, irritability, fatigue, or loneliness and have a negative evaluation of her ability and school performance. Kayla's Total CDI-2 score suggests that she may be experiencing a high level of self-reported depressive symptomology that incorporates both emotional (negative mood, physical symptoms, and negative self-esteem) and functional problems (not enjoying being with people, being uncooperative and irritable, and having disagreements and conflicts with others).

The ASEBA Child Behavior Checklist (CBCL) was completed by Kayla's mother to obtain her perceptions of Kayla's competencies and problems. She reported that although Kayla has an intense interest in several activity areas, she has no close friends and interacts with peers less than once a week outside of school. On the CBCL problem scales, Kayla's scores on the Somatic Complaints, Attention Problems, Rule-Breaking Behavior, and Aggressive Behavior syndrome scales were in the typical range. In contrast, her scores on the Anxious/ Depressed and Withdrawn/Depressed syndromes were in the clinical range and above the 97th percentile. Scores on the Social Problems and Thought Problems syndrome scales were also elevated and in the borderline clinical range (93rd to 97th percentiles). Overall, Kayla's mother reported more problems than are typically reported by parents of girls 6–11 years of age, particularly anxious, withdrawn, and depressed behavior, social problems, and thought problems. On the DSM-oriented scales, Kayla's scores on the Affective Problems and Anxiety Problems scales were in the clinical range and suggest that she may be at risk for co-occurring anxiety or mood disorders.

The ASEBA Teacher Report Form (TRF) was completed by Kayla's classroom teacher to obtain her perceptions of Kayla's adaptive functioning and problems in the classroom. Kayla's academic performance was rated below grade-level expectations. She was also rated as working less hard, behaving less appropriately, learning somewhat less, and being much less happy compared with typical students of the same age. Kayla's Total Adaptive Functioning score was in the clinical range below the 10th percentile. On the TRF problem scales, Kayla's Total Problems and Internalizing scores were both in the clinical range and above the 90th percentile. Her scores on the Anxious/Depressed, Withdrawn/Depressed, and Social Problems syndromes were all in the clinical range (97th percentile) and indicate more problems than are typically reported by teachers of girls 6–11 years of age. On the DSM-oriented scales, Kayla's scores on the Affective and Anxiety Problems scales were in the clinical range and suggest that she may be experiencing symptoms associated with internalizing problems such as anxiety and depression.

FAMILY SYSTEM

The Parenting Stress Index, Fourth Edition, Short Form (PSI-4-SF) was utilized to assess areas of stress in the parent–child relationship. Kayla's mother endorsed a high level of overall stress in her role as parent. Domain scores suggest that she may not be able to cope effectively with Kayla's behavior and feels anxious, depressed, and overwhelmed by the demands of parenting. This high level of self-reported distress may be a function of her own temperament or personal characteristics, as well as Kayla's functional impairments, and indicates a need for assistance in understanding and managing her daughter's social and communication deficits.

SUMMARY AND RECOMMENDATIONS

Kayla was referred for an individual evaluation to assess strengths and weaknesses in the areas of intellectual functioning, academic achievement, and social/behavioral adjustment. The results of the current assessment indicate that she is functioning in the average range of general intellectual ability. Kayla earned a Full Scale IQ (FSIQ) score of 108 on the Wechsler Intelligence Scale for Children, Fifth Edition (WISC-V), which places her at the 70th percentile compared with same-age peers. Kayla's cognitive profile indicates particular strength with fluid reasoning tasks compared with tasks involving verbal comprehension and language-based skills. She also demonstrated a significant weakness with executive function measures involving working memory and motor persistence, and planning and organization. The results of the Wechsler Individual Achievement Test, Third Edition (WIAT-III) indicate that, when compared with others at her age level, Kayla's performance is average in oral language, reading, writing, and mathematics. A relative weakness was noted in listening comprehension, expressive vocabulary, and short-term memory.

Observation and behavioral rating scales indicate significant problems in multiple domains of functioning. Kayla demonstrates a mild to moderate impairment in reciprocal social behavior and responsiveness across home and school contexts. Her social-communication (pragmatic) functioning is also positive for concerns related to social relationships and nonverbal communication skills. Kayla's social behavior and communication skills, including expressive vocabulary, listening, conversation, and nonverbal communication, are areas of weakness within her everyday adaptive functioning. Broad-based behavior rating scales completed both at home and school indicates clinically elevated problems in the areas of anxiety or depression, problems in social relationships, and cognitive inflexibility. Likewise, the intensity and frequency of Kayla's self-reported depressive symptoms may be significant enough to impair her adaptive functioning. Kayla's mother also reports a high level of stress in the parent–child relationship and with Kayla's adjustment difficulties within the family system.

Overall results of the current assessment indicate that Kayla presents with deficits in social interaction and communication, restrictive interests and repetitive behavior, resistance to change, and sensory sensitivities often observed with ASD in children and youth. Associated features include an uneven skill profile, with adaptive behavior skills measured well below intellectual ability, and a delay in fine-motor development. Kayla's parent also reports early developmental difficulties related to social interaction and communication skills, repetitive behaviors, and unusual sensory interests. These impairments and atypicalities in communication, social interaction, and behavior significantly affect Kayla's educational performance and progress across academic and social-emotional domains.

Kayla will require small-group and individualized services in language and social communication within a setting that provides support and exposure to typically developing peers. Strategies should be initiated to address social skills and reciprocal social behavior, in particular motivation to engage in social-interpersonal behavior and the interpretation of social cues. Educational planning should also focus on adaptive behavior concerns in the areas of communication, socialization, and daily-living skills. Special attention should be given to the socialization domain, especially interpersonal relationships. The use of social stories may help to improve Kayla's perspective-taking skills and enhance her social understanding and engagement. A comprehensive speech/language assessment is recommended to clarify her communication competence and pragmatic language functioning. Likewise, Kayla's high level of self-reported depressive symptomology indicates the need for further assessment and intervention. Kayla's restricted and repetitive pattern of behavior and sensory processing issues should also be the focus of attention. This should include attention to possible stressors, antecedent factors, and situational sensory demands across home and school contexts. Reducing auditory and visual stimulation in the classroom might reduce overstimulation and improve adaptability. Consultation from an occupational therapist will be helpful in formulating accommodations for Kayla's sensory issues and visual-motor weakness. Kayla's parents are in need of additional support to manage their child's behavioral challenges and should be referred to the appropriate community organizations and agencies for parenting assistance. Lastly, the assessment team should integrate the results of the current evaluation with multiple sources of information, including parent concerns and priorities, to determine the appropriate eligibility and program of special education and related services.

DISCUSSION OF CASE EXAMPLES

Daniel and Kayla's case examples illustrate many of the concepts and methods relevant to the assessment of students identified as at-risk for ASD described in Chapter 3. First and foremost, they demonstrate the best practice application of a comprehensive developmental approach to the evaluation of multiple domains of functioning. These sample reports also show, in addition to Kayla's and Daniel's histories and reports of autistic traits and symptoms, how these behaviors are assessed with multimethod measures across home and school settings.

Although Daniel's and Kayla's impairments in the communication, socialization, and behavioral domains are in keeping with many of the features associated with ASD, there are some important differences in their behavioral profiles. For example, while the most salient feature of both profiles is impairment in social reciprocity and restricted and repetitive behavior, Kayla's profile is one of internalizing behavior and social withdrawal, whereas Daniel's is characterized by externalizing behavior and problems with emotional regulation. Kayla's behavioral profile also provides an example of how it is often the absence of expected behavior (communication and social interaction) rather than atypical behavior that may characterize ASD. Likewise, her profile illustrates the importance of gender differences in the presentation of ASD. In terms of similarities, Daniel and Kayla both exhibit the uneven developmental profile and cognitive rigidity and adherence to routine and sameness often observed in children on the autism spectrum. They also have a consistent profile of adaptive functioning characteristic of ASD—specifically, delays and impairments in the social skills domain compared with age and cognitive ability. Additionally, both demonstrate the difficulties with executive functions related to flexibility, planning, organization, and other aspects of metacognition frequently reported in students with ASD. Their cases also show how co-occurring (comorbid) psychological liabilities such as anxiety and depression can have an adverse effect on social development and educational performance and productivity. Kayla's case example further illustrates how the identification of parental stress can be relevant to providing family support and improving outcomes for children with ASD. Finally, both case examples demonstrate the importance of focusing on social-communication competence and pragmatic skills, in addition to traditional language assessments, as well as assessing and targeting restrictive and repetitive behaviors, including sensory processing issues. Chapter 5 presents systematic research reviews of the evidence-based interventions and treatments for ASD.

BEST PRACTICE IN TREATMENT AND INTERVENTION

Supporting children with ASD requires individualized and effective intervention strategies. It is very important for teachers, administrators, and other school personnel to be knowledgeable about evidence-based approaches to adequately address the needs of students with autism and to help minimize the gap between research and practice. Although the resources for determining best practices in autism are more extensive and accessible than in previous years, school professionals face the challenge of being able to accurately identify these evidence-based strategies and then duplicate them in the classroom and other educational settings (Stansberry-Brusnahan and Collet-Klingenberg, 2010). The rapid growth of the scientific literature on ASD has also made it difficult for practitioners to stay up to date with research findings. Unfortunately, many proponents of ASD treatments make claims of cure or recovery, but provide little scientific evidence of effectiveness. These interventions appear in books and on websites that describe them as "cutting-edge therapies" for autism (Odom and Wong, 2015). Consequently, school-based personnel and families need to have a reliable source for identifying practices that have been shown, through scientific research, to be effective with children and youth with ASD. Evidence-based research provides a starting point for determining what interventions are most likely to be effective in achieving the desired outcomes for an individual. It is imperative not only for the field of special education, but specifically those educators responsible for teaching children with autism to have firsthand knowledge of evidence-based practices. This chapter provides professionals and families with the most current evidence to guide intervention planning and implementation. It presents findings from two nationally recognized systematic research reviews on evidence-based treatment and intervention for ASD, and describes an evidence-based approach to intervention selection, implementation, and progress monitoring. The term *intervention* is used here as an inclusive description of procedures used to improve outcomes for individuals with ASD, commonly described in the literature as treatments, programs, strategies, supports, or services.

BEST PRACTICE

There is a pressing need to train school personnel about ASD and the use of evidence-based methods for teaching and managing behavioral issues.

EVIDENCE-BASED PRACTICE

The term *evidence-based practice* (EBP) first appeared in the professional literature in early 1990s and is now the current benchmark for professionals in medicine, psychology, and education. For example, the American Psychological Association (APA) Task Force on Evidence-Based Practice with Children and Adolescents (2008) recommended that EBP be given priority and that children and adolescents receive the best available evidence-based mental health services based on the integration of science and practice. The use of evidence-based practice has also been emphasized in education policy and legislation such as the No Child Left Behind Act (NCLB; 2001) and the Individuals with Disabilities Education Act (IDEA) reauthorization of 2004 which call upon educational practitioners to use "scientifically-based research" to guide their decisions about which interventions to implement. According to IDEA (2004), scientifically based research means research that involves the application of rigorous, systematic, and objective procedures to obtain reliable and valid knowledge relevant to educational activities, programs, and strategies. Yet many practitioners have not been given the tools and information needed to distinguish interventions supported by scientifically rigorous evidence from those which are not.

BEST PRACTICE

Information about an intervention's effectiveness that is not supported by research, lacks peer review, and comes primarily from testimonials rather than empirical validation should be viewed with extreme caution.

Best practice procedures in various fields require the adherence to evidence-based practice. Developing and implementing effective interventions and treatment for students with autism requires that they be evidence-based and supported by science. All interventions and treatments should be based on sound theoretical constructs, robust methodologies, and empirical studies of effectiveness. An evidence-based practice can be defined as a strategy, intervention, treatment, or teaching program that has met rigorous peer review and other standards, and has a history of producing consistent positive results when experimentally tested and published in peer-reviewed professional journals (Mesibov and Shea, 2011; Simpson, 2005). It excludes evidence that is supported by anecdotal reports, case studies, and publication in non-refereed journals, magazines, internet, and other media outlets (Boutot and Myles, 2011). Evidence-based practices and procedures also have a knowledge base confirming both their efficacy and effectiveness. Treatment efficacy generally refers to whether a particular intervention/treatment has been found to work by means of experimental procedures (e.g. random assignment, control groups) whereas effectiveness involves determining whether a particular intervention has been found to produce a positive outcome in settings and conditions in which the intervention is implemented (e.g. classroom, clinic). Differences between the dimensions of research (efficacy) and typical practice (effectiveness) mean that interventions developed through efficacy trials may need to be adapted to real-world practice contexts. While a certain intervention/treatment may have a strong evidence base, it must also have "utility" and be effective in applied settings (Mash and Hunsley, 2005; Rogers and Vismara, 2008; Silverman and Hinshaw, 2008).

BEST PRACTICE

Evidence-based practice (EBP) requires the integration of professional expertise, family values, and the best research evidence into the intervention planning process.

COMPONENTS OF EVIDENCE-BASED PRACTICE

It is critically important to understand that there is no "one size fits all" approach to intervention for persons with ASD. Individual differences are the rule rather than the exception. Different approaches to intervention have been found to be effective for children and youth with autism, and no comparative research has been conducted that demonstrates one approach is superior to another. The selection of specific interventions should be based on goals developed from a comprehensive developmental assessment of each child's unique needs and family preferences. Although EBP indicates that research should be used as an important source of evidence to guide clinical and educational decision making, other factors must be considered as well. For example, intervention decisions must take into consideration not only the best available research, but each individual's unique presentation including specific strengths and needs, individual and family values and preferences, available family and community resources, and the expertise of the practitioner (Prizant, 2011). Consideration of individual characteristics includes cultural sensitivity and regard for the values, language, religion, education, socioeconomic, and social-emotional factors that influence the family's intervention preferences and participation. Practitioners must also use their training and experience to assist teachers and families in evaluating research data and selecting intervention approaches that are most likely to be effective.

EVIDENCE-BASED INTERVENTIONS

Two broad categories of effective interventions appear in the research literature and are described as either comprehensive or focused (Smith, 2013; Wong *et al.*, 2014). Comprehensive treatment models consist of a set of procedures that are designed to achieve a broad learning or developmental impact on the core deficits of ASD. Examples include the UCLA Young Autism Program, TEACCH Program, LEAP Model, and Denver Model. In contrast, focused interventions are individual instructional practices or strategies used to teach specific targets (i.e. skills, concepts, behaviors) to children and youth with ASD. They may be used in isolation or in combination with other focused interventions to address individual or multiple behavioral goals. This chapter is concerned with focused interventions as opposed to comprehensive treatment models as they are considered the essential building blocks of educational programs for children and youth with ASD.

BEST PRACTICE

Systematic reviews synthesize the results of multiple studies and provide school professionals with summaries of the best available research evidence to help guide decision making and support intervention practice.

SYSTEMATIC RESEARCH REVIEWS

Systematic research reviews play an important role in summarizing and synthesizing the knowledge base for determining what interventions are most likely to be effective in achieving the desired outcomes for children and youth with ASD. There are two major resources available to school professionals that provide a listing, along with systematic reviews, of evidence-based interventions and practices for students with ASD: the National Autism Center's (NAC; 2015b) second phase of the National Standards Project (NSP-2), which reviewed research studies to identify established interventions for individuals with ASD, and the National Professional Development Center on Autism Spectrum Disorders (NPDC on ASD (2015); Wong *et al.*, 2014), which also analyzed numerous research studies and identified evidence-based practices for students with autism. To be included in the NPDC and NAC systematic reviews, the interventions had to be behavioral, developmental, and/or educational in nature. They included interventions and practices that could be implemented in or by school systems, home, and across a variety of settings. Articles were included in the reviews only if they had been published in peer-reviewed journals. The NPDC excluded studies in which the independent variables were only medications, alternative/complementary medicine (e.g. chelation, hyperbaric oxygen therapy, acupuncture), or nutritional supplements/special diets (e.g. melatonin, gluten-free/casein-free, vitamins). Similarly, the NAC excluded studies examining medication trials, nutritional supplements, and complementary and alternative medical interventions, with the exception of therapeutic or modified diets. Both the NAC and NPDC included studies involving participants with conditions that commonly co-occur with ASD (e.g. intellectual disability, language impairment, ADHD, anxiety, depression). The NPDC tended to identify separate interventions, whereas the NAC reviews grouped substantially similarly focused interventions into an overall category or package. The NPDC identified 27 practices that met the research criteria for being evidence-based. Positive evidence was found in the following areas: prompting; antecedent-based interventions; time delay, reinforcement; task analysis; discrete trial training; functional behavior assessment; functional communication training; response interruption/redirection; differential reinforcement; social narratives; structured play group; video modeling; naturalistic interventions; peer-mediated intervention; Pivotal Response Training; visual support; self-management; parent-implemented interventions; social skills training; scripting; technology-aided instruction; Picture Exchange Communication System; and extinction (NPDC, 2015; Wong *et al.*, 2014, 2015). The NAC (2015b) identified 14 established interventions: behavioral interventions; cognitive-behavioral intervention package; comprehensive behavioral treatment for young children; language training; modeling; naturalistic teaching strategies; parent training package; peer training package; pivotal response treatments; schedules; scripting; self-management; social skills package; and story-based interventions. Emerging interventions were identified in 18 areas, while 13 interventions were identified as falling into the unestablished level of evidence (e.g. auditory integration training, facilitated communication, sensory interventions, gluten-free/casein-free diet, and social thinking intervention). According to the NAC (2015b), interventions falling in the established category have sufficient evidence to confidently determine that they are effective and produce favorable outcomes for individuals on the autism spectrum. Emerging interventions are those for which one or more studies suggest they may produce favorable outcomes but require additional high-quality studies. Unestablished interventions are those for which there is little or no evidence in the scientific literature to support their effectiveness with individuals with ASD or rule out the possibility that they may be harmful. The terms *effective practice* and *established intervention* indicate a high level of research support for a particular ASD intervention based on the findings of the two systematic reviews. The NAC and NPDC reports and specific information regarding the review process can be accessed through their respective websites. Brief descriptions of the NAC and NPDC evidence-based interventions/practices can be found in Appendix E.

Table 5.1 shows the overlap between the evidence-based practices and established interventions identified by the NAC and the NPDC reviews. Although both reviews were conducted independently, their findings are very similar and reflect a convergence across these two data sources. For example, the NAC established interventions include focused interventions that the NPDC identified as evidence-based practices. Similarly, several NPDC focused interventions that did not appear on the NAC list of established interventions, were identified as emerging interventions. One common finding among the systematic reviews is that the majority of the effective interventions and practices are derived from the behavioral literature and based on behavioral principles. The largest NAC category of established interventions is the behavioral intervention category, which also has the greatest overlap with NPDC evidence-based practices. This suggests that practitioners will need to have a good understanding of behavioral principles and applied behavioral analysis in order to implement interventions effectively and with fidelity (Suhrheinrich *et al.*, 2014). It must also be stated that these ratings are not intended as an endorsement or a recommendation as to whether or not a specific intervention is suitable for a particular child with ASD. The success of the intervention depends on the interaction between the age of the child, his or her developmental level and individual characteristics, strength of the intervention, and competency of the professional. Each child is different and what works for one may not work for another. As discussed earlier, research findings are only one component of evidence-based practice to consider when selecting interventions. The judgment of the professional with expertise in ASD must be taken into consideration in the decision-making process, together with family values and preferences.

TABLE 5.1 OVERLAP BETWEEN EVIDENCE-BASED INTERVENTIONS IDENTIFIED BY THE NAC AND NPDC

Evidence-based practices identified by the NPDC	Behavioral interventions	Cognitive-behavioral intervention package	Modeling	Naturalistic teaching strategies	Parent training package	Pivotal Response Training	Peer training package	Scripting	Self-management	Story-based intervention	Social skills package	Schedules
Behavioral interventions	X											
Cognitive-behavioral intervention		X										
Modeling			X									
Naturalistic interventions				X								
Parent-implemented intervention					X							
Pivotal Response Training						X						
Peer-mediated instruction							X					
Scripting								X				
Self-management									X			
Social narratives										X		
Social skills training											X	
Visual support												X
Technology-aided instruction	Technology-based intervention was identified as an emerging intervention by the NAC.											
Picture Exchange Communication System	Picture Exchange Communication System was identified as an emerging intervention by the NAC.											
Exercise	Exercise was identified as an emerging intervention by the NAC.											
Functional communication training	Functional communication training was identified as an emerging intervention by the NAC.											

Established interventions identified by the NAC

Structured play groups were identified as an evidence-based practice by the NPDC.

Language training (production) was identified as an established intervention by the NAC.

Comprehensive behavioral treatment for young children was identified as an established intervention by the NAC.

BEST PRACTICE
School professionals should strongly encourage parents and caregivers to investigate thoroughly any Complementary and Alternative Medicine (CAM) treatment approach or non-traditional therapy prior to implementing them with their child.

COMPLEMENTARY AND ALTERNATIVE MEDICINE (CAM) TREATMENTS

Controversial therapies and interventions continue to be a significant part of the history of children and youth with ASD, perhaps more so than any other childhood disorder. Given that autism has no known cure, parents and advocates will understandably pursue interventions and treatments that offer the possibility of helping the child with autism, particularly if they are perceived as unlikely to have any adverse effects and are generally accepted or popularized. Unfortunately, families are often exposed to unsubstantiated, pseudoscientific theories and related clinical practices that are ineffective and compete with validated treatments, or that have the potential to result in physical, emotional, or financial harm. Many CAM treatments are recommended to families based on anecdotal reports that make exaggerated claims, often appearing on the internet or in the popular media which do not qualify as scientific research. The time, effort, and financial resources spent on ineffective treatments can create an additional burden on families. School professionals play an important role in helping parents and caregivers to differentiate empirically validated treatment approaches from treatments that are unproven and potentially ineffective and/or harmful.

A significant number of children with ASD receive complementary and alternative medicine (CAM) treatments in place of, or in addition to, traditionally prescribed interventions or more conventional treatments.

The most commonly used CAM treatments for ASD fall into the categories of "non-biological" and "biological." Examples of non-biological interventions include treatments such as auditory integration training, sensory integration therapy, pet therapy, massage therapy, behavioral optometry, craniosacral manipulation, acupuncture, and facilitated communication. Biological therapies include immunoregulatory interventions (e.g. dietary restriction of food allergens or administration of immunoglobulin or antiviral agents), detoxification therapies (e.g. chelation), hyperbaric oxygen therapy (HBOT), gastrointestinal treatments (e.g. digestive enzymes, antifungal agents, probiotics, and gluten-free/casein-free diet), and dietary supplement regimens (e.g. vitamin A, vitamin C, vitamin B_6 and magnesium, folic acid, folinic acid, vitamin B_{12}, dimethylglycine and trimethylglycine, carnosine, omega-3 fatty acids, inositol, and various minerals).

BEST PRACTICE

Relying on ineffective and potentially harmful treatments puts the child at risk and uses valuable time that could be utilized in more productive educational or remedial activities.

At present, the empirical and treatment literature does not support and recommend the use of either biological or non-biological CAM treatments for children with ASD. There are no CAM interventions with sufficient evidence to suggest they are effective (Brondino *et al.*, 2015; Christon, Mackintosh, and Myers, 2010; Huffman *et al.*, 2011; Warren *et al.*, 2011). This includes modified diets (e.g. gluten-free/casein-free diet), sensory integration therapy, auditory integration training, hyperbaric oxygen therapy, and facilitated communication (American Academy of Pediatrics, 2012; Granpeesheh *et al.*, 2010; Hyman *et al.*, 2016; Lang *et al.*, 2012; Lange, Hauser, and Reissmann, 2015;

Mulloy *et al.*, 2010; National Autism Center, 2015b; National Research Council, 2001). The most extensively evaluated biological CAM treatment for autism, the hormone secretin, has been thoroughly evaluated and shown to be ineffective with respect to the core symptoms of ASD, including self-stimulatory behaviors, impaired communication, restrictive and repetitive behaviors, and gastrointestinal problems (Warren *et al.*, 2011). Additionally, research does not support the use of biological detoxification therapies such as chelation for ASD. According to the U.S. Food and Drug Administration (FDA) (2014), there are serious safety issues associated with chelation products. Similarly, the FDA has announced that hyperbaric oxygen treatment (HBOT) is not an approved or effective treatment for autism. The major risk of CAM treatments is not only the potential for harm (e.g. chelation products), but the time and resources devoted to ineffective therapies at the expense of evidence-based interventions that have demonstrated effectiveness. More methodologically sound research needs to be completed on CAM treatments, and this information disseminated to families by well-informed professionals, so that parents can make educated judgments in selecting interventions (Christon *et al.*, 2010). Lastly, professionals and parents should exercise caution when considering interventions and treatments that (a) are based on overly simplified scientific theories; (b) make claims of recovery and/or cure; (c) use case reports or anecdotal data rather than scientific studies; (d) lack peer-reviewed references or deny the need for controlled research studies; or (e) are advertised to have no potential or reported adverse effects.

BEST PRACTICE
School professionals should have a working knowledge of commonly prescribed medications for ASD and collaborate with parents, physicians, and therapists in evaluating the risks, benefits, and adverse effects of pharmacological interventions.

PHARMACOLOGICAL TREATMENTS

Prescription medications do not address the core symptoms of autism and are not considered to be "first-line" interventions or treatment for children with ASD. At present, early, intensive, and behaviorally based interventions are considered the benchmark interventions for autism. Pharmacologic interventions are often considered for maladaptive behaviors such as aggression, self-injurious behavior, repetitive behaviors, sleep disturbance, anxiety, mood lability, irritability, hyperactivity, inattention, destructive behavior, or other disruptive behaviors in children with ASD. The most commonly prescribed medications are selective serotonin reuptake inhibitors (SSRIs) such as Prozac, Zoloft, and Paxil; stimulants such as Concerta, Metadate, Methylin, Ritalin, and Adderall; and atypical neuroleptics such as risperidone (Risperdal) and aripiprazole (Abilify), both with FDA-approved labeling for the symptomatic (aggression and irritability) treatment of children and adolescents with ASD. Although methylphenidate (Ritalin) has been reported to be effective for reducing hyperactivity in some children with ASD, it has not found to be effective for treating restricted or repetitive behavior or irritability (Huffman et al., 2011). Some marginal evidence of benefit has been reported for various SSRIs in the treatment of restricted, repetitive behaviors, but more study is needed (Huffman et al., 2011; Warren et al., 2011). Although Risperdal and Abilify have been reported by caregivers to reduce problem behaviors such as irritability, hyperactivity, tantrums, abrupt changes in mood, emotional distress, aggression, repetitive behaviors, and self-injury, the risk of adverse (side) effects is considered to be quite high (Warren et al., 2011).

Research indicates increasing rates of psychotropic use and the simultaneous use of multiple psychotropic medications (polypharmacy) among children with ASD. For example, a research study involving a large sample of children with ASD found 64 percent used psychotropic medications and 35 percent had evidence of polypharmacy

(Spencer *et al.*, 2013). Although co-occurring problems such as hyperactivity, inattention, aggression, and anxiety or depression may respond to a medication regimen, as well as relieve family stress and enhance adaptability, there are general concerns about these medications. For example, there is a lack of evidence clearly documenting the safety or effectiveness of psychotropic treatment during childhood. Likewise, there is a paucity of information about the safety and effectiveness of psychotropic polypharmacy and potential interactions between and among medications that may affect individuals with complex psychiatric disorders, including ASD (Spencer *et al.*, 2013). Further research is needed to assess the value of these medications when weighed against their potential for harm. Because school-based professionals may not be aware of the extent and effects of psychotropic use and polypharmacy when working with children with ASD, they should collaborate with parents, primary care providers, and others to carefully obtain medication histories and monitor treatment effects.

BEST PRACTICE
Parents and family members should be involved in the intervention planning process, including setting goals and priorities for their child's treatment and supporting their child's newly acquired skills in home and community activities.

STEPS IN THE INTERVENTION PROCESS

This section describes the steps in the intervention process and how to integrate evidence-based interventions into an effective individualized educational or behavioral program. The complicated nature of intervention planning and implementation requires the participation of an intervention team to plan the intervention(s), arrange supports for the intervention process, monitor progress, and evaluate the student's response to intervention. Members of the team may include but are not limited to the parent(s), student, general education and exceptional education teacher(s), site-based administrator, reading coach, school psychologist, social worker, occupational therapist, speech/language pathologist, and other professionals as needed. ASD intervention should be considered to be a dynamic and ongoing process that occurs within the context of the following three steps.

BEST PRACTICE

It is important to establish goals with specific predicted outcomes before selecting and implementing an intervention.

STEP 1: IDENTIFY GOALS

The first step prior to choosing a specific strategy is conducting an assessment of the student's current skills to create measurable goals. As described in Chapter 4, a comprehensive developmental assessment identifies the unique intervention needs of each individual with ASD. School professionals and families use this information to collaborate and to identify intervention priorities. Goal selection includes consideration of characteristics such as the student's level of cognitive functioning, communication skills, and the severity of social impairment. Intervention goals not only reflect the individual's strengths and needs, but family values and preferences as well. At this first step in the intervention planning process, primary attention is given to current objectives and short-term goals in order to select effective interventions to address those specific needs. Goals and objectives typically are identified in the following broad areas: (a) improving core ASD symptoms in communication, social interaction, and behavioral flexibility; (b) decreasing challenging behaviors such as intrusive RRBs, self-injury, inattention, or aggression; (c) improving academic engagement and achievement; (d) addressing co-occurring emotional/behavioral problems; and (e) accessing related and community services.

Whenever possible, the intervention goal should clearly identify what the student should do (instead of what he or she should not do). It should also be relevant and developmentally appropriate. In other words, the goal should be achievable and lead to meaningful improvements. For example, learning to communicate and socialize appropriately with peers often leads to significant improvements in a student's classroom performance. Similarly, reducing challenging behavior may enhance a student's social interaction with peers and increase the amount of time spent on task. Once the goal is identified, the behavior targeted for change should be very specific, observable, and easily measured. The team then discusses how to measure the target behavior, using what type of collection procedures, the type of data, where, by whom, and how often. Next, a decision is made on a data collection system that provides the most accurate picture of student performance in the classroom. It is important to use manageable techniques for collecting data; if procedures are too burdensome, data may not be collected or the quality or usefulness of the data may be compromised.

Data should be collected both before and during implementation of the intervention to help assess whether the student is making progress toward the selected goal(s). The data collected prior to the intervention are called "baseline" data. Without collecting baseline data, it will be impossible to clearly show whether the intervention has led to student improvement. Although various techniques may be used to collect information (e.g. direct observation, informant questionnaires, practitioner-rated measures, self-report, self-monitoring systems, permanent products), direct systematic observation is one of the most widely used assessment procedures. Observational data collection procedures include counting the number of times a behavior has occurred within a given time period (frequency), determining whether or not behaviors occur within a specific interval of time (time sampling), recording when the behavior begins and stops (duration data), and determining length of time before a behavior occurs (latency data). Direct observation procedures are flexible and can be tailored to suit the specific needs of the assessment situation. They are also one of the most useful strategies for linking assessment to intervention. Although anecdotal evidence may seem helpful, it is often unreliable and should only be used alongside data-based evidence. The reader is referred to the NAC (2015) publication, *Evidence-Based Practice and Autism in the Schools: An Educator's Guide to Providing Appropriate Interventions to Students with Autism Spectrum Disorder* (Second Edition) for a comprehensive discussion and example of procedures for collecting data in the classroom.

BEST PRACTICE

Intervention selection should include consideration of each child's unique presentation including specific strengths and needs, individual and family values and preferences, and available family and community resources.

STEP 2: INTERVENTION SELECTION

Once the goal(s) have been identified and the target behavior(s) operationally defined, the team tries to determine the function or purpose of the problem behavior based on the data collected. Questions include: What are the most likely reasons for this problem and why it is occurring? At this step, the goal is to identify the right match between the student's problem and the intervention. It is important when developing an intervention that planning be directly linked to the problem identified at the outset of the intervention process.

Understanding individual variation in responses to environmental features also plays an important role in intervention planning. Identifying environmental features that are aversive or are highly motivating for a specific individual can be used to make environmental modifications and select interventions that improve individual functioning across home and school settings. This is also a good time to discuss what has worked and what hasn't worked in the past. Next, families and school-based professionals collaboratively review available research evidence from reliable resources (i.e. NAC and NPDC) to identify effective interventions that can address individual intervention goals and provide a good match with other individual characteristics. Once the intervention is selected, this step also identifies who is responsible for implementing the intervention, including the role of parent or caregiver involvement, and provides other relevant details such as the intervention setting, required components, observation system, and frequency or duration of the intervention.

Although the NPDC and NAC provide a strong foundation upon which to base intervention decisions, selection should not be made in a cookbook fashion. Peer-reviewed, empirical research should be considered but one source of evidence in guiding practice. Professional judgment and family input are also essential. Professional judgment involves (a) integrating information about a student's unique history; (b) an awareness of current research findings; and (c) the need to make data-based intervention decisions (NA Center, 2015b). For example, if a family asks about a specific intervention that has been shown to be ineffective or unestablished, the practitioner may discuss the goals the family hopes to address and recommend alternative interventions with a higher level of research support. It is the training and experience of the school-based professional that guides the content of this conversation.

It should also be emphasized here that parent/caregiver involvement is necessary to maximize the effectiveness of interventions because of their central role both in determining the child or individual's environment and experiences and in facilitating coordination of intervention services. Thus, families are treated as partners throughout the intervention process.

STEP 3: MONITOR PROGRESS

Progress monitoring is critical in order to determine whether the intervention is working. Professional judgment and decision making should always be informed by data. Data collected prior to beginning the intervention serve as a baseline or yardstick by which progress is measured. Comparison of the data between the baseline and intervention implementation phases helps professionals and families determine if the intended changes in behavior are occurring and whether the student is progressing toward the intended goal identified in the initial step of the intervention process. During progress monitoring, a decision is made about continuing, modifying, or discontinuing interventions, or introducing new interventions. The team considers questions such as: If progress is noted, does the amount or degree of progress justify continuation of the intervention? Alternatively, if there is no progress or only minimal improvement, are there components of the intervention that need adjustment or is selection of a new intervention most appropriate? Professionals should be prepared to recommend other intervention options if the data show that an intervention does not result in timely progress for the student's target(s). Likewise, interventions often require revision and adjustments to further tailor the intervention to the specific individual student.

BEST PRACTICE

Regardless of the method, school professionals and interventionists should make a determined effort to collect data related to intervention integrity (fidelity).

TREATMENT INTEGRITY

Treatment integrity or fidelity refers to the accuracy and consistency with which each component of a treatment or intervention plan is implemented as intended. It is an important link between the use and effectiveness of interventions in school settings and one of the key aspects of scientific investigation (Elliott and Busse, 1993). Identifying an evidence-based intervention or treatment for ASD is a necessary but insufficient provision for producing behavior change (Wickstrom *et al.*, 1998; Wilkinson, 2006). Intervention plans implemented with poor integrity make it difficult to draw accurate inferences about the effects of individual strategies. In other words, a lack of treatment integrity information compromises the professional's knowledge of what interventions (or components) are responsible for improvement. For example, absent or weak treatment effects might be the result of the poor integrity of interventions, despite their demonstrated empirical support. Unfortunately, this construct has largely been ignored in research and practice (Gresham, Gansle, and Noell, 1993; Lane *et al.*, 2004). The failure to provide treatment integrity information makes it particularly difficult to conclude whether an intervention was ineffective because of the intervention or because the strategy was poorly implemented. Thus, it is essential that treatment integrity information be collected when implementing interventions so as to distinguish between ineffective treatments and potentially effective interventions implemented with poor integrity. The most frequently reported methods of treatment integrity measurement include direct observation; self-reports; rating scales; checklists; interviews; and permanent products resulting from the intervention (Gresham, 1989; Kabot and Reeve, 2014; Wilkinson, 2006).

BEST PRACTICE
Evidence-based strategies such as self-management have shown considerable promise as a method for teaching students with ASD to be more independent and self-reliant, and less dependent on external control and continuous adult supervision.

RESEARCH TO PRACTICE

This section provides a real-world case example of an evidence-based intervention implemented in the classroom to reduce a student's challenging behavior. Self-management is an effective instructional strategy and a component of positive behavioral support that has been shown to facilitate the generalization of adaptive behavior, promote independence, and produce broad behavioral improvements across various contexts for many children with ASD (Lee, Simpson, and Shogren, 2007; NAC, 2015b; Wilkinson, 2005, 2008b; Wong *et al.*, 2014). Self-management procedures are cost-efficient and can be especially effective when used as a component of a comprehensive intervention program (e.g. functional assessment, social groups, curricular planning, sensory accommodations, and parent–teacher collaboration) for ASD.

SELF-MANAGEMENT
One of the salient features of students with ASD is an absence or poorly developed set of self-management skills. This includes difficulty directing, controlling, inhibiting, or maintaining and generalizing behaviors required for adjustment both in and outside of the classroom without external support and structure from others. Many children with ASD do not respond well to typical top-down approaches involving the external manipulation of antecedents and consequences. Self-management provides an opportunity to participate in the development and implementation of their behavior management

programs and teaches students to be more independent and self-reliant, and less dependent on external control and continuous supervision. This can also help minimize the potential for the power struggles and confrontations often encountered with the implementation of externally directed techniques.

Self-management generally involves activities designed to change or maintain one's own behavior. In its simplest form, students are instructed to (a) observe specific aspects of their own behavior; and (b) provide an objective recording of the occurrence or non-occurrence of the observed behavior. This self-monitoring procedure involves providing a cue or prompt and having students discriminate whether or not they engaged in a specific behavior at the moment the cue was supplied. Research indicates that the activity of focusing attention on one's own behavior and the self-recording of these observations can have a positive reactive effect on the behavior being monitored. Designing and implementing a self-management strategy need not be a complicated or difficult undertaking. However, there are several questions to consider:

- What is the target behavior(s)?

- In what setting(s) will the student self-monitor?

- What type of prompt (cue) is most appropriate?

- How often will the student self-monitor?

- What external incentive or rewards will be used?

The following steps provide a general guide to preparing and implementing a self-management plan in the classroom. They should be modified as needed to meet the individual needs of the student.

STEP 1: IDENTIFY PREFERRED BEHAVIORAL TARGETS

The initial step is to identify and operationally define the target behavior(s). This involves explicitly describing the behavior so that the student can accurately discriminate its occurrence and non-occurrence. For example, target behaviors such as "being good" and "staying on task" are broad and relatively vague terms, whereas "raising hand to talk" and "eyes on paper" are more specific. When developing operational definitions, it is also useful to provide exact examples and non-examples of the target behavior. This will help students to recognize when they are engaging in the behavior(s).

While self-management interventions can be used to decrease problem behavior, it is best to identify and monitor an appropriate, desired behavior rather than a negative one. Describe the behavior in terms of what students are supposed to do, rather than what they are not supposed to do. This establishes a positive and constructive alternative behavior. Here are some examples of positive target behaviors:

- Cooperate with classmates on group projects by taking turns

- Follow teacher directions and raise hand before speaking

- Sit at desk and work quietly on the assignment.

STEP 2: DETERMINE HOW OFTEN STUDENTS WILL SELF-MANAGE THEIR BEHAVIOR

An interval method is usually recommended for monitoring off-task behavior, increasing appropriate behavior and compliance, and decreasing disruptive behavior. Typically, the interval will depend on the student's characteristics, such as age, cognitive level, and severity of behavior. Some students will need to self-monitor more frequently than others. For example, if the goal is to decrease a challenging behavior that occurs frequently, then the student will self-monitor a positive, replacement behavior more often. Teachers may wish to establish interval lengths based on their students' individual ability levels and degree of behavioral control.

Once the frequency of self-monitoring is determined, a decision is made as to the type of cue that will be used to signal students to self-observe and record their behavior. In classroom settings, this generally involves the use of a verbal or nonverbal external prompt. There are several types of prompts that can be used to signal students and help teachers monitor their own instructional time in the classroom: verbal cue; silent cue, such as a hand motion; physical prompt; timing device with a vibrating function; kitchen timer; watch with an alarm function; or prerecorded cassette tape with a tone. The type of cue will depend on the ecology of the classroom and the students' individual needs and competencies. Regardless of the prompt selected for the student, it is important that it be age-appropriate, unobtrusive, and as non-stigmatizing as possible.

STEP 3: MEET WITH THE STUDENT TO EXPLAIN THE SELF-MANAGEMENT PROCEDURE

Active student participation is a necessity as it increases proactive involvement in the plan. Once the target behavior has been defined and frequency of self-monitoring decided, discuss the benefits of self-management, behavioral goals, and specific rewards or incentives for meeting those goals with the student. Providing the student with a definition of behaviors to increase and decrease, as well as commenting on the benefits of managing one's own behavior will increase the likelihood of a successful intervention. Students might be told: "Self-management means being responsible for your own behavior so that you can succeed in school and be accepted by others." Asking students to select from a menu of reinforcers or identify at least three preferred school-based activities also helps to ensure that the incentives are truly motivating and rewarding.

STEP 4: PREPARE A STUDENT SELF-RECORDING SHEET

The most popular self-management recording method in school settings is the creation of a paper-and-pencil checklist or form. This form lists the appropriate academic or behavioral targets students will self-observe when they are cued at a specified time interval.

For example, a goal statement such as "Was I paying attention to my seatwork?" would be included as a question to which the student records a response. When developing the form, it is important to consider each student's cognitive ability and reading level. For students with limited reading skills, pictures can be used to represent the target behaviors or response to the goal statement/question. Figure 5.1 provides an example of a self-recording sheet with behavioral goal questions.

Name:			
Date:	**My Self-Monitoring Form**		
Today in class…	Was I paying attention to my assigned work? Was I following the classroom rules?	Y Y	N N
	Was I paying attention to my assigned work? Was I following the classroom rules?	Y Y	N N
	Was I paying attention to my assigned work? Was I following the classroom rules?	Y Y	N N
	Was I paying attention to my assigned work? Was I following the classroom rules?	Y Y	N N
	Was I paying attention to my assigned work? Was I following the classroom rules?	Y Y	N N
	Total number of Y (yes) = _____ My Goal = _____		
Signed:	_____ _____ _____		
	Student *Teacher* *Parent*		

Figure 5.1 Self-Monitoring Form
Source: Adapted from Wilkinson, 2008b

STEP 5: MODEL THE SELF-MANAGEMENT PLAN AND PRACTICE THE PROCEDURE

The use of modeling, practice, and performance feedback is critical in training students to self-manage their behavior. After the target behaviors and goals are identified, frequency of self-monitoring determined, and the data recording form developed, the self-management process is demonstrated for the student. This includes modeling the procedure and asking students to observe while the teacher simulates a classroom scenario. Students are encouraged to role-play both desired and undesired behaviors at various times during practice, and to accurately self-observe and record these behaviors. The teacher also practices rating the target behavior to become familiar with the self-monitoring form and make students aware that others are checking their monitoring. Accuracy is determined by comparing student ratings with those of the teacher made on the same self-recording form. Students are provided with feedback on their progress and, when necessary, given further opportunity to practice. Students practice until they demonstrate mastery of the procedure by meeting a minimum criterion for accuracy (e.g., 80% accuracy for two out of three consecutive instructional sessions).

STEP 6: IMPLEMENT THE SELF-MANAGEMENT PLAN

Once reliability with the self-monitoring procedure is firmly established, the students rate their behavior on the self-recording sheet at the specified time interval in the natural setting. For example, students might be prompted (cued) to record their behavior at ten-minute intervals during independent or small-group instruction in their general education classroom. When cued, the student responds to the self-observation question (e.g. Was I paying attention to my seat work?) by placing a plus "+" (yes) or minus "–" (no) on the recording sheet. Students may also be required to maintain a designated level of accuracy (e.g. no more than one session per week with less than 80% accuracy) during implementation of the self-management procedure. If the level is not maintained, booster sessions are provided to review target behavior definitions and the self-monitoring process.

STEP 7: MEET WITH THE STUDENT TO DETERMINE WHETHER GOALS WERE ATTAINED

A brief conference is held with the student each day to determine whether the behavioral goal was met and to compare teacher and student ratings. Students are rewarded from their reinforcement menus or with the agreed-upon incentives when the behavioral goal is met for the day. If the behavioral goal is not reached, students are told they will have an opportunity to earn their reward during the next day's self-monitoring session. When the students' ratings agree with their teacher (e.g., 80% of the time), they are provided with verbal praise for accurate recording. Accuracy checks can occur more frequently at the beginning of the intervention and reduced once the target behavior is established.

It is important to remember that the teacher's ratings are always the accepted standard. It is not unusual, especially at the beginning of a self-management plan, for the teacher and student to have honest disagreements about the accuracy of the ratings. If this occurs, it is best to initiate a conference with the student to help clarify the target behavior and attempt to resolve the conflict. Occasionally, students may continue to argue with the teacher about the ratings. If this problem persists, then the self-monitoring procedure is discontinued, as it is unlikely to be an effective intervention.

STEP 8: PROVIDE THE REWARDS WHEN EARNED

An important component of self-management is the presence of a reward. Although self-monitoring can be effective without incentives, goal-setting and student selection of reinforcement makes the intervention more motivating and increases the likelihood of positive reactive effects. Therefore, it is critically important that the agreed-upon incentives be provided when students have met their daily behavioral goal.

STEP 9: INCORPORATE THE PLAN INTO A SCHOOL–HOME COLLABORATION SCHEME

Parents play an essential role in developing and implementing behavior management plans for students with ASD. The self-recording sheet is sent home each day for their signature to ensure that the student receives positive reinforcement across settings. It is usually best to have a phone or personal conference with parents before beginning the intervention to explain the purpose of self-monitoring and how they can positively support the intervention at home (such as using their child's special interest as a reward).

STEP 10: FADE THE INTERVENTION

The procedure may gradually be faded once the desired behavior is established in order to reduce reliance on external cueing. This typically involves extending the interval between prompts or reducing the number of intervals. The target behaviors are continuously monitored to determine compliance with the procedures and the need to readjust the fading process. The ultimate goal is to have students self-monitor their behavior independently and without prompting. Once students achieve competency with self-management, they can apply their newly learned self-regulation skills to other situations and settings, thereby facilitating generalization of appropriate behaviors in future environments with minimal or no feedback from others.

CASE EXAMPLE: JASON

Jason was a nine-year-old student with a history of difficulty in the areas of appropriateness of response, task persistence, attending, and topic maintenance. Challenging social behaviors reported by his teacher included frequent off-task behavior, arguing with adults and peers, temper tantrums, and non-compliance with classroom rules. Among Jason's strengths were his well-developed visual memory skills. Several interventions had been tried, but without success, including verbal reprimands, time-out, and loss of privileges. Jason's teacher decided to implement a self-management intervention in an effort to reduce Jason's challenging classroom behavior.

Behavior ratings completed by Jason's teacher indicated that Jason was disengaged and non-compliant more than 60 percent of the time during independent seatwork and small-group instruction. She identified on-task behavior and compliance with classroom rules as the target behaviors. The self-management procedure consisted of two primary components: (a) self-observation and (b) self-recording. Self-observation involved the covert questioning of behavior (e.g. Was I paying attention to my assigned work?) and self-recording the overt documentation of the response to this prompt on a recording sheet. Jason was told: "Self-management means accepting responsibility for managing and controlling your own behavior so that you can accomplish the things you want at school and home." He was also given an example of the target behaviors to be self-monitored. "On-task" behavior was defined as (a) seated at own desk; (b) work materials on desk; (c) eyes on teacher, board, or work; and (d) reading or working on an assignment. "Compliant" was defined as following classroom rules by (a) asking relevant questions of teacher and neighbor; (b) raising hand and waiting turn before speaking; (c) interacting appropriately with other students; and (d) following adult requests and instructions. Jason was trained to accurately self-observe and record the target behaviors. His teacher read the goal questions on the self-recording form and provided examples of behavior indicating their occurrence or non-occurrence. She also modeled the behaviors Jason needed to increase and demonstrated how to use the self-recording form to respond to the behaviors observed. Jason then practiced self-monitoring the target behaviors until he demonstrated proficiency with the procedure.

Following three days of training, the self-monitoring procedure was incorporated into Jason's daily classroom routine. A self-recording form was taped to the upper right-hand corner of his desk. Because he was the only student who was self-monitoring in the class and other students might be disturbed by a verbal cue, his teacher physically cued Jason by tapping the corner of his desk at ten-minute intervals during approximately 50 minutes of independent and small-group instruction. When cued, Jason covertly asked himself: "Was I paying attention to my assigned work?" and "Was I following my teacher's directions and classroom rules?" He then marked the self-recording sheet with a "plus" (Yes) or "minus" (No), indicating his response to the questions regarding the target behaviors. Jason and his teacher then held a brief meeting to determine whether his behavioral goal was met for that day, compare ratings, and sign the self-recording sheet. Jason was provided with the agreed-upon rewards when he met his behavioral goal and provided with verbal praise for accurately matching his teacher's ratings. When he met his daily behavioral goals, Jason could make a selection from a group of his preselected incentives such as additional computer game time and access to a preferred game or activity before school dismissal. The self-recording sheet was then sent home for his parent's signature, so they could review Jason's behavior and provide a reward contingent upon meeting his behavioral goals. The self-monitoring intervention continued for approximately three weeks during which time Jason's teacher continued to collect performance data. She also completed a treatment integrity checklist each day to ensure that all components of the self-monitoring intervention were implemented as planned.

When his teacher determined that Jason's task engagement and compliant behavior had increased to 90 percent, the procedure was slowly faded by increasing the intervals between self-monitoring cues (e.g. 10 minutes, 15 minutes, and 20 minutes). Jason's teacher continued to monitor the target behaviors to determine whether additional support (e.g. booster sessions) was needed to maintain his performance. The goal of the final phase of the plan was to eliminate the prompts to self-monitor and instruct Jason to keep track of his "own" behavior. Home–school communication continued via a daily performance report to help maintain his self-management independence and positive behavioral gains. Periodic behavioral ratings by Jason's teacher indicated that task engagement and compliant behavior remained at significantly improved levels several weeks after the self-monitoring procedure was completely faded.

LIMITATIONS

Despite the potential uses and benefits of self-management, this strategy is not without some limitations. Self-management procedures are intended to complement, not replace, positive behavioral support strategies already in place in the classroom. They are not static and inflexible procedures, but rather a framework in which to design and implement effective interventions. For example, the self-monitoring plan described in Jason's case example represents only one of the many possible ways that self-management procedures can be utilized in the classroom. School professionals are encouraged to use their creativity in applying the components of self-management to their own classroom situations.

Shifting from an external teacher-managed approach to self-management can present some obstacles. As with other interventions, self-management strategies can fail due to student and teacher resistance, poor training, and/or a lack of appropriate reinforcement. Successful implementation of self-management procedures requires that students be motivated and actively involved in the self-monitoring activities. Likewise, teachers considering implementation of a self-management intervention will need to invest the time required to identify behavior needs, establish goals, determine reinforcers, and teach students how to recognize, record, and meet behavioral goals. In order for self-management to be an effective intervention, the procedures must be acceptable to all parties and implemented with integrity. If not fully supported, it is better to focus on a more suitable behavior management approach.

Self-management interventions are not appropriate for every child with ASD. Some procedures will meet the needs of individual students better than others. For example, seriously challenging behaviors may require a comprehensive approach using multiple intervention strategies. Students may also react differently to self-management procedures. A number of students will find being in control a motivating and reinforcing activity. For others, self-management procedures may actually prove to be a time-consuming distraction. As with any behavioral intervention, a thorough understanding of the student's problems and needs should precede and dictate selection of a specific behavior management strategy.

BEST PRACTICE
Different approaches to intervention have been found to be effective for children with autism, and no comparative research has been conducted that demonstrates one approach is superior to another. The selection of a specific intervention should be based on goals developed from a comprehensive developmental assessment and systematic research reviews.

CONCLUSION

In order to meet the challenging and diverse needs of students with ASD, school professionals must be able to access ongoing research, systematic reviews, and the tools to implement effective interventions and supports. Research findings are not the only factor involved when selecting an intervention. Professional judgment, and values and preferences of parents and caregivers, and the individual's unique needs and abilities are also important. Although children with ASD share a number of similar behavioral and other characteristics, intervention approaches must be sensitive to a child's uniqueness and individuality. Unfortunately, intervention research cannot predict, at the present time, which particular intervention approach works best with which children. It cannot be emphasized too often that no single approach, intervention strategy, or treatment is effective for all children with ASD, and not all children will receive the same level of benefit. The most effective programs are those that incorporate a variety of empirically supported practices and are designed to address and support the unique needs of individual students and families (National Research Council, 2001). Chapter 6 examines best practice procedures in special education eligibility and planning for children with ASD.

BEST PRACTICE IN SPECIAL EDUCATION

Mental health professionals, educators, and policy makers recognize that educational programs are essential to providing effective services to children with ASD. Educational provision is considered to be the most effective treatment for children with autism. However, educators are faced with some unique challenges. Children with autism have intellectual and academic profiles that can differ to a large degree. No two children are alike. As a result, no one program exists that will meet the needs of every child with autism. Additionally, children with autism learn differently from typical peers or children with other types of developmental disabilities. To meet the needs of the individual child, it is critical to examine the child's strengths, weaknesses, and unique needs when determining the appropriate educational placement and developing a program of special education services. This chapter focuses on special education law, eligibility and placement, individualized educational programs (IEPs), family support, and legal issues. Several evidence-based strategies and supports designed to improve academic and communication skills, promote social interaction, and decrease challenging behavior are also described.

BEST PRACTICE
A clinical or medical diagnosis of ASD alone is not sufficient to qualify a child for special education services under the IDEA disability category of autism. It is state and federal education codes and regulations (not clinical criteria) that determine eligibility and IEP planning decisions.

SPECIAL EDUCATION LAW

INDIVIDUALS WITH DISABILITIES EDUCATION ACT (IDEA)

Two federal laws, the Individuals with Disabilities Education Act (IDEA) and Section 504 of the Rehabilitation Act of 1973 (Section 504), regulate the services to children and youth identified with disabilities in public schools. These laws are differentiated by their eligibility requirements and the benefits they provide. State laws complement the coverage of IDEA and Section 504, with the general rule being that they may add to, but not subtract from, the foundational requirements in these federal laws. Thus, states may provide additional rights and benefits to those provided under federal law. For those children who meet eligibility criteria, IDEA provides special education and related services from birth to 36 months of age under Part C of the Act and ages three to 21 years or until graduation from high school under Part B of the Act. Under IDEA, school-based professionals determine a child's eligibility for special education services in one or more of the 13 categories (see Appendix B) mandated in the law, including the autism category. As described earlier, the educational classification of autism is defined as

> a developmental disability significantly affecting verbal and nonverbal communication and social interaction, generally evident before age three, that adversely affects a child's educational performance. Other characteristics often associated with autism are engagement in repetitive activities and stereotyped movements, resistance to environmental change or change in daily routines, and unusual responses to sensory experiences. (IDEA, 2004)

As previously noted, a medical/clinical diagnosis of ASD does not directly translate into eligibility for special education under the autism category. Although clinical diagnoses, psychiatric reports, and treatment recommendations can be helpful in educational planning, the provisions of IDEA are the controlling authority (not DSM-5) with regard to decisions for special education eligibility and placement. The child is eligible for services only by meeting the criteria for autism or another disability category under IDEA, and any applicable state criteria that are consistent with the IDEA definition. However, a child who receives a clinical diagnosis of ASD that adversely affects his or her educational performance may be referred for special education eligibility under the IDEA category of autism. If clinical/medical information or reports are available, they should be considered as part of the assessment information that is reviewed during the special education eligibility process. Once again, it is the child's educational team (including his or her parent/family) that determines the appropriate, if any, special education category for the individual student.

Two legal mandates, free appropriate public education (FAPE) and least restrictive environment (LRE), exist within the context of IDEA to protect children and youth with disabilities and ensure their access to the educational environment. The guiding principle of IDEA is FAPE, which states that all children with disabilities must have available to them a free appropriate public education program that emphasizes special education and related services designed to meet their unique needs and prepare them for employment and independent living. This means that any program and placement offered to parents must be at no cost and take into consideration the unique needs of the individual student, and not be based solely on factors such as category of disability, availability of special education and related services, extent of the service delivery system, administrative fiat, funding formula, or other factors external to the unique needs and abilities of the individual student (Kurth, 2015; Twachtman-Cullen and Twachtman-Bassett, 2011). LRE is also a major tenet of the IDEA and mandates that:

> To the maximum extent appropriate, children with disabilities, including children in public or private institutions or other care facilities, are educated with children who are not disabled, and

special classes, separate schooling, or other removal of children with disabilities from the regular educational environment occurs only when the nature or severity of the disability of a child is such that education in regular classes with the use of supplementary aids and services cannot be achieved satisfactorily. (IDEA, 2004)

Thus, every effort must be made to have the child learn alongside typically developing students in general education classes with appropriate aids and supports when recommending placement and services. If this is not possible, schools have the responsibility of providing a continuum of alternative services and placements to educate students in the setting that provides them with the least restriction. This continuum requirement emphasizes the importance of meeting the unique needs of the student, rather than a "one size fits all" approach in determining the LRE placement for each student with a disability. Educational placements can range from full inclusion in general education classrooms with supports, to itinerant or co-taught classes (both a special and general education teacher in the classroom), to pull-out resource classes (assistance for selected, core academic subjects), to special education classrooms (either full or partial day), and to specialized school placements outside of the public school setting (specialized residential behavioral treatment programs) (Kabot and Reeve, 2014; Wagner, 2014). It is especially important to understand that LRE is not a specific placement. IDEA 2004 clearly states that special education is a service for children with disabilities rather than a place, and recognizes that some students may require a more comprehensive program to meet their unique needs. Consequently, the general education classroom may not always be the least restrictive environment in which the student with ASD can derive the most educational benefit.

SECTION 504

Section 504 of the Rehabilitation Act of 1973 is also a federal law that protects the rights of students with disabilities. There are a number of differences between Section 504 and IDEA, which have different, but complementary, objectives. The key differences from IDEA are that Section 504 is a civil rights law rather than an educational benefit and funding law, and has a broader definition of disability. Section 504 is designed to "level the playing field" for individuals with disabilities by eliminating barriers that exclude them from participating in protected activities, regardless of the nature or severity of the disability. Like IDEA, Section 504 requires schools to provide evaluations for eligibility, FAPE for eligible children, and impartial hearings as one of the procedural safeguards. However, the administering agency within the U.S. Department of Education is the Office for Civil Rights (OCR), which provides both policy interpretations and a complaint resolution process. The definition of a disability is also much broader under Section 504 than it is under IDEA. Section 504 defines a person with a disability as (a) having a physical or mental impairment which limits one or more major life activity; (b) having a record of such impairment; or (c) being regarded as having an impairment. Major life activities include caring for one's self, performing manual tasks, walking, seeing, hearing, speaking, breathing, learning, and working. The list of examples of major life activities is not exclusive, and an activity or function not specifically listed in the Section 504 regulatory provision can be considered a major life activity. For example, social interaction qualifies as a major life activity under Section 504 and may provide protection for children and youth with ASD (Zirkel, 2014). Another major difference between Section 504 and IDEA is that, unlike IDEA, Section 504 does not ensure that an eligible student will receive an IEP designed to meet his or her unique learning needs. Rather, Section 504 provides accommodations based on the child's disability and resulting weaknesses that are intended to afford the same access to education as individuals without disabilities. These accommodations may be detailed in a written plan (504 Accommodation Plan) and include, but are not limited to, extra time on tests, larger text, reduced work load, supplemental materials, specialized curricula, preferential seating, use of a computer, visual supports, one-to-one instruction, oral reading of materials, short work sessions, peer note takers, and pre-teaching. It should also be noted that some students will be covered under both IDEA and Section 504. For example, students who are eligible for special educational services under IDEA are automatically included under Section 504. Although school professionals and parents of children with disabilities are more often familiar with the provisions of IDEA, they should also have an understanding of Section 504 of the Rehabilitation Act. Knowledge of both statutes, particularly their implementing regulations, is important to ensure an appropriate education for children and youth identified with disabilities in the schools.

BEST PRACTICE

The determination of an eligibility for autism should include a variety of assessment tools and information sources, and should not be based on a single process or approach.

RESPONSE TO INTERVENTION (RTI)

Response to intervention, commonly referred to as RTI, is defined as "the practice of providing high-quality instruction and interventions matched to student need, monitoring progress frequently to make decisions about changes in instruction or goals, and applying child response data to important educational decisions" (Batsche *et al.*, 2005, p.3). It is considered a prevention-oriented approach to linking assessment and instruction that can inform educators' decisions about how best to teach their students. Schools use RTI data to identify students at risk for poor learning outcomes, monitor student progress, provide evidence-based interventions, and adjust the intensity and nature of those interventions depending on a student's responsiveness (National Center on Response to Intervention, 2010). RTI employs a multi-level prevention system including three levels of intensity or three levels of prevention (primary, secondary, and tertiary), which represent a continuum of supports. As students move through the framework's specified levels of prevention, their instructional program becomes more intensive and more individualized to target their specific areas of learning or behavioral need. Progress monitoring is used to assess students' performance over time, to quantify student rates of improvement or responsiveness to instruction, to evaluate instructional effectiveness, and, for students who are least responsive to effective instruction, to formulate effective individualized programs.

IDEA 2004 allows states to use a process based on a student's response to scientific, research-based interventions (i.e. RTI) to determine if the child has a specific learning disability (SLD). However, federal law does not require schools to use RTI to determine eligibility for all disabilities. The Office of Special Education Programs (OSEP) has clarified that the IDEA does not address the use of an RTI model for children suspected of having disabilities other than SLD and has emphasized that although RTI may be used to determine if a child responds to scientific, research-based intervention as part of the evaluation process, RTI is not, in itself, the equivalent to or replacement for a comprehensive evaluation (U.S. Department of Education, 2007; Hale, 2008). Schools must use a variety of assessment tools and strategies to gather relevant functional, developmental, and academic information about the child, including information provided by the parent, which may assist in determining eligibility, and not use any single measure or assessment as the sole criterion for determining whether a child has a disability, and for determining an appropriate educational program. This requirement applies to all children suspected of having a disability (IDEA, 2004).

Although RTI is an important advance in educational practice, there are serious concerns about identifying a child with autism utilizing the RTI process. The heterogeneity of needs and high level of co-occurring problems demonstrated by children and youth with autism may affect the overall use and generalizability of the RTI model. For example, intervention research cannot predict, at the present time, which particular intervention approach works best with which children. Similarly, the needs of children with ASD are complex and often more difficult to identify than those with other disabilities. A lack of understanding of ASD and some of the more subtle symptoms of ASD might also result in the use of interventions and teaching methods that are inappropriate for this group of children (Twachtman-Cullen and Twachtman-Bassett, 2011). Moreover, some intervention and assessment procedures for ASD require a specific knowledge base and skills for successful implementation. Teachers may not have the skills to implement scientifically based instructional practices and assessments. For example, research indicates that school personnel's (i.e. general education and special education teachers, school counselors, and paraprofessionals) factual knowledge about the assessment/diagnosis and treatment of autism is low and that few teachers receive training on evidence-based practices for students with ASD (Hendricks, 2011; Williams *et al.*, 2011). Even with adequate teacher training, it is difficult to determine if the interventions were implemented with integrity (i.e. accurately and consistently). In addition, measures used to identify response to intervention may not have adequate reliability and validity (Hale, 2008). Although evidence-based interventions delivered across the levels of RTI might be considered as part of the assessment process, RTI is not a substitute for a comprehensive evaluation in determining a student's eligibility for special education under the IDEA disability category of autism. The determination of autism should include a variety of information sources and measures, and should not be based on a single measure, process, or information source. At present, the comprehensive development assessment model described in Chapter 3 represents best practice in the evidence-based assessment and identification of ASD in the school context.

BEST PRACTICE
The IEP is the cornerstone for the education of a child with ASD and the vehicle for planning and implementing education objectives and services.

INDIVIDUALIZED EDUCATION PROGRAM (IEP)

For school-aged children, the special education process begins with the screening and identification of students who may have the need for special programs and services. The evaluation process is comprehensive and results in a profile of the child's unique pattern of abilities. A team of qualified professionals and the child's parents then review the child's evaluation, and the team decides if the child meets eligibility criteria as defined by IDEA and their respective state and local education agencies. Once again, it is the student's educational team (including his or her parent/caregiver) that determines the appropriate, if any, educational eligibility category for the individual student. When a student is determined eligible for special education services, a team is formed to develop an individualized education program or plan (IEP) and recommend the appropriate classroom placement based on the child's unique learning needs (Wagner, 2014).

The IEP is the cornerstone for the education of a child with a disability which details not only how, but where a student's disability will be addressed in the school system in order to provide progress in an educational program. Regardless of the service delivery option recommended by the team, an effective education placement for children with ASD should include the following elements: (a) highly structured physical environments; (b) consistent and predictable classroom schedules and routines for engaging both students and staff; (c) visual supports to facilitate independence, receptive language, self-regulation, and academic achievement, and to enhance participation in classroom and learning activities; (d) an integration of the curriculum with individual needs; (e) specialized instructional strategies that address the student's unique learning style; (f) a systematic review of the student's progress through periodic curriculum-based assessment, and regular data collection and analysis to inform instruction; and (g) specialized training and support to all school staff involved in educating the student with ASD (Iovannone *et al.*, 2003; Kabot and Reeve, 2014; National Research Council, 2001).

BEST PRACTICE
A comprehensive IEP should be based on the student's unique strengths and weaknesses. Goals for a student with ASD usually include the areas of communication, social interaction, challenging behavior, and academic and functional skills.

CONTENT OF THE IEP
The key to any child's education program lies in the objectives specified in the IEP and the manner in which they are addressed. Parents, teachers, and support professionals play a key role in the development, implementation, and evaluation of the child's IEP. Educational legislation supports the involvement of family members in the educational process. Parents should be involved both in their child's assessment and in decisions that are made regarding service delivery needs. In addition, parents and teachers should collaborate when identifying skills to target for development (IDEA, 2004). All parties share the responsibility for monitoring the student's progress

toward meeting specific academic, social, and behavioral goals and objectives in the IEP. Although the type and intensity of services will vary, depending on the student's age, cognitive and language levels, behavioral needs, and family priorities, the IEP should address all areas in which a child needs educational assistance, together with the specific setting in which the services will be provided and the professionals who will provide the service (Twachtman-Cullen and Twachtman-Bassett, 2011; Wagner, 2014). Goals for a child with ASD commonly include the areas of communication, social behavior, adaptive skills, challenging behavior, and academic and functional skills. Evidence-based instructional strategies should also be adopted to ensure that the IEP is implemented appropriately. The content of an IEP must include the following (IDEA, 2004):

- A statement of the child's present level of educational performance (both academic and non-academic aspects of his or her performance).

- Specific goals and objectives designed to provide the appropriate educational services. This includes a statement of annual goals that the student may be reasonably expected to meet during the coming academic year, together with a series of measurable, intermediate objectives for each goal.

- Appropriate objective criteria, evaluation procedures and schedules for determining, at least annually, whether the child is achieving the specific objectives detailed in the IEP.

- A description of all specific special education and related services, including individualized instruction and related supports and services to be provided (e.g. counseling; occupational, physical, and speech/language therapy; transportation) and the extent to which the child will participate in regular educational programs with typical peers.

- Accommodations should be specifically documented in the IEP. Adjustments may be made to (a) instructional methods, teaching style, and curricular materials; (b) classroom and homework assignments; (c) assessment tools and ways of responding; (d) time requirements; and (e) environmental setting.

- Provision for extended school year (ESY) services, if special education and related services are needed beyond the usual school year to meet the student's unique needs.

- The initiation date and duration of each of the services to be provided (including ESY services).

- If the student is 16 years of age or older, the IEP must include a description of transitional services (coordinated set of activities designed to assist the student in movement from school to post-school activities).

The IEP team should review the child's IEP periodically, but not less than annually, to determine whether the annual goals for the child are being achieved. School districts should ensure that progress monitoring of students with ASD is completed at specified intervals by an interdisciplinary team of professionals who have a knowledge base and experience in autism. This includes collecting evidence-based data to document progress toward achieving IEP goals and to assess program effectiveness. School districts should also provide ongoing training and education in ASD for both parents and professionals. Professionals who are trained in specific methodology and techniques will be most effective in providing the appropriate services and in modifying curriculum based upon the unique needs of the individual child. Appendix F provides examples of IEP goals and objectives.

BEST PRACTICE
The development of a formal transition plan is critical for youth with ASD and includes a coordinated set of activities and objectives to address new developmental challenges such as independent living, vocational engagement, post-secondary education, and family support.

TRANSITION PLAN

Once the young person with autism leaves the school system, the educational entitlements of the IDEA are no longer available. The lack of supports and services available to help adolescents transition to greater independence has become a critical issue as the prevalence of ASD continues to grow and as children identified with ASD reach adolescence and young adulthood. A growing number of youth face significant challenges as they transition to adulthood, with many on the spectrum unemployed, isolated, and lacking services (Orsmond *et al.*, 2013). Research indicates that outcomes are almost universally lower for youth on the autism spectrum compared with their peers who have other types of disabilities. For example, a recent report (Roux *et al.*, 2015) found that only about one in five lived independently (without parental supervision) in the period between high school and their early 20s. Sixty percent of youth had at least two health or mental health conditions in addition to ASD, and nearly 50 percent of youth experienced threats and bullying during high school. Unfortunately, transition planning, a key process for helping youth build skills and access services as they enter adulthood, was frequently delayed. Just 58 percent of youth had a transition plan by the federally required age.

The transition from school to adulthood is a process for all students, regardless of their disability, and begins when students and their parents begin planning for their life after high school. A transition plan is critical for young people with ASD to be successful and participate to the fullest extent possible in society. The focus of intervention/ treatment must shift from addressing the core deficits in childhood to promoting adaptive behaviors that can facilitate and enhance ultimate functional independence and quality of life in adulthood. This includes new developmental challenges such as independent living, vocational engagement, post-secondary education, and family support. IDEA requires that transition plan activities for students with disabilities begin no later than the first IEP to be in effect when the child turns 16, or younger if determined appropriate by the IEP team or state education agency. Transition services are considered to be a coordinated set of activities that focus on improving the academic and functional achievement of the child with a disability to facilitate the movement from school to post-school activities, including post-secondary education, vocational education, integrated employment (as well as supported employment), continuing and adult education, adult services, independent living, or community participation. Responsibilities of the IEP team include coordinating communication and services between school and community-based service providers; addressing environmental, sensory, behavioral, and/or mental health concerns; identifying potential careers and employers; and teaching work behaviors, job skills, and community living skills (Virginia Department of Education, 2010). Just as with other educational services in a student's IEP, schools must provide the services necessary for the student to achieve the transition goals stated in the IEP. The IEP must include: (a) appropriate measurable post-secondary goals based upon age-appropriate transition assessments related to training, education, employment, and, where appropriate, independent living skills; (b) the transition services (including courses of study) needed to assist the child in reaching those goals; and (c) beginning not later than one year before the child reaches the age of majority under state law, a statement that the child has been informed of the child's rights under Part B, if any, that will transfer to the child on reaching the age of majority. The school must also invite the student to his or her IEP meeting if a purpose of the meeting will be the consideration of the post-secondary goals for the child and the transition services needed to assist the child in reaching these goals (IDEA, 2004).

BEST PRACTICE

Functional behavior assessment (FBA) is a well-established tool for identifying and developing behavior intervention plans for students with ASD. Interventions developed from FBA information are more likely to result in a reduction of challenging behavior.

BEHAVIOR INTERVENTION PLAN (BIP)

The IDEA amendments require that a functional behavior assessment (FBA) be completed and a behavior intervention (or support) plan (BIP) implemented for students with disabilities when they are the subject of school discipline proceedings or being considered for an alternative placement. IDEA also requires that the IEP team include "positive behavioral interventions, strategies, and supports" when addressing the needs of students who demonstrate persistent challenging behavior that impedes their learning or the learning of others (IDEA 2004). If the child's behavior is not addressed in the IEP, the IEP team must review and revise the IEP to ensure that the child receives appropriate behavioral interventions and supports.

A behavior intervention plan or BIP is a written individualized support plan based on a functional assessment of the child's challenging behavior that utilizes behavioral interventions and supports in order to reduce behaviors that interfere with the learning progress and/or to increase adaptive, socially appropriate behaviors that lead to successful learning for the student. A BIP is considered a legal document that incorporates a comprehensive set of procedures and support strategies that are selected on the basis of the individual student's needs, characteristics, and preferences, and supports the goals and objectives of the IEP. Positive behavioral intervention plans include (a) modifications to the environment; (b) teaching skills to replace problem behaviors; (c) effective management of consequences; and (d) promotion of positive life-style changes. If the child needs a BIP to improve learning and socialization, the BIP can be included as part of the IEP and aligned with the goals in the IEP.

Functional behavior assessment (FBA) is an important component of providing positive behavior support and for developing a BIP for students with ASD. FBA methods are considered best practice in identifying and designing behavioral interventions, and must be conducted prior to the development and implementation of a BIP. A consistent finding has been that intervention plans developed from

FBA information are more likely to result in a significant reduction of challenging behavior (Carr *et al.*, 1999; Dunlap and Fox, 1999; Horner *et al.*, 2002). The process of conducting an FBA is best described as (a) a strategy to discover the purposes, goals, or functions of a student's behavior; (b) an attempt to identify the conditions under which the behavior is most likely and least likely to occur; (c) a process for developing a useful understanding of how a student's behavior is influenced by or relates to the environment; and (d) an attempt to identify clear, predictive relationships between events in the student's environments and occurrences of challenging behavior and the contingent events that maintain the problem behavior. For example, students might exhibit challenging behaviors with the goal of escape or the goal of seeking attention. When the curriculum is difficult or demanding, students may attempt to avoid or escape work through their behavior (e.g. refusal, passive aggression, disruption). Similarly, they may also use challenging behavior to get focused attention from parents, teachers, siblings, and peers, or to gain access to a preferred item or participate in an enjoyable activity. Challenging behavior may also occur because of sensory aversions. Because students with ASD have significant social and pragmatic skills deficits, they may experience difficulty effectively communicating their needs or influencing the environment. Thus, challenging classroom behavior may serve a purpose for communicating or a communicative function. Understanding the goal of student behavior can help develop and teach alternative replacement behavior and new interactional skills.

An FBA can be conducted in a variety of ways. There are two general assessment tools to assist in the collection of information about the variables and events that surround the occurrence (or non-occurrence) of the student's challenging behavior. The first are interviews and rating scales (see Chapter 3) that provide information from the individuals (parents, teachers) who know the student best, along with the student themselves. The second method is direct observation of the student in his or her natural daily environments.

Data collection through direct observation focuses on recording patterns of behavior and events in the environment as they are actually occurring. Two particularly useful tools are ABC (Antecedent-Behavior-Consequence) recording and scatter plots. The ABC format involves recording the A or antecedent to the behavior (what happens right before the behavior occurs) and the C or consequence of the behavior (what happens directly after the behavior). With scatter plots, the observer notes instances of behaviors on a chart or grid, which often allows patterns of behavior to be more quickly observed.

The following are a general guide to developing a student behavior intervention or support plan:

- Behavioral support plans should be developed collaboratively with input from the student's entire IEP team and begin with a functional behavioral assessment of the problem behavior to understand the student and the nature of the challenging behavior in the context of the environment.

- The team examines the results of the FBA and develops hypothesis statements as to why the student engages in the challenging behavior. The hypothesis statement is an informed, assessment-based explanation of the challenging behavior that indicates the possible function or functions served for the student. This includes a description of the behavior, triggers or antecedents for the behavior, maintaining consequences, and the purpose of the problem behavior.

- Once developed, the hypothesis provides the foundation for the development of intervention strategies. The focus of the intervention plan is not only on behavior reduction, but for also teaching appropriate, functional skills that serve as alternative/replacement behaviors for the undesirable behavior. Changes should be identified that will be made in classrooms or other environments to reduce or eliminate problem behaviors.

Prevention strategies may include environmental arrangements, personal support, changes in activities, new ways to prompt a child, changes in expectations, etc. These strategies should be integrated into a student's overall program and daily routines, rather than being separate from the educational curriculum. Goals for teaching replacement skills, for example, should be addressed in the student's IEP.

- A positive behavior intervention plan must be implemented as planned (with integrity) and effects monitored. Once the plan has been implemented, the team regularly reviews and evaluates its effectiveness and makes modifications as needed.

The development and implementation of BIPs should be considered as a dynamic process rather than one with a specific beginning and ending. Over time, they will need to be adjusted as the student's needs and circumstances change. Readers interested in a comprehensive discussion of issues related to school-based functional assessment and positive behavioral intervention are referred to Alberto and Troutman, 2012; Chandler and Dahlquist, 2010; Crone, Hawken, and Horner, 2015; and O'Neill *et al.*, 2015.

BEST PRACTICE
A variety of evidence-based interventions and strategies should be used to support the student's IEP goals and objectives.

STRATEGIES AND SUPPORTS

The following evidence-based strategies and supports may be used in developing and implementing a comprehensive special education program for learners with ASD.

ASSISTIVE TECHNOLOGY

Assistive technology (AT) refers to a number of accommodations and adaptations which enable individuals with disabilities to function more independently. AT includes any type of technology that provides students with disabilities greater access to the general education curriculum and increases the potential to master academic content, interact with others, and enhance functional independence and quality of life. While AT is not necessary or required for every student receiving special education services, schools are required to provide the appropriate AT system when it supports the child's access to a free and appropriate public education (FAPE). There are various types of technology ranging from "low" to "high" tech that might be incorporated into the educational setting to increase children's independent functioning skills and reduce barriers that may prevent them from performing at a similar level to their peers. For example, students may use software with word prediction capabilities that allow them to have more success with written composition. Hardware such as portable keyboards, laptop computers, and tablets may lessen the physical demand of writing for students with weak fine-motor skills or difficulty coordinating ideas with writing. Similarly, a speech-generating device or voice output communication aids may meet the needs of children with limited expressive language, by providing an effective means of verbal communication.

BEST PRACTICE

The Picture Exchange Communication System (PECS) is a widely used form of augmentative and alternative communication (AAC) that has been shown to produce positive improvements in communication and interpersonal skills for some children with ASD.

Communication impairments can impact an individual's ability to communicate with others (expressive communication) and/or receive communication from others (receptive communication). Augmentative and alternative communication (AAC) is a type of assistive technology that can help children with communication impairments to increase skills in this area and to become more competent communicators. Some students with ASD who have difficulty with expressive communication may be successful in social interaction and expressing their wants and needs with a low-technology AAC system such as the Picture Exchange Communication System (PECS; Frost and Bondy, 2002). PECS is considered an evidence-based practice that incorporates both behavioral and developmental-pragmatic principles to teach functional communication to children with limited verbal and/or communication skills (National Professional Development Center on Autism Spectrum Disorders, 2015). PECS-based methods have been used to successfully improve functional communication, play, and behavioral skills (Charlop-Christy *et al.*, 2002; Ganz *et al.*, 2012; Hart and Banda, 2010; Sulzer-Azaroff *et al.*, 2009).

It is important for educational teams to consider AAC for any student with ASD. For some students, AAC may act as the primary mode of communication. For others, it may be a secondary form. A referral to an assistive technology specialist or speech/language pathologist for an evaluation should be made for a student who may benefit from assistive technology and/or an augmentative communication system (Kabot and Reeve, 2014). As with all assessment and intervention procedures, a team approach is necessary to determine the child's strengths and limitations, and the range and scope of potential assistive technology options to address his or her specific needs.

BEST PRACTICE

Educational programs for children with ASD should incorporate appropriately structured physical and sensory environments within the context of functional educational goals to accommodate any unique or problematic sensory processing patterns.

OCCUPATIONAL THERAPY

Occupational therapy (OT) may be included in a child's IEP if he or she requires these services to benefit from special education and/or to access the general education curriculum. The OT practitioner employs strategies, adaptations, modifications, and/or assistive technology to reduce barriers that limit student participation and increase success throughout the school day.

Services for children with ASD may include: (a) facilitating play activities that instruct as well as aid in interacting and communicating with others; (b) devising strategies to help transition from one setting to another, from one person to another, and from one developmental phase to another; (c) collaborating with the family to identify safe methods of community mobility; and (d) developing or adapting daily activities that are meaningful to enhance the child's performance and quality of life (American Occupational Therapy Association, 2010).

Unusual sensory responses (i.e. sensory over-responsivity, sensory under-responsivity, and sensory seeking) are relatively common in children with ASD and, when present, may interfere with performance in many developmental and functional domains across home and school contexts. The use of sensory integration therapy (SIT) for treatment of ASD has been both popular and controversial. Although SIT is often used individually or as a component of OT services for children with ASD, this intervention is best described as unsupported. For example, a systematic review of intervention studies involving the use of SIT concluded that the current evidence base does not support its use in the education and treatment of children with ASD (Lang *et al.*, 2012).

The National Autism Center's National Standards Project (2015b) also identifies SIT as an "Unestablished Treatment." Likewise, the NPDC (Wong *et al.*, 2014) found "insufficient evidence" for sensory diets and sensory integration and fine-motor intervention. Further, the American Academy of Pediatrics Section on Complementary and Integrative Medicine and Council on Children with Disabilities (2012) has issued a policy statement indicating that although OT with the use of sensory-based therapies may be acceptable as one of the components of a comprehensive treatment plan, parents and professionals should be informed that the research regarding the effectiveness of SIT is limited and inconclusive. They recommend that, when utilized, interventions to address sensory-related problems should be integrated at various levels into the student's IEP. The American Occupational Therapy Association (2010) also suggests that practitioners utilizing an SIT approach use clinical reasoning, existing evidence, and outcomes to create a comprehensive, individualized approach for each client, rather than employing isolated, specific sensory strategies. It is important to recognize that other OT treatments which focus on improving functional skills (e.g. activities of daily living) are essential for a range of neurodevelopmental disorders, and therefore children with ASD should have access to those interventions when indicated.

Best practice guidelines indicate that, when needed, comprehensive educational programs for children with ASD should integrate an appropriately structured physical and sensory milieu in order to accommodate any unique sensory processing patterns. Students with ASD frequently require accommodations and modifications to prevent the negative effects that school and community environments can have on their sensory systems. Although many schools may find it difficult to make major environmental changes, relatively simple adaptations and accommodations can be implemented to lessen the impact of sensory issues on the student with ASD. These include (a) reducing the amount of material posted on classroom wall for a student who has problems with excessive visual stimulation;

(b) teaching the student to recognize the problem and ask in their mode of communication to leave the area; (c) providing a low distraction, visually clear area for work; (d) providing alternative seating and a quiet/calming space when students become overwhelmed; and (e) using headphones or similar device to minimize high noise levels. The accommodations and modifications needed to address sensory issues should be specified in the student's individualized educational program (IEP). The collaboration of knowledgeable professionals (e.g. occupational therapists, speech/language therapists, physical therapists, adaptive physical educators) is necessary to provide guidance about supports and strategies for children whose sensory processing and/or motoric difficulties interfere with educational performance and access to the curriculum.

BEST PRACTICE

Peer-mediated strategies can be used to teach typically developing peers ways to help learners with ASD acquire new social skills by increasing social opportunities in natural environments.

PEER-MEDIATED STRATEGIES

Difficulty interacting appropriately with peers is a common feature of ASD. Children on the spectrum frequently try to interact with peers, but may do so in unexpected or socially inappropriate ways. There has been a shift away from relying solely on standard social skills training and toward greater emphasis on teaching classmates how to interact with children who have social challenges (Kasari *et al.*, 2012). Peer-mediated strategies facilitate skill growth for children with ASD by training peers on how to initiate and respond during social interactions with a child on the spectrum. They involve systematically teaching typically developing students ways of engaging learners with ASD in positive and meaningful social interactions, and encouraging the

179

use of desired communicative and social behaviors. Peers are taught how to gain the attention of the child with ASD, facilitate sharing, model appropriate play skills, and help organize play activities. After training, peers interact with the individual with ASD in a structured setting during a familiar activity which allows them to practice their new skills in a comfortable environment. Types of peer-mediated instruction and intervention include integrated play groups, circle of friends, peer buddy and peer tutors, group (classroom) training, peer networks, and peer initiation training.

An important benefit of peer-mediated interventions is their ability to promote generalization and maintenance of skills, as opposed to adult-managed interventions, which may not often generalize. Peer-mediated strategies are also proactive, require little teacher planning time, and can be easily adapted to the classroom. The available research evidence on peer-mediated strategies indicates that having trained peers promotes both acceptance of the child with ASD and skill development in all children. Peer-mediated strategies have been shown to be a successful and evidence-based method of building social responsiveness and increasing interactions among students (DiSalvo and Oswald, 2002; Kasari *et al.*, 2012; National Autism Center, 2015b; Owen-DeSchryver *et al.*, 2008; Williams, Johnson, and Sukhodolsky, 2005; Wong *et al.*, 2014).

BEST PRACTICE

The components of Pivotal Response Training® (PRT) can be adapted and utilized in the classroom setting to improve the communication, language, play, and social behaviors of learners with ASD.

PIVOTAL RESPONSE TRAINING®

Pivotal Response Training®, also referred to as Pivotal Response Teaching® and Pivotal Response Treatment®, focuses on targeting behaviors in which certain aspects of a child's development are considered to be "pivotal" or critical. PRT is one of the best-studied and validated behavioral treatments for autism. It is a naturalistic intervention model that uses both a developmental approach and applied behavior analysis (ABA) procedures to provide learning opportunities in the child's natural environment, such as the home, community, and school setting (Koegel *et al.*, 2006; Koegel, Robinson, and Koegel, 2009; Suhrheinrich *et al.*, 2014). A primary objective of PRT is to shift children with autism toward a more typical developmental path by focusing on the following pivotal learning variables: (a) motivation, (b) responding to multiple cues, (c) self-management, and (d) self-initiation. These are important foundational skills upon which learners with ASD can make widespread and generalized improvements in a variety of social-communicative functions and reduce inappropriate, maladaptive behaviors. Motivational procedures including child choice, task variation, interspersing maintenance and acquisition tasks, rewarding attempts, and the use of direct natural reinforcers are incorporated to make the intervention more effective and efficient. The outcome research for PRT has shown positive effects on language and communicative interaction, and social engagement and play for children with ASD (Bryson *et al.*, 2007; Hardan *et al.*, 2015; National Autism Center, 2015b; Suhrheinrich *et al.*, 2014).

BEST PRACTICE
Positive behavioral support (PBS) strategies have been shown to be an effective proactive approach to eliminate, minimize, and prevent challenging behavior by designing effective environments and teaching students appropriate social and communication skills.

POSITIVE BEHAVIOR SUPPORT (PBS)

The problem behaviors of children with ASD are among the most challenging and stressful issues faced by schools and parents. The current best practice in addressing and preventing unwanted or challenging behaviors utilizes the principles and practices of positive behavior support (PBS). PBS has been demonstrated to be effective with a wide range of problem behavior and disability classifications. PBS is not a specific intervention per se, but rather an approach that has evolved from traditional behavioral management methods that are intended to decrease problem behaviors by designing effective environments and teaching students appropriate social and communication skills (Dunlap *et al.*, 2008). Instead of reacting to students' negative behaviors and giving subsequent consequences, desired behaviors are explicitly taught and the school environment reorganized to prevent the unacceptable behavior. Arranging the environment and using instructional strategies to promote success and prevent failure offers a powerful yet relatively simple tool for promoting positive behavior and preventing challenging behavior.

PBS utilizes primary (school-wide), secondary (targeted group), and tertiary (individual) levels of intervention, each level providing increasing intensity and support (Sugai *et al.*, 2000). Although functional behavior assessment (FBA) is required for students with serious and persistent challenging behaviors (see "Behavior Intervention Plan" in this chapter), teachers may prevent the possibility of problematic behavior through the implementation of class-wide and targeted group PBS strategies. Strategies such as arranging the classroom environment and/or adapting instruction and the curriculum to fit within the framework of the classroom, when used consistently, help promote positive student behavior by reducing the triggers or events that set off the challenging behavior. Teaching effective social interaction and communication as replacements for challenging behavior is also a preventive strategy for improving student adjustment. For example, teachers can model, demonstrate, coach, or role-play the appropriate interaction skills and teach students to ask for help during difficult activities or negotiate alternative times to finish work. Encouraging positive social interactions such as conversational skills will also help students with problem behavior to effectively obtain positive peer attention. Because students with ASD often lack the social skills to communicate and interact effectively with peers and adults, they may use challenging or disruptive behavior to communicate their needs. The following examples illustrate how PBS provides a proactive framework for addressing social interaction and communication needs and for teaching new, effective skills that replace the challenging behavior (Vaughn *et al.*, 2005; Wilkinson, 2012).

INITIATING INTERACTIONS

Teachers might notice that when a student with ASD enters the classroom, group activity, or other social interaction, he or she may have particular difficulty greeting others students or starting a conversation. For example, they may joke, call another student a name, laugh, or say something inappropriate. In this situation, the student may have trouble initiating interactions or conversations. Teachers might talk to the student individually and offer suggestions for ways he or she can provide an appropriate greeting or introduce a topic of conversation. The student might then be asked to practice or role-play the desired behavior.

> Example: "Why don't you ask students what they did last night, tell them about a TV show you watched, or ask if they finished their homework, rather than shouting or saying, 'Hey, Stupid.' Other students in the class want to be your friend, but you make it difficult for them to talk to you. Let's practice the next time the class begins a new group activity."

MAINTAINING INTERACTIONS

Many students with ASD struggle to maintain a conversation (e.g. turn-taking). Some may dominate the conversation and make others feel that they have nothing to contribute, whereas other students may experience difficulty keeping up with the flow of conversation and asking questions. Students may also have limited topics of interest and discuss these topics repetitively.

> Example: "I've noticed that other students cannot share their thoughts and ideas with you when you start a conversation because you do all the talking. It may seem to them that you don't care what they have to say. Other students will be more willing to talk if you stop once you've stated your idea or opinion and allow them a turn to talk. When you stop, they know you are listening. You can say to them, 'What do you think?' or 'Has this ever happened to you?'"

TERMINATING INTERACTIONS

Some students with ASD may not know how to appropriately end a conversation. They may abruptly walk away, start talking with another student, or bluntly tell a student they don't know what they're talking about. Other students may interpret this as rude and impolite behavior. Teachers might point out to the student some acceptable ways of ending a conversation.

> Example: "You just walked away from that student when they were talking. Rather than walk away, you might say, 'I have to go now,' 'It's time for my next class,' or 'I'll see you later and we can finish our talk.'"

RECOGNIZING BODY LANGUAGE

The recognition of body language or nonverbal cues is critical to successful social interactions. Students with ASD typically have difficulty interpreting these cues from teachers or other students. Body language tells students when they violate a person's personal space, a person needs to leave, or they need to change behavior. Teachers can incorporate these skills into their class time or school day.

> Example: Before leaving the classroom, demonstrate nonverbal cues by holding a finger to your lips and telling students that means "quiet," a hand held up with palm facing outward means "wait" or "stop," and both hands pushing downward means "slow down." You may need to demonstrate facial expressions you use to "deliver messages" and what they mean. Other students can demonstrate nonverbal cues they use. When students move through the halls, you may want to teach them the "arm's length" rule for personal space.

TRANSITIONS

Many students with ASD have significant problems changing from one activity to the next or moving from one location to another. They may be easily upset by abrupt changes in routine and unable to estimate how much time is left to finish an activity and begin the next one. Poor executive function skills such as disorganization may also prevent them from putting materials away from the last activity or getting ready for the next activity. They may also need closure and preparation time for the transition. Problems arise if the teacher tries to push them to transition at the last minute. Some of these problems can be avoided if:

- the routine for making transitions is consistent and rehearsed ahead of time

- students are given five- or ten-minute warnings before the transition must be made

- a daily visual schedule is posted and reviewed throughout the day or class period

- students' individual schedules are kept on or near their desks and are reviewed with students after each activity or period

- changes are made on the posted classroom schedule and students' individual schedules to reflect any changes in the routine

- materials for activities are organized and easily accessible.

Example: About ten minutes prior to the transition, refer to the classroom schedule and announce when the bell will ring or when the next activity will begin. Provide a five-minute and then a one-minute warning. This countdown helps students finish assignments or end favorite activities. For students who have difficulty getting started after a transition, place assignment folders on their desks so that they have their assignments and don't have to wait for instructions or materials. They can use the same folder to submit assignments (the folders can be left on their desks at the end of the period).

BEST PRACTICE
Social skills training is an essential component of educational programming for students with ASD and should be delivered throughout the day in various natural settings, using specific activities and interventions designed to meet age-appropriate social interaction goals.

SOCIAL SKILLS TRAINING
Impairment in social communication and interaction is a core feature of ASD. Social skills deficits include difficulties with initiating

interactions, maintaining reciprocity, taking another person's perspective, and inferring the interests of others. Social impairment may result in negative outcomes, such as poor academic achievement, social isolation, and peer rejection. Because social skills deficits interfere with the ability to establish meaningful social relationships, they may also lead to withdrawal and co-occurring (comorbid) anxiety and depression. Research evidence indicates that, when appropriately planned and delivered, social skills training programs have the potential to produce positive effects in the social interactions of children with ASD (NAC, 2015b; Wong *et al.*, 2014). Since social skills are critical to successful social, emotional, and cognitive development and long-term outcomes, best practice indicates that social skills programming should be an integral component of educational programming for all children with ASD (National Research Council, 2001).

The general objective of any social skills intervention is to provide individuals with ASD the skills necessary to meaningfully participate in the social environments of their homes, schools, and communities. Social skills training is typically offered as small-group instruction with a shared goal or outcome of learned social skills in which participants can learn, practice, and receive feedback. These interventions seek to build social interaction skills in children and adolescents with ASD by targeting basic responses (e.g. eye contact, name response) as well as complex social skills (e.g. how to initiate or maintain a conversation). The overarching goal of social skills instruction should be the development of social and communicative competency through direct teaching, modeling, coaching, and role-playing activities in real-world situations. The effectiveness of social skills training can be enhanced by increasing the quantity (or intensity) of social skills interventions, providing instruction in the child's natural setting (classroom), matching the intervention strategy with the type of skill deficit, and ensuring treatment integrity (Bellini *et al.*, 2007; Rao, Beidel, and Murray, 2008). Regardless of the specific method or strategy used to teach social skills, the format should include the following: (a) identify the social skill to be taught; (b) explain the importance of the social skill; (c) model the skill; (d) provide examples; (e) allow for guided practice; (f) provide opportunities for independent practice; and (g) continue to monitor student progress. Although there is no single approach that will help children to be socially successful, the following are general strategies for facilitating and reinforcing social-communication competency in the classroom (White, Koening, and Scahill, 2007; Wilkinson, 2012).

- *Increase social motivation by encouraging self-awareness.* Begin with simple, easily learned skills and intersperse new skills with those previously mastered. Provide social skills training and practice opportunities in a number of settings to encourage students to apply new skills to multiple real-life situations.

- *Increase social initiations and improve age-appropriate social responding by making social rules clear and concrete.* Teach simple social response scripts for common situations, and use natural reinforcers for social initiations and response attempts. In addition, utilize modeling and role-play to teach and reinforce prosocial skills, and build social activities around preferred activities/interests. Employ primarily positive strategies and focus on facilitating the desirable social behavior as well as eliminating undesirable behavior.

- *Promote skill generalization and coordinate peer involvement (e.g. prompting and initiating social interactions; maintaining physical proximity).* Use several individuals with whom to practice skills, including parents, and provide opportunities to apply learned skills in safe, natural settings (e.g. field trips). Look for opportunities to teach and reinforce social skills as often as possible throughout the school day. Include parents and caregivers as significant participants in developing and selecting interventions (they can help reinforce the skills taught at school to further promote generalization across settings).

- *Teach effective social interaction and communication as replacements for challenging behavior).* Model, demonstrate, coach, and/or role-play the appropriate interaction skills. Teach students to ask for help during difficult activities or to negotiate alternative times to finish work. Encourage positive social interactions such as conversational skills to help students with challenging behavior obtain positive peer attention. Use assessment strategies, including functional assessments of behavior, to identify children in need of more intensive interventions as well as target skills for instruction.

Social relationship skills are critical to successful social, emotional, and cognitive development and to long-term outcomes for students with ASD. Social skills training is an evidence-based intervention/practice with both preventive and remedial effects that can help reduce the risk for negative outcomes not only for children on the autism spectrum but for all children.

BEST PRACTICE
The provision of speech/language therapy is important at all levels and ages for children with ASD and should focus on the social (pragmatic) communication and interaction skills necessary to build and sustain positive relationships within family, peers, and community environments.

SPEECH/LANGUAGE THERAPY
Deficits in verbal and nonverbal social communication are a core feature of ASD. Although many children with ASD may have some delay in the form and content of language, communication problems are primarily in the area social (pragmatic) language. When typical children engage in reciprocal conversation, they are aware of the knowledge, interests, and intentions of the other person, as well as the

social rules that determine pragmatic competence. These "unspoken rules" of social engagement involve the use of the pragmatic, social-communicative functions of language (e.g. turn-taking, understanding of inferences and figurative expressions) as well as nonverbal skills needed to communicate and regulate interaction (e.g. eye contact, gesture, facial expression). Children with ASD tend to interpret language literally and may be puzzled by the common everyday expressions used by a typical peer or adult. They may fail to use appropriate nonverbal communication skills such as eye contact and have impairments in comprehension, or generally have difficulty communicating with others. As a result, peers often feel ineffective when engaged in social exchanges with a child with ASD and may avoid that person and/or react in a negative way (e.g. teasing or bullying), further impacting the development of appropriate social skills.

Because pragmatic language is a critical part of everyday social interaction, it is imperative that speech/language services for children with ASD include a focus on social-communication skills (National Research Council, 2001; Prizant and Wetherby, 2005; Twachtman-Cullen and Twachtman-Bassett, 2014). Although speech/language pathologists (SLPs) may address these pragmatic deficits via several service delivery options, interventions are likely to be most effective when they are developed and delivered in natural settings such as the classroom. Not only do natural learning environments encourage higher rates of initiation and generalization, they also enhance the strength of the intervention. As Twachtman-Cullen and Twachtman-Bassett (2014, p.121) comment, "pragmatically based communication deficits require pragmatically based intervention."

BEST PRACTICE

Story-based interventions are considered an effective approach for facilitating social skills in children with ASD and may be integrated into the student's IEP or behavior support plan on a daily basis to complement other interventions and strategies.

STORY-BASED INTERVENTIONS

Story-based interventions are an evidence-based strategy for teaching children with ASD to manage challenging situations in a wide variety of settings. These interventions identify a target behavior and involve a written description of the situations under which specific behaviors are expected to occur. The objective is to enhance a child's understanding of social situations and teach an appropriate behavioral response that can be practiced. The most well-known story-based intervention is Social Stories™ (Gray, 2010). A social story is a short story describing a situation, skill, or concept in terms of relevant social cues, perspectives, and common responses presented in a specifically defined style and format. They are designed to help the child learn how others perceive various social actions and to facilitate the understanding of important social cues and the unwritten rules (or hidden curriculum) of social interaction. Each story describes where the activity will take place, when it will occur, what will happen, who is involved, and why the child should behave in a certain way. In essence, social stories seek to answer the who, what, when, where, and why aspects of a social situation in order to improve the child's perspective taking. Most social stories are written from an "I" or "some people" viewpoint and follow an explicit format of 5–10 sentences describing the social skill, the appropriate behavior, and others' perspective of the behavior. These sentences are written in a way that ensures accuracy of interpretation, using vocabulary and print size appropriate for the child's ability. Pictures illustrating the concept can be included for children who have difficulty reading text without cues. They can be simple line drawings, clip art, or actual photographs. Although a number of commercial publications offer generic social stories for common social situations, it is best to individualize the content of the story according to the child's unique behavioral needs. There is evidence from a large number of studies that the social story approach can help increase the social interaction and communication of children with ASD (NAC, 2015b; Wong *et al.*, 2014). However, story-based interventions are not intended to address all of the behavioral and social challenges of the child with ASD and should not be used in isolation. Rather, they should be integrated into the student's IEP or behavior support plan on a daily basis, and used as part of a multi-component intervention strategy in classroom settings (Ozdemir 2008; Sansosti, Powell-Smith, and Kincaid, 2004; Spencer, Simpson, and Lynch, 2008).

BEST PRACTICE
Classroom interventions and programs should capitalize on the preferences of children with ASD for visual structure, routines, schedules, and predictability.

VISUAL SCHEDULES/SUPPORTS

Visual schedules and supports are an evidence-based intervention/practice and an integral part of most comprehensive programs for children with ASD. Because school-age children with ASD routinely experience new learning environments and a lack of consistency in classroom routines, schedules provide a way to handle transitions more effectively and engage in appropriate task-related behaviors with minimal adult prompting. They allow students to anticipate upcoming events, develop an understanding of time, and reduce fear of the unknown. A schedule can make the day more predictable and less anxiety-provoking, which can in turn reduce interfering behavior.

A schedule may consist of photographs, pictures, written words, physical objects, or any combination of these items, and communicates a series of activities or the steps of a specific activity. A daily or across-task schedule shows the child all of the activities he or she will undertake during a single day. A within-task (or mini-schedule) illustrates all of the steps the student needs to take to complete a specific activity. Schedules can be used once per day, multiple times per day, or once per week and should be followed by access to preferred activities. Successful implementation of visual schedules has been shown to decrease challenging behaviors, to improve transitioning, enhance on-task behavior, and to teach daily-living skills to children with autism (NAC, 2015b; Wong et al., 2014).

BEST PRACTICE
School professionals should be sensitive to the everyday challenges faced by families of children with ASD and work closely with parents to provide support and help them advocate, problem-solve, plan for the future, and locate the resources that meet the developmental needs of the child and family.

FAMILY SUPPORT

Supporting the family and ensuring the system's emotional and physical health is a critical aspect of overall management of ASD (Myers and Johnson, 2007). Professionals working with families of children with an ASD should be aware of the negative effects of stress and anxiety, and assist in offering services that directly address parental needs and support mental health. Studies indicate that the demands placed on parents caring for a child with autism contribute to a higher overall incidence of parental stress, depression, and anxiety, and adversely affect family functioning and marital relationships compared with parents of children with other disabilities (Estes *et al.*, 2009; Giallo *et al.*, 2013). Negative outcomes include (a) increased risk of marital problems; (b) decrease in father's involvement; (c) greater parenting and psychological distress; (d) higher levels of anxiety and depression; (e) added pressure on the family system; (f) more physical and health-related issues; (g) decrease in adaptive coping skills; and (h) greater stress on mothers than fathers (Barnhill, 2014; Feinberg *et al.*, 2014; Lee, 2009; Pottie and Ingram, 2008; Weiss *et al.*, 2012). Parents often experience stress as they decide how to allocate their attention and energy across family members. For example, they may feel guilty about the limited time they spend with their spouse and other children, when so much of their attention is focused on the child with ASD. Mothers, in particular, may experience high levels of psychological distress, depressive symptoms, and social isolation (Hoffman *et al.*, 2009). Research found that nearly 40 percent of mothers reported clinically significant levels of parenting stress and between 33 percent and 59 percent experienced significant depressive symptoms following their child's diagnosis of ASD (Feinberg *et al.*, 2014). Challenges in obtaining a timely ASD diagnosis and lack of appropriate treatment services and education were also contributors to parental stress and dissatisfaction. When families receive a diagnosis of autism, a period of anxiety, insecurity, and confusion often follow. Some autism specialists have suggested that parents go through stages of grief and mourning similar to the stages experienced with the loss of a loved one (e.g. fear, denial, anger, bargaining/guilt, depression, and acceptance). Understanding this process can help school professionals provide support to families during the critical period following the child's autism diagnosis when parents are learning to navigate the complex system of autism services (Feinberg *et al.*, 2014).

It is well established that social support is protective of optimal parent well-being and, therefore, is an important component of any intervention to address the well-being of parents of children with ASD. Parents with limited assistance to share the daily demands of caregiving and family life are likely to be at greater risk of experiencing stress than parents with more support. For these parents, there might also be fewer opportunities to engage in self-care behaviors that are likely to alleviate or protect them from stress (Giallo *et al.*, 2013). Parents of children with ASD are also now more likely to be involved in the provision of early intervention and learning activities to promote positive outcomes for their children. However, parental stress and a lack of time and energy often present a barrier to providing early intervention activities and support. Thus, understanding parent perspectives and targeting parental stress is critical in enhancing well-being and the parent–child relationship. Parent concerns about their children include (a) poor long-term outcomes; (b) protection and safety; (c) self-injurious behaviors and aggression; (d) eating problems; (e) poor sleeping habits and personal care skills; (f) poor language skills; (g) disruptive behavior in home and community; (h) social rejection and stigma for both parent and child; (j) future and independent living; and (k) limited time available to care for siblings and themselves (Barnhill, 2014; Gray, 2002; Ivey, 2004). School professionals who have knowledge and understanding of the stressors parents face are in a position to provide more effective assistance and support to the family.

Practitioners can support parents by educating them about ASD, providing guidance and training, assisting them in obtaining access to resources, offering emotional support by listening and talking through problems, and helping them advocate for their child's needs (National Research Council, 2001). It is especially important to acknowledge the value of parents' unique and important perspective, validate their observations and concerns, and reinforce their roles as important contributors to the educational process (Barnhill, 2014). Professionals should also help the family understand what the identification or diagnosis of ASD means and what the next steps are in addressing the issues of support and educational planning. This includes helping parents achieve a better understanding of how their child thinks and learns differently, and become familiar with strategies that might help both at home and school. For example, parents can be taught evidence-based strategies that successfully support their children with ASD. Parent-implemented interventions have the potential to improve the child's communication skills and reduce aggression and disruptive behaviors, as well as increase the functioning of the family system (NAC, 2015b). Parents can learn to implement story-based interventions, visual supports/schedules, and PRT strategies in their home and/or community through individual or group training formats (Hardan *et al.*, 2015). Professionals can also assist families by offering parents training in behavior management, which has been shown to increase parents' self-efficacy and decrease their child's problematic behaviors (Barnhill, 2014).

Another major strategy for helping families with children with ASD is providing information on access to ongoing supports and services. This includes publicly funded, state-administered programs such as early intervention, special education, vocational and residential/living services, and respite services. Professionals and family advocates need to be aware of the various programs and their respective eligibility requirements, and help parents to access these services. Parents will also need timely and appropriate information regarding their children's programs and services, and may have questions about long-term educational planning. It is important to openly communicate the student's strengths and weaknesses, and encourage parents to play an active role in developing and implementing intervention plans and IEPs (Myers and Johnson, 2007; Rogers and Vismara, 2008; Wagner, 2014). Professionals should also remember that parents have a life-long role in their child's development and realize that the family's needs will change over time, and that they have other family responsibilities in addition to their child with autism (Barnhill, 2014). When schools use a family-centered approach and work to increase parental involvement and support, not only do the parents and children benefit, but school personnel do as well (NAC, 2015a).

BEST PRACTICE

School professionals should establish effective communications with parents and investigate the use of various alternate dispute resolution methods such as mediation and IEP facilitation to address legal issues associated with special education eligibility and placement.

LEGAL ISSUES

Research indicates that the proportion of published court decisions attributable to the autism classification under IDEA has risen rapidly. For example, children with autism were found to account for nearly one-third of a comprehensive sample of published court decisions concerning the core concepts of free appropriate public education (FAPE) and least restrictive environment (LRE) under IDEA. Overall, the FAPE/LRE court cases were over ten times more likely to concern a child with autism than the proportion of these children in the special education population (Zirkel, 2011). The disproportionate growth of autism litigation is likely due in part to school systems' challenges in effectively addressing this complex disability and providing effective programs for individual children with autism. As more children are identified with autism, school districts are facing significant budgetary constraints and shortages of qualified personnel while parents are requesting additional and more expensive services. FAPE also invites autism litigation due to the uncertainty of the complexity and the diversity of the condition. Likewise, confusion between the legal (educational) classification of autism and the clinical definition of ASD has contributed to eligibility and placement controversies. Given the disparity between parent concerns and school practices, together with high costs, treatment/intervention controversies, and the complexity of ASD, it is understandable why parents of children with autism tend to be more prone to litigation than the parents of children with other disabilities (Zirkel, 2014).

In order to address these legal issues, state and local policymakers must become more knowledgeable and sensitive about the legal and appropriate educational supports critical to children with autism and their families. For example, school districts should ensure that the IEP process follows the procedural requirements of IDEA and that parents are notified of their due process rights. This includes actively involving parents in the IEP process and adhering to the time-frame requirements for assessment, and developing and implementing the student's IEP. School professionals should also be thoroughly familiar with state and federal education codes and regulations regarding the eligibility criteria for ASD. Special education leaders need to pay particular attention to establishing effective communications and trust building with parents to maximize the use of alternative approaches to dispute resolution, with the use of the legal system being the last option (Mandlawitz, 2002; Zirkel, 2011, 2014). Likewise, parents must understand that school districts, much like families, do not have unlimited resources. Parents and schools must work together and make a serious effort to achieve a realistic understanding of the child's needs and to address them in a mutually agreeable and appropriate manner. Lastly, schools must balance but not confuse ethical and legal duties, and effectively facilitate open communication among parents, teachers, administrators, and support personnel for the common interest of the child and the school system (Zirkel, 2014).

CONCLUSION

Education is the most effective treatment for children with ASD. School professionals most likely to be involved with assessments and the determination of autism eligibility (e.g. school psychologists, speech/language pathologists, special education teachers) are advised to become familiar with the criteria for autism specified in the IDEA and to keep in mind that when it comes to special education, it is state and federal education codes and regulations (not clinical criteria) that determine eligibility and IEP planning decisions (Zirkel, 2014). The following are the key components of a comprehensive educational program for children with ASD (Mandlawitz, 2002; National Research Council, 2001; Wagner, 2014; Yell *et al.*, 2003; Zirkel, 2014):

- An effective, comprehensive educational program should reflect an understanding and awareness of the challenges presented by autism.

- Parent–professional communication and collaboration are key components for making educational and intervention/ treatment decisions.

- Comprehensive, individualized evaluations should be completed by professionals who have knowledge, experience, and expertise in ASD. If qualified personnel are not available, schools should provide the appropriate training or retain the services of a consultant.

- Ongoing training and high-quality professional development education for teachers is necessary to ensure that personnel have the skills and knowledge necessary to provide evidence-based instruction to children with ASD. Professionals who are trained in specific methodology and techniques will be most effective in providing the appropriate services and in modifying curriculum based upon the unique needs of the individual child.

- Inclusion with typically developing peers is important for a child with ASD as peers provide the best models for language and social skills. However, inclusive education alone is insufficient; evidence-based intervention and personnel training are also required to provide the necessary supports. Although the LRE provision of IDEA requires that efforts be made to educate students with special needs in less restrictive settings,

IDEA also recognizes that some students may require a more comprehensive program.

- Assessment and progress monitoring of a student with ASD should be completed at specified intervals by an interdisciplinary team of professionals who have a knowledge base and experience in autism.

- A comprehensive IEP should be based on the child's unique pattern of strengths and weaknesses. Goals for a child with ASD commonly include the areas of communication, social behavior, adaptive skills, challenging behavior, and academic and functional skills. Evidence-based instructional strategies should also be adopted to ensure that the IEP is implemented appropriately and the identified goals and objectives met.

- The IEP must address appropriate instructional and curricular accommodations and/or modifications, together with related services such as counseling, occupational therapy, speech/ language therapy, physical therapy, and transportation needs. Transition goals must be developed when the student reaches 16 years of age. A positive behavior intervention plan is also required when a student's behavior interferes with learning.

Chapter 7 provides a discussion of the current status of the field, including intervention issues, programs, policy and training, and recommendations for future research and practice.

FUTURE DIRECTIONS FOR RESEARCH AND PRACTICE

The dramatic rise in reported numbers of children and youth with autism in public schools and an expansion of knowledge of educational practices effective with this group of students has created a sense of urgency among educators and parents to ensure students are provided an appropriate education. The multifaceted nature of autism, including co-occurring disabilities, has significant implications for planning and intervention across school, home, and community. Because the knowledge base in ASD is changing so rapidly, school-based professionals are challenged to stay current with the latest methods of evaluation and intervention/treatment, acquire and become skilled with the most up-to-date screening and assessment tools, and maintain an awareness of community resources. This requires that they engage in a periodic review of current best practices. This final chapter describes several critical directions for future research and practice.

SCHOOL PERSONNEL

One of the most critical practice needs is for both personnel preparation and ongoing education and training opportunities for all school professionals. The autism landscape has changed dramatically over the past 20 years due to an increase in the awareness of autism among the general public, educators, and healthcare professionals. It is vital that school personnel understand this complex disorder in order to help students achieve positive outcomes, especially since they share the responsibility of educating the increasing number of children being identified with ASD. In addition to recognizing the red flags of autism, service providers such as teachers (regular and special education), speech/language pathologists, school psychologists, and other support personnel must be familiar with current best practice guidelines for assessment and intervention. Unfortunately, there appears to be a discrepancy between best practice parameters and reality in the schools. For example, there is research to suggest that both general and special education teachers who serve students with autism are not implementing evidence-based strategies at a satisfactory level (Hendricks, 2011; Williams *et al.*, 2011). Even though many children with ASD are served in general education classrooms, few general education teachers receive training on evidence-based practices for students on the autism spectrum. In order to facilitate access to general education environments, it is imperative to increase the skills of all school personnel who provide service and supports to students with ASD. Professionals must be competent in a range of strategies including applied behavior analysis (ABA), natural environment teaching, assistive technology, augmentative and alternative communication, as well as assessment and data collection, and be able to apply evidence-based intervention strategies based on student need with integrity (National Autism Center, 2015a; National Research Council, 2001). Although the literature suggests that school personnel are receiving some specialized training related to autism, there continues to be a pressing need for more continuing education opportunities and improved preparation (Williams *et al.*, 2011). These issues should be addressed through multiple levels of pre-service instruction, including coursework specifically centering on autism, integration of evidence-based content into current preparation courses, and opportunities for hands-on experience with students with ASD through practicums and student teaching (Hendricks, 2011).

Federal statutes require that school districts ensure that comprehensive, individualized evaluations are completed by school professionals who have knowledge, experience, and expertise in ASD. School psychologists play a central role in the assessment process and are now more likely to be asked to participate in the screening, identification, and educational planning for students with ASD than at any other time in the past. The call for greater use of evidence-based practice has increased demands that school psychologists be knowledgeable about evidence-based assessment and intervention strategies for students with ASD. Although surveys suggest an adequate knowledge base regarding the signs and symptoms of autism, there is a need for school psychologists to develop greater levels of competency in evidence-based assessment and identification practices with children who have or may have an ASD (Wilkinson, 2013). This includes more in-depth, formal training complete with supervision and consultation, especially regarding best practice guidelines for evaluation and intervention, at the pre-service level through graduate school (e.g. practicums and internships), as well as at the practitioner level through professional development opportunities. School psychologists can help to ensure that students with ASD receive an effective educational program by participating in continuing education and in-service programs designed to increase their understanding and factual knowledge about best practice approaches in assessment and intervention.

POLICY ISSUES

There is also a need to address state and federal policy issues going forward. For example, the dramatic increase in the number of students qualifying for special education under the autism category in schools may be related, in part, to vague definitions together with ambiguous, variable, and inappropriate evaluation procedures. Research indicates that despite similar foundations, state education agency (SEA) definitions of autism display considerable variability and are often too vague to be of much utility (MacFarlane and Kanaya, 2009; Pennington, Cullinan, and Southern, 2014). Evaluation procedures also vary significantly across SEAs with little agreement between the definition (what autism is) and evaluation procedures (how autism is recognized). Definition components are often not addressed by evaluation features. For example, one of the least recommended evaluation features is the requirement to administer an autism-specific measure as part of the eligibility process (Pennington *et al.*, 2014). The publication of DSM-5 provides SEAs with the opportunity to expand and update their state definitions of autism, as well as revise the corresponding evaluation procedures used for special education eligibility determination. Improved, more specific definitions and assessment procedures will allow SEAs and school districts to better serve students with autism and more efficiently allocate resources. Likewise, IDEA is due for reconsideration and possible amendment, which presents an opportunity to update and clarify the federal educational definition of autism.

A related policy issue involves inclusive education for students with autism. IDEA requires that students be educated in the least restrictive environment. However, there is some research to suggest that factors external to child characteristics have a significant influence on educational placement decisions for students with ASD (Kurth, 2015). In other words, the child's unique needs may not be the primary determinant of placement. Although students with ASD should be considered for an inclusive setting with appropriate supports, it appears that many states are not including them in general education settings for significant portions of the day (Kurth, 2015). The focus must now shift from whether children with ASD should be included in general education to understanding how to include students with ASD meaningfully in inclusive settings. It is critical to investigate how evidence-based practices, including structure (visual supports, communication supports, and social supports), positive behavior supports, and systematic instruction, can be implemented successfully in general education settings. Lastly, those involved with recommending placement for students with ASD should consider the unique needs of the child, and be certain to match those needs to specific supports and services that will be provided in the least restrictive setting (Kurth, 2015).

COMORBIDITY

It is well documented that in addition to the core symptoms of social interaction and communication deficits and restricted and repetitive behaviors, children with ASD often experience other comorbid (co-occurring) conditions, with rates significantly higher than would be expected from the general population. The most common co-occurring diagnoses are anxiety and depression, attention problems, and disruptive behavior disorders. This has important implications for school-based practitioners. The core symptoms of ASD can often mask the symptoms of a comorbid condition. A challenge for practitioners is to determine if the symptoms observed in ASD are part of the same dimension (i.e. the autism spectrum) or whether they are associated with another condition (Mazzone *et al.*, 2012). Assessment of co-occurring behavior/emotional problems can be especially difficult, because there is a paucity of autism-specific tools designed and validated for this purpose. Although various psychometric instruments, such as clinical interviews, self-report questionnaires and third-party checklists, are widely used to assist in identifying comorbid problems, these tools are designed and standardized to identify symptoms in the general population. Nevertheless, school-based professionals should give greater attention to co-occurring conditions in children and youth with ASD because they are common and can interfere significantly with educational performance and adaptive behavior (Doepke *et al.*, 2014) Thus, assessment of comorbid problems such as anxiety, depression, and attention problems might be included as a standard and integrated part of the assessment of ASD. School professionals will also need to be knowledgeable about evidence-based interventions that can be implemented in the school context to address these problems. Reducing comorbid symptoms in children with ASD, in addition to treating the core symptoms, may result in greater improvement in social-emotional functioning. More research is needed in order to better understand the characteristics and longitudinal course of different co-occurring conditions, as well as effective intervention/treatment strategies for these problems.

RESTRICTED AND REPETITIVE BEHAVIOR (RRB)

Restricted and repetitive behavior (RRB) is a core diagnostic feature of ASD. Although these behaviors present a major barrier to learning and social adaptation, most of the research on ASD has focused on social and communication deficits, with less attention given to the RRB symptom domain (Boyd, McDonough, and Bodfish, 2012; Leekam, Prior, and Uljarevic, 2011). Further research is needed to better understand the development, expression, assessment, and related clinical features (e.g. cognitive ability, adaptive functioning, comorbid disorders) of RRBs (Stratis and Lecavalier, 2013). For example, it is important to understand how RRBs in typical development vary across time in order to compare atypical trajectories in children with ASD across intellectual and adaptive levels. Future research should also be directed to understanding the RRB subtypes and their relationship to comorbid psychiatric symptoms. Compared with the relatively large number of evidence-based, behavioral interventions for the social-communication and interaction symptoms of ASD, RRBs are less likely to be included in intervention planning. There is a need to develop evidence-based interventions that are effective in treating the continuum of repetitive behaviors in order to provide support in this domain and improve RRBs before these behaviors become well established (Leekam *et al.*, 2011). In terms of assessment, RRB measures such as the RBS-R and RBQ-2 (see Chapter 3) should be used to provide a more complete understanding of specific RRBs and their impact on adaptive functioning, as well as inform intervention selection. It will also be important to provide parents with education and training on how to effectively address these inflexible and repetitive patterns of behaviors that affect their everyday lives.

TRANSITION PLANNING

Students with autism face significant challenges as they transition to adulthood. Post-secondary outcome studies reveal poor long-term outcomes in living arrangements, employment, and community integration when compared with their peers with other types of disabilities. Research indicates that many are socially isolated and that the vast majority of young adults with ASD will be residing in the parental or guardian home during the period of emerging adulthood (Anderson *et al.*, 2014; Orsmond *et al.*, 2013). The lack of services available to help prepare young adults on the autism spectrum transition to greater independence has become an increasingly important issue as the prevalence of ASD continues to grow and as these children reach adolescence. A consistent theme for parents of adolescents with autism is the fear that their child will "fall through the cracks" when transitioning from child to adult services. Comprehensive transition planning and support for students leaving high school and exiting special educational programming, each with unique strengths, interests, and challenges, is an especially urgent task facing our society (Roux *et al.*, 2015). Greater emphasis should be placed on transition planning in schools as a key process for helping youth build skills and access services as they enter adulthood. This includes a focus on independent living skills, vocational engagement, post-secondary education, family support, and a continuum of mental health services for those experiencing comorbid psychiatric problems (Lake, Perry, and Lunsky, 2014).

INTERVENTION PRACTICES

Although there has been substantial progress in our understanding and treatment of children with autism over the past two decades, research is needed to improve screening measures, identify valid autism-specific instruments, and develop more effective intervention strategies. There are several research directions that are needed to help improve intervention and treatment practices for children with autism. Although special education programs and the various evidence-based practices all have a place in the management of ASD, further inquiry is needed to understand which children are likely to benefit from a particular intervention or program. To date, studies have failed to adequately describe the characteristics of interventions (or the children receiving them) in a way that helps clarify why certain children show more positive outcomes than others. Research is needed to enhance our understanding of which interventions are most effective for specific children with ASD, and to isolate the elements or components of interventions associated with positive effects. Likewise, the literature lacks studies that directly compare interventions or utilize combinations of interventions, despite the fact that most children receive multiple treatments (Weitlauf *et al.*, 2014).

A related area of investigation involves the accessibility of scientifically supported interventions. Research is needed to examine the generalizability and transportability of interventions shown to be efficacious in research settings to the applied settings of home and school. Although many effective approaches are described in the literature, they may not be readily available to parents and educators. Teachers frequently have difficulty developing effective intervention plans because empirical procedures used in research do not translate into real-world classroom application. Most are published in peer-reviewed scientific journals, which abbreviate the descriptions of the interventions and do not provide enough detail to permit replication in school and community settings. There is a need to develop effective and efficient consumer-friendly intervention strategies that are specifically designed and packaged for utilization in schools, community settings, and at home. Research should inform practice. Utilizing a research-to-practice framework will do much to enhance the development of effective interventions for children with ASD across real-world environments.

SOCIAL SKILLS

The ability to relate and interact with others is the foundation for successful human connection and adjustment to the social world. One of the best childhood predictors of adult adaptation and well-being is not IQ or school grades, but rather the competence with which the children relate to both peers and adults. Deficits in social interaction and communication are the core, underlying feature of ASD. Children with ASD faces many challenges with transitions to new learning and social environments, and contact with new peers and adults as they progress through school. The social-communication domain becomes increasingly divergent from typical expectations with age and grade. Social skills training has been shown to produce positive effects in the social interactions of children with ASD. Both the National Professional Development Center on Autism (NPDC) and the National Autism Center (NAC) have identified social skills instruction/training as an evidence-based intervention and practice. Most often, schools are expected to assume the responsibility of delivering social skills training programs to children with social skills deficits, because these impairments significantly interfere with social relationships and have an adverse effect on academic performance. However, implementing social skills programming can be challenging for school personnel (e.g. teachers, counselors, psychologists, social workers), who often have limited training, time, and resources to successfully implement this intervention strategy.

Given the life-long consequences of poor social functioning, schools should devote greater efforts and resources to social skills programming and make social learning an educational priority across age and grade levels (Wilkinson, 2012). Although there is support to suggest that social skills training increases a student's awareness of social cues and understanding of how to interact appropriately with peers, further research is needed to examine how this knowledge is applied in the context of everyday situations. Thus, an important area for future research is to evaluate the generalization of social skills from training groups to other environments. There is also a need to conduct follow-up studies to document the longer-term outcomes of social skills interventions for children and youth with ASD.

GENDER ISSUES

Both clinical practice and research indicate an urgent need to examine the similarities and differences between boys and girls with ASD (Wilkinson, 2008a). Although boys are being referred and identified in greater numbers, this is not the case for girls (Centers for Disease Control and Prevention, 2014). Girls are also diagnosed with ASD at later ages relative to boys (Goin-Kochel *et al.*, 2006). This gender gap should be empirically investigated as it raises serious questions regarding identification practices and delivery of services. If girls process language and social information differently to boys, then assessment and intervention strategies based largely on research with boys may be inappropriate.

Girls on the autism spectrum are at risk for developing significant affective symptoms (i.e. anxiety and depression) in adolescence, indicating the need for increased awareness, screening, identification, and intervention (Solomon *et al.*, 2012). An understanding of elevated levels of internalizing symptoms in girls with ASD and how to treat comorbid affective symptoms is essential to help improve interpersonal functioning and quality of life, as well as reduce the negative outcomes frequently associated with adolescent mental health issues. Girls who are identified with ASD might be screened for internalizing problems and closely monitored for symptoms of anxiety and depression.

Research also indicates that parenting stress is higher for parents of girls than for parents of boys (Zamora *et al.*, 2014). Parents of female children with ASD experience challenges not only in obtaining a timely and accurate diagnosis, but also in connecting to treatment services and identifying sources of social support. Understanding and targeting parental stress is critical to supporting the parent–child relationship. Future research and practice should focus on specific challenges experienced by parents of female children with ASD, including ways to increase access to comprehensive treatment services and educational and social support. Differences in parental stress experienced between mothers and fathers should also be examined.

TREATMENT INTEGRITY

The success of an intervention is largely dependent on the extent to which it is implemented as intended or planned, or what has been termed *treatment integrity* (Gresham, 1989; Lane *et al.*, 2004; Wilkinson, 2006). Identifying an evidence-based treatment or intervention is a necessary but inadequate condition for producing behavior change. Knowing that an intervention is effective and understanding how to use it does not guarantee its accurate implementation and use. Unfortunately, the measurement of treatment integrity tends to be more the exception than the rule. For example, a review of published behavioral intervention research studies with children with autism found that only 18 percent actually assessed and reported treatment integrity data (Wheeler *et al.*, 2006). Reporting treatment integrity is essential not only from a methodological point of view but from practical one as well. The absence of treatment integrity data makes it very difficult to determine whether a particular intervention was unsuccessful because it is an ineffective strategy for the child or because key components of the intervention were omitted or poorly implemented. Without treatment integrity, even evidence-based interventions may fail (Wilkinson, 2006). The social significance of the intervention outcomes or social validity is also of critical importance. Consumers (parents and teachers) must feel assured that the selected intervention strategies are effective and appropriate, and that the social objectives are important for the child to achieve. If the intervention lacks social validity, consumers are less likely to apply the effort necessary to implement the intervention, thus reducing intervention fidelity. Educators, parents, and families expect (and hope) that research will produce interventions and treatments that will improve quality of life of children affected by autism. Thus, the measurement of treatment integrity and social validity should be a standard feature of intervention research and practice.

CONCLUSION

The majority of children with autism are educated within the public school system, most often in general education classes, either full- or part-time. Teachers are now expected to instruct children with special educational needs who are included in their classroom. However, many lack formal training in educating and intervening with children with ASD. Among the most pressing challenges is the need for more coordinated efforts among the various professionals for the training of teachers in evidence-based instruction and behavioral management practices, and for greater attention to the emotional and social adjustment of children with ASD. As our scientific knowledge and thinking about ASD continues to develop, professionals such as school psychologists, behavior interventionists, counselors, social workers, occupational therapists, and speech/language pathologists will play an increasingly important role in the educational programming of children with ASD by providing support, information, and recommendations to teachers, administrators, and families regarding best practice procedures in assessment and intervention. Therefore, it is critically important to remain current with the research and up to date on scientifically supported approaches that have direct application to the educational setting. School professionals can help form cohesive educational support networks for children with ASD and ensure that they receive an effective educational program by being knowledgeable about best practice assessment and intervention/ treatment approaches, including their strengths and limitations. It is hoped that the current edition of this book will continue to make a meaningful contribution toward this important objective.

GLOSSARY OF TERMS

Accommodations Changes made to reduce the effects of a disability without altering the instructional content or learning expectations for the student. Accommodations are intended to enable a student with a disability to fully access the general education curriculum. (Compare with "Modifications" below.)

Adaptive behavior The age-appropriate or typical performance of daily activities based on social standards and expectations. It refers to an individual's ability to adjust to and apply new skills to other situations (e.g. different environments, tasks, objects, and people).

Applied behavior analysis (ABA) A methodology that involves the application of behavioral principles to facilitate the development of language, positive skills, and social behavior. ABA strategies include discrete trial training, prompting, differential reinforcement, modeling, shaping, fading, and task analysis. Many of the evidence-based interventions identified in this book are based on ABA principles (see Chapter 5).

Assessment for intervention planning The process of evaluating an individual's functioning across several domains in order to develop a profile of strengths and challenges that informs intervention planning, including selection of goals and specific intervention strategies (see Chapter 3).

Assistive technology (AT) Any device, materials, product system, or piece of equipment that provides students with disabilities greater access to the general education curriculum and increases their ability to master academic content, interact with others, and enhance functional independence.

Augmentative and alternative communication (AAC) Communication methods used to support, enhance, supplement, or replace speech or writing for students with impairments in the production or comprehension of spoken or written language

Autism spectrum disorder (ASD) A neurodevelopmental disorder characterized by deficits in social communication and social interaction, and the presence of restricted and repetitive behaviors. Symptoms are present during the early developmental period and cause clinically significant impairment in social, occupational, or other important areas of functioning. For the purpose of this book, the terms *ASD* and *autism* are used interchangeably.

Behavioral intervention A strategy designed to reduce problem behaviors and teach functional alternative behaviors or skills through the application of basic principles of behavior change.

Behavior intervention plan (BIP) A written plan with multiple components, specifying the procedures and supports which will be implemented to decrease problem behavior and increase alternative, positive behavior.

Best practice A technique, strategy, or methodology that, through experience and evidence-based research, has proven to reliably lead to a desired outcome.

Broader autism phenotype (BAP) Refers to individuals with mild impairments in social interaction and communication skills that are similar to those shown by individuals with ASD, but exhibited to a lesser degree. Includes close relatives (parents, siblings) of people diagnosed with ASD and who have mild autistic traits themselves.

Comorbidity The presence of one or more disorders that co-occur with a primary condition or diagnosis and that share a focus of clinical and educational attention.

Complementary and alternative medicine (CAM) A group of diverse medical and healthcare practices, products, and treatment approaches that are not presently considered to be part of conventional medicine. CAM treatments include, but are not limited to, botanicals, vitamins, minerals, other natural products, mind-body medicine, and manipulative practices.

Comprehensive behavioral intervention programs for young children (CBTYC) Programs that involve intensive early behavioral interventions that target a range of skills that define or are associated with ASD (e.g. communication, social, and pre-academic/academic skills).

Comprehensive developmental approach An approach to assessment that emphasizes multiple areas of functioning and the reciprocal impact of abilities and disabilities in order to understand the departure from normal developmental expectations that characterize ASD.

Core symptoms A description of the central clinical features of ASD: impaired social interaction and communication, and restricted, repetitive patterns of behavior, interests, or activities.

Diagnostic and Statistical Manual of Mental Disorders (DSM) A publication by the American Psychiatric Association containing descriptions, symptoms, and other criteria for diagnosing mental and neurodevelopmental disorders.

Diagnostic evaluation The process of gathering information via interview, observation, and specific testing in order to arrive at a clinical diagnosis or categorical conclusion.

Discrete trial teaching (DTT) A specific treatment approach or method of instruction based on applied behavior analysis (ABA) that consists of a highly structured series of repeated lessons or "trials" taught on a one-on-one basis.

Discriminant validity An instrument's accuracy in predicting group membership (e.g. ASD versus non-ASD). Discriminant validity can be expressed through metrics such as sensitivity and specificity, measures of a test's ability to correctly identify someone as having a given disorder (sensitivity) or not having the disorder (specificity).

Early intensive behavioral intervention (EIBI) A comprehensive behavioral intervention program for young children (generally under the age of eight) delivered on an intensive basis that involves a combination of applied behavior analysis (ABA) procedures.

Evidence-based interventions Interventions derived from high-quality, independently replicated scientific research studies that show sufficient evidence of effectiveness (see Chapter 5).

Evidence-based practice (EBP) A practice that bridges the science-to-practice gap by using evidence-based research to inform practice. EBP requires the integration of research findings with (a) professional judgment and data-based decision making; (b) values and preferences of families, including the student with ASD; and (c) the capacity to implement interventions with a high degree of integrity.

Executive function A set of higher-order mental processes that are required to regulate, control, and manage goal-directed problem-solving behavior, including response inhibition, working memory, cognitive flexibility, emotional control, self-regulation, and planning and organization.

Expressive language A description of how a person communicates their wants and needs. Expressive language skills include facial expressions, gestures, intentionality, vocabulary, semantics (word/sentence meaning), morphology, and syntax (grammar rules).

Focused interventions Individual strategies designed to address specific behavioral or developmental outcomes for individuals with ASD. They may be used alone or in combination for a specified period of time to change a specific behavior or teach a specific skill.

Free appropriate public education (FAPE) A term used to describe the federal mandate that schools must provide students with an educational program that is individualized to a specific child, is designed to meet that child's unique needs, provides access to the general curriculum, meets the grade-level standards established by the state, and from which the child receives educational benefit.

Functional behavior assessment (FBA) A process for identifying clear, predictive relationships between events in the student's environment and the occurrences of a target behavior. Specific behaviors are described in terms of the purposes of the behavior and the function the behaviors serve for the individual exhibiting the behavior.

Functional communication training (FCT) A systematic practice designed to replace inappropriate or ineffective behavior serving a communicative function with a more appropriate or effective behavior or skill.

Gluten- and casein-free diet (GF/CF) A complementary and alternative treatment for ASD in which all foods containing gluten (found in wheat, barley, and rye) and casein (found in milk and dairy products) are removed from the child's daily food intake.

Hyperlexia An ability to learn to read at an early age and advanced level without instruction.

Hypersensitivity An over-responsivity to everyday, common stimuli of sound, sight, taste, touch, or smell.

Hyposensitivity An insensitivity or under-responsivity to sensory input or stimulation.

Inclusion A teaching approach that focuses on including students with special education needs with typical peers in general education classrooms and the school community (see "Least restrictive environment").

Individualized education program (IEP) A federally mandated plan or program developed to ensure that a child who has a disability identified under the law and is attending an elementary or secondary educational institution receives specialized instruction and related services. An IEP contains specific information regarding a child's present level of functioning, educational needs, goals, service levels and providers, appropriate placements, and measurable outcomes and data.

Individuals with Disabilities Education Act (IDEA) A U.S. federal law that governs how states and public agencies provide early intervention, special education, and related services to children with disabilities.

Interdisciplinary team A group of professionals from various disciplines with specialized skills and expertise who collaborate during the assessment and intervention planning process to achieve consensus on identification and eligibility, appropriateness of interventions, programs, and services, and define goals and outcome measures

Intervention Any strategy, technique, method, therapy, treatment, model, or program that is primarily intended to bring about developmental improvement in the core symptoms of ASD. In this book, the terms *intervention* and *treatment* are used interchangeably.

Least restrictive environment (LRE) A requirement in federal law that students with disabilities receive their education, to the maximum extent appropriate, with non-disabled peers.

Modifications Changes in the instructional level, content or curriculum, performance criteria (objective), or assignment structure for students with disabilities. (Compare with "Accommodations" above.)

National Autism Center (NAC) A non-profit organization dedicated to serving children and adolescents with ASD by providing reliable information, promoting best practices, and offering comprehensive resources for families, practitioners, and communities. The NAC is the sponsor of one of the research reviews in this book (see Chapter 5).

National Professional Development Center on Autism Spectrum Disorder (NPDC) A multi-university center that promotes the use of evidence-based practice through the development of training materials and provision of training and technical assistance to teachers and practitioners who serve individuals from birth through 22 years with ASD. The NPDC is the sponsor of one of the research reviews in this book (see Chapter 5).

National Standards Project (NSP) An effort funded by the National Autism Center (NAC) to produce a set of standards for effective, research-validated education and behavioral interventions for children with ASD (see Chapter 5).

Packaged interventions Interventions that are substantially similar are combined into a single category or package.

Pervasive developmental disorders (PDD) A group of five disorders (in the DSM-IV-TR) characterized by severe and pervasive impairment in several areas of development: reciprocal social interaction skills, communication skills, or the presence of stereotyped behavior, interests, and activities. The five pervasive developmental disorders are: (1) autistic disorder, (2) Asperger's disorder, (3) Rett's disorder, (4) childhood disintegrative disorder, and (5) pervasive developmental disorder not otherwise specified (PDD-NOS).

Picture Exchange Communication System (PECS) A form of augmentative and alternative communication (AAC) in which people use pictures to communicate their interests, needs, and spontaneous thoughts, ask and answer questions, and schedule activities.

Pivotal Response Training (PRT) An intervention based on principles of applied behavior analysis (ABA) that is designed to teach pivotal behaviors, including motivation, responding to multiple cues, social interaction, social communication, self-management, and self-initiation within a naturalistic framework.

Positive behavior support (PBS) A systematic approach to preventing or reducing challenging behaviors and, eventually, to enhancing the quality of life for individuals and support providers. A key objective in PBS is to determine the function of the problem behavior, and then to teach socially acceptable alternative/replacement skills and behaviors.

Pragmatic language The social rules for using functional spoken language in a natural and meaningful context or conversation (knowing what to say, how to say it, when to say it, and where to say it). Pragmatic language includes both the verbal and nonverbal aspects of communication and is a common feature of the social-communication difficulties in children with ASD.

Prosody The rhythm and melody of spoken language expressed through rate, pitch, stress, inflection, or intonation to convey a meaning.

Receptive language The comprehension of language, which includes the areas of attention, receptive vocabulary, following directions, and understanding questions.

Related services The supportive services needed by a child with a disability in order to benefit from special education (e.g. speech/language therapy, occupational and physical therapy, counseling services, interpreting services, recreation, social work services, transportation).

Restricted and repetitive behavior (RRB) A core feature of ASD that encompasses a wide range of behaviors such as stereotyped or repetitive motor movements, use of objects, or speech; insistence on sameness, inflexible adherence to routines, or ritualized patterns of behavior; highly restricted, fixated interests; and hyper- or hypo-reactivity to sensory input or unusual sensory interests.

Section 504 A civil rights law (Rehabilitation Act of 1973) that prohibits discrimination on the basis of disability and requires school districts provide a free appropriate public education (FAPE) to qualified students in their jurisdictions who have a physical or mental impairment that substantially limits one or more major life activities, regardless of the nature or severity of the disability.

Screening The use of specific standardized instruments to identify an individual's risk for having ASD and the need for further evaluation and assessment for intervention planning (see Chapter 2).

Sensory integration therapy (SIT) A therapeutic approach that incorporates the use of sensory materials and physical input in order to help children increase focus, regulate moods, and tolerate frustration and environmental change, as well as reduce negative reactions to sensory stimuli in order to facilitate participation in daily routines and social interactions.

Sensory processing The way the nervous system receives, detects, and integrates incoming sensory information for use in producing adaptive responses to one's environment. Sensory processing is also referred to as sensory integration or SI.

Social (pragmatic) communication disorder (SCD) A DSM-5 disorder characterized by deficits in understanding and following social rules of verbal and nonverbal communication in naturalistic contexts which affects the development of social relationships and discourse comprehension, and cannot be explained by low abilities in the domains of word structure and grammar or general cognitive ability. SCD is distinguished from ASD by the absence of any history (current or past) of restricted and repetitive patterns of interest or behavior.

Social reciprocity The back-and-forth flow of social interaction or how the behavior of one person influences and is influenced by the behavior of another person and vice versa. Also, mutual responsiveness in the context of interpersonal contact, such as awareness of and ability to respond appropriately to other people.

Social validity The social importance, acceptability, and satisfaction of treatment goals, intervention procedures, and outcomes, usually assessed by requesting opinions from the people who receive and implement them.

Special education Refers to the practice of providing specially designed instruction and learning experiences to meet the unique needs of a child with a disability.

Supplementary aids and services The supports provided in regular education classes that enable children with disabilities to be educated with non-disabled children to the maximum extent appropriate.

Target behavior The behavior(s) to be increased or decreased in some measurable way, such as frequency, intensity or duration.

Treatment integrity (fidelity) A scientific term that describes the degree to which an intervention is implemented in the way in which it was designed to be implemented.

Visual supports Any visual display, including schedules, that increases an individual's communication skills and understanding of expectations by providing graphic models, prompts, or reminders of how to participate successfully in interactions and routines throughout the day. The terms *visual supports*, *visual strategies*, or *visual cues* are often used interchangeably.

APPENDIX A

COMPARISON OF DSM-IV-TR AND DSM-5 CRITERIA

DSM-IV-TR	DSM-5
Diagnostic Classification	
Pervasive Developmental Disorders (PDD)	**Autism Spectrum Disorder (ASD)**
Diagnostic Categories	
• Autistic Disorder • Asperger's Disorder • Rett's Disorder • Childhood Disintegrative Disorder • PDD-NOS	• Autism Spectrum Disorder *Specify:* • With or without intellectual impairment • With or without language impairment • Associated with a known genetic or environmental factor • Additional neurodevelopmental, mental, or behavioral conditions
Domains	
• Social interaction • Communication • Restricted, repetitive, and stereotyped patterns of behavior	• Social interaction and social communication • Restricted, repetitive patterns of behavior, interests, or activities *Specify level of severity for each domain*
Age of Onset	
• Delays or abnormal functioning with onset prior to age 3 years	• Symptoms must be present in the early developmental period (but may not become fully manifest until social demands exceed limited capacities)

223

APPENDIX B

IDEA DISABILITY CATEGORIES

1. **Autism** means a developmental disability significantly affecting verbal and nonverbal communication and social interaction, generally evident before age three, that adversely affects a child's educational performance. Other characteristics often associated with autism are engagement in repetitive activities and stereotyped movements, resistance to environmental change or change in daily routines, and unusual responses to sensory experiences.

   a. Autism does not apply if a child's educational performance is adversely affected primarily because the child has an emotional disturbance, as defined by IDEA.

   b. A child who manifests the characteristics of autism after age three could be identified as having autism if the above criteria are satisfied.

2. **Deaf-blindness** means concomitant hearing and visual impairments, the combination of which causes such severe communication and other developmental and educational needs that they cannot be accommodated in special education programs solely for children with deafness or children with blindness.

3. **Deafness** means a hearing impairment that is so severe that the child is impaired in processing linguistic information through

hearing, with or without amplification that adversely affects a child's educational performance.

4. **Emotional disturbance** means a condition exhibiting one or more of the following characteristics over a long period of time and to a marked degree that adversely affects a child's educational performance:

   a. An inability to learn that cannot be explained by intellectual, sensory, or health factors.

   b. An inability to build or maintain satisfactory interpersonal relationships with peers and teachers.

   c. Inappropriate types of behavior or feelings under normal circumstances.

   d. A general pervasive mood of unhappiness or depression.

   e. A tendency to develop physical symptoms or fears associated with personal or school problems.

   Emotional disturbance includes schizophrenia. The term does not apply to children who are socially maladjusted, unless it is determined that they have an emotional disturbance.

5. **Hearing impairment** means an impairment in hearing, whether permanent or fluctuating, that adversely affects a child's educational performance but that is not included under the definition of deafness in this section.

6. **Intellectual disability**, formerly labeled "mental retardation" means significantly subaverage general intellectual functioning, existing concurrently with deficits in adaptive behavior and manifested during the developmental period, that adversely affects a child's educational performance. There are two key components within this definition, a student's IQ and his or her capability to function independently, usually referred to as adaptive behavior.

7. **Multiple disabilities** means concomitant impairments (such as intellectual disability-blindness or intellectual disability-orthopedic impairment), the combination of which causes such severe educational needs that they cannot be accommodated in special education programs solely for one of the impairments. Multiple disabilities does not include deaf-blindness.

8. **Orthopedic impairment** means a severe orthopedic impairment that adversely affects a child's educational performance. The term includes impairments caused by a congenital anomaly, impairments caused by disease (e.g. poliomyelitis, bone tuberculosis), and impairments from other causes (e.g. cerebral palsy, amputations, and fractures or burns that cause contractures).

9. **Other health impairment** means having limited strength, vitality, or alertness, including a heightened alertness to environmental stimuli, that results in limited alertness with respect to the educational environment, that—

   a. Is due to chronic or acute health problems such as asthma, attention deficit disorder or attention deficit hyperactivity disorder, diabetes, epilepsy, a heart condition, hemophilia, lead poisoning, leukemia, nephritis, rheumatic fever, sickle cell anemia, and Tourette syndrome; and

   b. Adversely affects a child's educational performance.

10. **Specific learning disability** means a disorder in one or more of the basic psychological processes involved in understanding or in using language, spoken or written, that may manifest itself in the imperfect ability to listen, think, speak, read, write, spell, or to do mathematical calculations, including conditions such as perceptual disabilities, brain injury, minimal brain dysfunction, dyslexia, and developmental aphasia.

a. Disorders not included. Specific learning disability does not include learning problems that are primarily the result of visual, hearing, or motor disabilities, of intellectual disability, of emotional disturbance, or of environmental, cultural, or economic disadvantage.

11. **Speech or language impairment** means a communication disorder, such as stuttering, impaired articulation, a language impairment, or a voice impairment, that adversely affects a child's educational performance.

12. **Traumatic brain injury** means an acquired injury to the brain caused by an external physical force, resulting in total or partial functional disability or psychosocial impairment, or both, that adversely affects a child's educational performance. Traumatic brain injury applies to open or closed head injuries resulting in impairments in one or more areas, such as cognition; language; memory; attention; reasoning; abstract thinking; judgment; problem-solving; sensory, perceptual, and motor abilities; psychosocial behavior; physical functions; information processing; and speech. Traumatic brain injury does not apply to brain injuries that are congenital or degenerative, or to brain injuries induced by birth trauma.

13. **Visual impairment** including blindness means an impairment in vision that, even with correction, adversely affects a child's educational performance. The term includes both partial sight and blindness.

Source: Individuals with Disabilities Education Improvement Act of 2004.
Pub. L. No. 108-446, 108th Congress, 2nd Session (2004).

APPENDIX C

ASD ASSESSMENT WORKSHEET

Date: _____ Student Name: _____

Birth Date: _____ Age: _____
Grade: _____

Pre-Eval. Meeting Date: _____

Eval. Meeting Date: _____ Eval. Due Date: _____

Sensory Status

☐ Record/File Review

☐ Vision Screening

☐ Pure Tone and Tympanometry Screening

Intellectual/Cognitive Functioning

☐ Record/File Review

☐ Informal Interviews: Parent, Teacher, and Student

☐ Wechsler Intelligence Scale for Children, Fifth Edition (WISC-V)

☐ Wechsler Preschool and Primary Scale of Intelligence, Fourth Edition (WPPSI-IV)

☐ Differential Ability Scales, Second Edition (DAS-II)

☐ Stanford-Binet Intelligence Scale, Fifth Edition (SB-5)

☐ Leiter International Performance Scale, Third Edition (Leiter-3)

Academic Achievement

☐ Record/File Review

☐ Wechsler Individual Achievement Test, Third Edition (WIAT-III)

☐ Woodcock-Johnson IV Tests of Achievement (WJ IV ACH)

☐ Kaufman Test of Educational Achievement, Third Edition (KTEA-3)

☐ Classroom Observation

☐ Informational Assessments

☐ Other _____

ASD Assessment

☐ Record/File Review

☐ Parent/Teacher Interviews

☐ Behavioral Observation

☐ Childhood Autism Rating Scale, Second Edition (CARS-2)

☐ Social Responsiveness Scale, Second Edition (SRS-2)

☐ Autism Diagnostic Interview, Revised (ADI-R)

☐ Autism Diagnostic Observation Schedule, Second Edition (ADOS-2)

☐ Autism Spectrum Rating Scales (ASRS)

☐ Social Communication Questionnaire (SCQ)

Communication (Language)

- ☐ Record/File Review
- ☐ Clinical Evaluation of Language Fundamentals, Fifth Edition (CELF-5)
- ☐ Expressive One-Word Picture Vocabulary Test, Fourth Edition (EOWPVT-4)
- ☐ Peabody Picture Vocabulary Test, Fourth Edition (PPVT-4)
- ☐ Test of Pragmatic Language, Second Edition (TOPL-2)
- ☐ Children's Communication Checklist, Second Edition (CCC-2)
- ☐ Pragmatic Language Skills Inventory (PLSI)
- ☐ Test of Auditory Comprehension of Language, Fourth Edition (TACL-4)
- ☐ Comprehensive Assessment of Spoken Language (CASL)
- ☐ Social Language Development Test, Elementary (SLDT-E)
- ☐ Language Sample
- ☐ Observation

Restricted and Repetitive Behavior (RRB)

- ☐ Repetitive Behavior Scale, Revised (RBS-R)
- ☐ Repetitive Behavior Questionnaire, Second Edition (RBQ-2)

Sensory Processing

- ☐ Sensory Profile, Second Edition (SP-2)
- ☐ Sensory Processing Measure (SPM)

Motor Skills

☐ Record/File Review

☐ Bruininks-Oseretsky Test of Motor Proficiency, Second Edition (BOT-2)

☐ Developmental Test of Visual-Motor Integration, Sixth Edition (Beery VMI)

Executive Function, Memory, and Attention

☐ Record/File Review

☐ Conners Third Edition (Conners 3)

☐ Developmental Neuropsychological Assessment, Second Edition (NEPSY-II)

☐ Delis-Kaplan Executive Function System (D-KEFS)

☐ Wide Range Assessment of Memory and Learning, Second Edition (WRAML-2)

☐ Behavior Rating Inventory of Executive Function, Second Edition (BRIEF-2)

☐ California Verbal Learning Test, Children's Version (CVLT-C)

Emotional/Behavior Functioning

☐ Record/File Review

☐ Informal Interviews: Parent, Teacher, and Student

☐ Achenbach System of Empirically Based Assessment (ASEBA)

☐ Behavior Assessment System for Children, Third Edition (BASC-3)

☐ Children's Depression Inventory, Second Edition (CDI-2)

☐ Revised Children's Manifest Anxiety Scale, Second Edition (RCMAS-2)

☐ Other _____

Adaptive Behavior

☐ Record/File Review

☐ Behavioral Observation

☐ Informal Interviews: Parent, Teacher, and Student

☐ Vineland Adaptive Behavior Scales, Second Edition (VABS-II)

☐ Adaptive Behavior Assessment System, Third Edition (ABAS-3)

☐ Developmental Profile, Third Edition (DP-3)

Family System

☐ Interview

☐ Parenting Stress Index, Fourth Edition (PSI-4)

Comments

_____

_____

_____

_____

_____

APPENDIX D

ASD OBSERVATION CHECKLIST

Deficits in Social Interaction

_____ absence of interest in peers

_____ trouble with back-and-forth social interactions

_____ inability to respond to social cues

_____ inability to understand how someone else might feel (perspective taking)

_____ difficulty in sharing imaginative play

_____ impaired imitation—not engaging in simple games

_____ not accepting cuddling, hugging, touching unless self-initiated

_____ difficulty making friends

_____ little sense of other people's boundaries

_____ engaging in stereotypic question asking as interaction pattern

_____ inappropriately intrusive in social situations

_____ reduced sharing of interests or emotions

_____ inappropriate use of eye contact, avoidance, or extended staring

_____ poor use of nonverbal gestures

Deficits in Social Communication

_____ problems with pronouns

_____ problems getting the order of words in sentences correct

_____ inappropriate repetitive language

_____ difficulty following the rules of conversation (initiating, terminating, turn-taking)

_____ problems understanding jokes

_____ problems understanding multiple meaning of words

_____ problems understanding sarcasm, idioms, and figurative speech

_____ echoing what is said directly, later, or in a slightly changed way (echolalia)

_____ difficulty initiating topics of shared interest

_____ difficulty understanding abstract concepts

_____ difficulty understanding nonverbal communication (facial expression)

_____ difficulty making inferences

_____ preference for topics of special interest

_____ problems with pedantic speech

_____ problems using speed, tone, volume appropriately (prosody)

Restricted and Repetitive Patterns of Behavior, Interests or Activities

_____ repeatedly watching videos or video segments

_____ lining up and/or ordering objects

_____ strong attachment to inanimate objects (e.g. strings, bottles)

_____ fascination with movement (e.g. spinning wheels, fans, doors, and drawers)

_____ pacing or running back and forth

_____ excessive smelling or touching of objects

_____ adverse reaction to specific sounds or textures

_____ insistence on adherence to routines, resisting change

_____ negative reaction to small changes in environment

_____ highly fixated, restricted interests

_____ difficulty with unstructured time

_____ difficulty with transitions

_____ apparent indifference to temperature or pain

_____ staring at patterns, lights, or shiny surfaces

_____ lack of fear of real danger

_____ excessive fearfulness of some harmless objects or situations

_____ defensive to touch

Learning Characteristics

_____ uneven profile of skills

_____ well-developed memory for detail and long-term recall

_____ difficulty with executive function skills (working memory, planning, organization)

_____ over- and under-generalization of learning

_____ good visual skills

_____ difficulty with reading comprehension

_____ short attention span with some activities and not others

_____ impulsivity

_____ difficulty with fine- and/or gross-motor skills

_____ limited flexibility

_____ sequential learner

_____ needs help to problem-solve

Observable Problem Behaviors

_____ aggression (physical or verbal)

_____ anxiety or social withdrawal

_____ self-injurious behaviors

_____ temper tantrums

_____ non-compliance or oppositional behavior

_____ eating problems

_____ sleeping problems

Note: This checklist should be used as part of the assessment process when observing, interviewing parent/teacher, and/or directly interacting with the student. It should not be used as the sole measure for making a decision regarding eligibility classification or educational programming.

APPENDIX E

DESCRIPTION OF EVIDENCE-BASED INTERVENTIONS

Intervention	Descriptor
Behavioral interventions	These interventions are designed to reduce problem behavior and teach functional alternative behaviors or skills through the application of basic principles of behavior change.
Cognitive-behavioral intervention	Cognitive-behavioral interventions are designed to change negative or unrealistic thought patterns and behaviors with the goal of positively influencing emotions and life functioning.
Comprehensive behavioral treatment for young children (CBTYC)	These programs involve intensive early behavioral interventions that target a range of essential skills which define or are associated with ASD. They are often described as ABA (applied behavior analysis) or EIBI (early intensive behavioral intervention) programs.
Exercise	Exercise is a strategy that involves an increase in physical exertion as a means of increasing desired behaviors (time on task, correct responding) and reducing inappropriate behaviors (aggression, self-injury).
Functional communication training (FCT)	Functional communication training (FCT) is a systematic practice of replacing inappropriate or ineffective behaviors with more appropriate or effective behavior that serves the same function.
Language training (production)	Language training (production) targets the ability of the individual with ASD to emit a verbal communication (i.e. functional use of spoken words). Strategies may include oral communication training, structured discourse, simultaneous communication, and individualized language remediation.

Modeling	This intervention relies on an adult or peer providing a demonstration (live and video) of a target behavior to the person learning a new skill, so that person can then imitate the model. Modeling can include simple and complex behaviors and is often combined with other strategies such as prompting and reinforcement.
Naturalistic interventions/ teaching strategies	These interventions primarily involve child-directed interactions to teach real-life skills (communication, interpersonal, and play skills) in natural environments. Strategies often involve providing a stimulating environment, modeling how to play, encouraging conversation, providing choices and direct/natural reinforcers, and rewarding reasonable attempts.
Parent training/ intervention	Parents provide individualized intervention to their child to improve/increase a wide variety of skills such as communication, play, or self-help, and/or to reduce challenging behavior. Parent training can take many forms, including individual training, group training, support groups with an educational component, and training manuals.
Peer-mediated training/ intervention	Teachers/service providers systematically teach typically developing peers to interact with and/ or help children and youth with ASD to acquire new behavior, communication, and social skills by increasing social and learning opportunities within natural environments.
Picture Exchange Communication System (PECS)	PECS is an augmentative and alternative communication system (AAC) based on behavioral principles that uses pictures and other symbols to teach functional communication to children with limited verbal and/or communication skills.
Pivotal Response Treatment/Training (PRT)	PRT is a naturalistic intervention model that targets pivotal areas of a child's development, such as motivation, responsivity to multiple cues, self-management, and social initiations that enable learners with ASD to make widespread and generalized improvements in communication, social, and behavioral domains.

Scripting	This intervention involves developing a verbal and/or written script about a specific skill or situation which serves as a model for the child with ASD. Scripts are usually practiced repeatedly before the skill is used in the actual situation and are typically used in conjunction with behavioral interventions such as reinforcement, modeling, and prompting.
Self-management	Self-management strategies involve teaching individuals with ASD to evaluate and record the occurrence/non-occurrence of a target behavior and secure reinforcement. The objective is to be aware of and regulate their own behavior so they will require little or no direct assistance from adults.
Social skills training	Social skills training involves group or individual instruction designed to teach learners with ASD ways to appropriately interact with peers, adults, and other individuals by targeting basic responses (e.g. eye contact, name response) and complex social skills (e.g. how to initiate or maintain a conversation).
Story-based intervention/ social narratives	These interventions identify a target behavior and involve a written description of the situation under which specific behaviors are expected to occur. Most stories aim to improve perspective-taking skills and may be supplemented with additional components (e.g. reinforcement, prompting, and discussion). The most well-known story-based intervention is Social Stories™.
Structured play group (SPG)	A structured play group is an intervention that uses a small-group activity to teach a broad range of outcomes. The goal of SPG is to move children with ASD from a repetitive, solitary pattern of play to one that involves interaction and imagination.
Technology-aided instruction (TAI)	Instruction or interventions in which technology is the central feature supporting the acquisition of a goal for the learner. TAI includes the use of computers to teach academic skills and to promote communication and language development.
Visual support/schedules	Any visual display that supports the learner engaging in a desired behavior or skills independent of prompts. Examples of visual supports include pictures, written words, schedules, maps, labels, organization systems, scripts, and timelines.

APPENDIX F

EXAMPLES OF IEP GOALS AND OBJECTIVES

I. _____ will increase social interaction skills as measured by the benchmarks listed below:

a. Will raise their hand and wait to be called on before talking out loud in group settings given 4 out of 5 opportunities to do so.

b. Will work cooperatively with peers in a small-group settings (i.e. share materials, allow peers to share different thoughts) given 4 out of 5 opportunities to do so.

c. Will develop an understanding of the relationship between his or her verbalizations or actions and effect on others given 4 out of 5 opportunities to do so.

d. Will engage in appropriate cooperative social play interactions initiated by others given 4 out of 5 opportunities to do so.

e. Will engage in cooperative social play interactions by allowing others to make changes or alter the play routine given 4 out of 5 opportunities to do so.

f. Will engage in appropriate turn-taking skills by attending to a peer's turn and waiting for own turn given 4 out of 5 opportunities to do so.

g. Will appropriately acknowledge an interaction initiated by others by giving an appropriate response, either verbal or nonverbal given 4 out of 5 opportunities to do so.

h. Will develop an understanding of the rationale for various social skills by stating the reason when asked (e.g. why do we say excuse me?) given 4 out of 5 opportunities to do so.

i. Will increase social awareness of environment by stating what is taking place or imitating actions of others given 4 out of 5 opportunities to do so.

j. Will increase safety awareness by stating the effect of various situations given 4 out of 5 opportunities to do so.

k. Will identify the appropriate social rules and codes of conduct for various social situations given 4 out of 5 opportunities to do so.

l. Will not interrupt others by exhibiting appropriate social interaction skills given 4 out of 5 opportunities to do so.

2. _____ will increase perspective-taking skills as measured by the benchmarks listed below:

a. Will identify various emotional states in others given 4 out of 5 opportunities to do so.

b. Will state why a person might be feeling a particular emotion given 4 out of 5 opportunities to do so.

c. Will identify various simple emotional states in his or her self given 4 out of 5 opportunities to do so.

d. Will state why he or she might be feeling a particular emotion given 4 out of 5 opportunities to do so.

e. Will state what would be an appropriate emotional/behavioral response to specific social situations given 4 out of 5 opportunities to do so.

3. _____ will increase social-communication skills as measured by the benchmarks listed below:

a. Will initiate communicative interactions with others given 4 out of 5 opportunities to do so.

b. Will initiate varied appropriate topics with others given 4 out of 5 opportunities to do so.

c. Will initiate communicative interactions with others by asking questions given 4 out of 5 opportunities to do so.

d. Will engage in conversational turn-taking with others across 3 to 4 conversational turns, given 4 out of 5 opportunities to do so (topics initiated by self or others).

e. Will call attention to communicative partner prior to communicating given 4 out of 5 opportunities to do so.

f. Will ask questions of others regarding topics initiated by self or others to sustain conversation for conversational turn-taking given 4 out of 5 opportunities to do so.

g. Will identify and understand various nonverbal social-communication behaviors (i.e. tone of voice, personal space, vocal volume, body orientation, facial expressions) by stating their implied meaning given 4 out of 5 opportunities to do so.

h. Will spontaneously seek assistance/ ask for help/ seek additional information given visual prompts given 4 out of 5 opportunities to do so.

i. Will spontaneously use a verbal or nonverbal message to indicate to the speaker that he or she needs additional "wait" time to process information editorially given 4 out of 5 opportunities to do so.

j. Will identify breakdowns in communication and make appropriate adjustments given 4 out of 5 opportunities to do so.

4. _____ will increase adaptive skills within the school environment as measured by the benchmarks listed below:

a. Given visual and verbal prompts, participate in tasks and activities to completion by exhibiting appropriate behaviors ___% of the time.

b. Will transition appropriately from classroom tasks and activities ___ % of the time given visual and verbal prompts.

c. Will accept changes in routine/schedule by exhibiting appropriate behaviors when given visual and verbal cues ___ % of the time.

d. Will follow classroom rules and directives given visual and verbal prompts ___% of the time.

e. Will independently ask to take a break given visual and verbal prompts ___% of the time.

Evidence-based strategies to support the above goals:

- Social narratives

- Visual schedule

- Self-monitoring

- Peer-mediated training

- Social skills group

- Pivotal Response Training (PRT)

- Modeling.

INDEX TO BEST PRACTICE GUIDELINES

SCREENING

A standardized screening tool should be administered at any point when concerns about ASD are raised by a parent or teacher, or as a result of school observations or questions about developmentally appropriate social, communicative, and play behaviors.   41

Students who screen negative should be carefully monitored so as to minimize misclassification and ensure access to intervention services.   42

Gender differences should be taken into consideration when screening and evaluating children for ASD.   44

ASSESSMENT

The identification of autism should be made by a professional team using multiple sources of information, including, but not limited to, an interdisciplinary assessment of social behavior, language and communication, adaptive behavior, motor skills, sensory issues, and cognitive functioning.   47

Evidence-based assessment tools must not only demonstrate adequate psychometric properties, but also have relevance and utility to the delivery of services to students with ASD.   50

A comprehensive developmental assessment should include evaluation of multiple domains of functioning across multiple contexts/settings in order to differentiate ASD from other conditions and provide a complete student profile to facilitate intervention planning.   53

An important step in the core assessment process is to review the student's early developmental and medical history and current concerns with his or her parents. This should include a review of communication, social, and behavioral development.   54

All students diagnosed with ASD should receive a medical screening or examination to assist in determining the presence of any associated medical conditions or health risk factors. This includes a vision and hearing screening and referral for a formal assessment if concerns are present. 55

The parent or caregiver interview plays an important role in evaluating a child's early developmental history and identifying behaviors associated with ASD. 56

Direct behavioral observation of the student in both structured and natural settings should be included in the assessment process as this improves accuracy in the identification of ASD. 58

Parent and teacher ratings are one of the most important sources of information about deficits in the core ASD domain of social communication and social interaction across home and school contexts. 61

Formal assessment should include standardized evaluation tools with established reliability and validity to determine present levels of performance and identify priority educational needs. 63

The measurement of cognitive ability is critical for making a determination of ASD and for intervention planning purposes. Evaluation of cognitive functioning in both verbal and nonverbal domains is necessary to develop a profile of strengths and weaknesses. 64

Although intelligence test profiles can be helpful in understanding cognitive strengths and weaknesses, they should never be used to determine or confirm the presence of ASD. 65

Assessment of academic achievement is important for the purposes of educational decision making and intervention planning. Areas of strength and weakness can often go unrecognized. 68

The identification of parenting stress and parent–child relationship problems can alert the assessment team to the need for additional family support or counseling. 93

Professional judgment and experience is essential for the accurate identification of ASD, regardless of the strengths and limitations of an evidence-based instrument. 95

TREATMENT AND INTERVENTION

There is a pressing need to train school personnel about ASD and the use of evidence-based methods for teaching and managing behavioral issues. 112

Information about an intervention's effectiveness that is not supported by research, lacks peer review, and comes primarily from testimonials rather than empirical validation should be viewed with extreme caution. 126

Evidence-based practice (EBP) requires the integration of professional expertise, family values, and the best research evidence into the intervention planning process. 127

Systematic reviews synthesize the results of multiple studies and provide school professionals with summaries of the best available research evidence to help guide decision making and support intervention practice. 128

School professionals should strongly encourage parents and caregivers to investigate thoroughly any CAM treatment approach or non-traditional therapy prior to implementing them with their child. 133

Relying on ineffective and potentially harmful treatments puts the child at risk and uses valuable time that could be utilized in more productive educational or remedial activities. 134

School professionals should have a working knowledge of commonly prescribed medications for ASD and collaborate with parents, physicians, and therapists in evaluating the risks, benefits, and adverse effects of pharmacological interventions. 135

Parents and family members should be involved in the intervention planning process, including setting goals and priorities for their child's treatment and supporting their child's newly acquired skills in home and community activities. 137

It is important to establish goals with specific predicted outcomes before selecting and implementing an intervention. 138

Intervention selection should include consideration of each child's unique presentation including specific strengths and needs, individual and family values and preferences, and available family and community resources. 140

Regardless of the method, school professionals and interventionists should make a determined effort to collect data related to intervention integrity (fidelity). 142

Evidence-based strategies such as self-management have shown considerable promise as a method for teaching students with ASD to be more independent and self-reliant, and less dependent on external control and continuous adult supervision. 143

Different approaches to intervention have been found to be effective for children with autism, and no comparative research has been conducted that demonstrates one approach is superior to another. The selection of a specific intervention should be based on goals developed from a comprehensive developmental assessment and systematic research reviews. 155

SPECIAL EDUCATION

A clinical or medical diagnosis of ASD alone is not sufficient to qualify a child for special education services under the IDEA disability category of autism. It is state and federal education codes and regulations (not clinical criteria) that determine eligibility and IEP planning decisions.   157

The determination of an eligibility for autism should include a variety of assessment tools and information sources, and should not be based on a single process or approach.   162

The IEP is the cornerstone for the education of a child with ASD and the vehicle for planning and implementing education objectives and services.   165

A comprehensive IEP should be based on the student's unique strengths and weaknesses. Goals for a student with ASD usually include the areas of communication, social interaction, challenging behavior, and academic and functional skills.   166

The development of a formal transition plan is critical for youth with ASD and includes a coordinated set of activities and objectives to address new developmental challenges such as independent living, vocational engagement, post-secondary education, and family support.   168

Functional behavior assessment (FBA) is a well-established tool for identifying and developing behavior intervention plans for students with ASD. Interventions developed from FBA information are more likely to result in a reduction of challenging behavior.   170

A variety of evidence-based interventions and strategies should be used to support the student's IEP goals and objectives.   174

The Picture Exchange Communication System (PECS) is a widely used form of augmentative and alternative communication (AAC) that has been shown to produce positive improvements in communication and interpersonal skills for some children with ASD.   175

Educational programs for children with ASD should incorporate appropriately structured physical and sensory environments within the context of functional educational goals to accommodate any unique or problematic sensory processing patterns.   177

Peer-mediated strategies can be used to teach typically developing peers ways to help learners with ASD acquire new social skills by increasing social opportunities in natural environments.   179

The components of Pivotal Response Training (PRT) can be adapted and utilized in the classroom setting to improve the communication, language, play, and social behaviors of learners with ASD.   180

Positive behavioral support (PBS) strategies have been shown to be an effective proactive approach to eliminate, minimize, and prevent challenging behavior by designing effective environments and teaching students appropriate social and communication skills.   181

Social skills training is an essential component of educational programming for students with ASD and should be delivered throughout the day in various natural settings, using specific activities and interventions designed to meet age-appropriate social interaction goals.   186

The provision of speech and language therapy is important at all levels and ages for children with ASD and should focus on the social (pragmatic) communication and interaction skills necessary to build and sustain positive relationships within family, peers, and community environments.   189

Story-based interventions are considered an effective approach for facilitating social skills in children with ASD and may be integrated into the student's IEP or behavior support plan on a daily basis to complement other interventions and strategies.   191

Classroom interventions and programs should capitalize on the preferences of children with ASD for visual structure, routines, schedules, and predictability.   192

School professionals should be sensitive to the everyday challenges faced by families of children with ASD and work closely with parents to provide support and help them advocate, problem-solve, plan for the future, and locate the resources that meet the developmental needs of the child and family.   193

School professionals should establish effective communications with parents and investigate the use of various alternate dispute resolution methods such as mediation and IEP facilitation to address legal issues associated with special education eligibility and placement.   197

REFERENCES

Abidin, R.R. (2012) *Parenting Stress Index* (4th edn). Lutz, FL: PAR.

Achenbach, T.M. and Rescorla, L.A. (2001) *Manual for the ASEBA School-age Forms and Profiles*. Burlington, VT: University of Vermont, Research Center for Children, Youth, and Families.

Akshoomoff, N., Corsello, C., and Schmidt, H. (2006) "The role of the Autism Diagnostic Observation Schedule in the assessment of autism spectrum disorders in school and community settings." *The California School Psychologist 11*, 7–19.

Alberto, P. and Troutman, A. (2012) *Applied Behavior Analysis for Teachers* (9th edn). Upper Saddle River, NJ: Pearson Education.

Alpern, G., Boll, T., and Shearer, M. (2007) *Developmental Profile* (3rd edn). Torrance, CA: Western Psychological Services.

American Academy of Pediatrics (2012) "Policy Statement: Sensory integration therapies for children with developmental and behavioral disorders. Section on Complementary and Integrative Medicine and Council on Children with Disabilities." *Pediatrics 129*, 6, 1186–1189. Available at http://pediatrics.aappublications.org/content/early/2012/05/23/peds.2012-0876.full.pdf+html (accessed June 23, 2016).

American Occupational Therapy Association (2010) "The scope of occupational therapy services for individuals with an autism spectrum disorder across the life course." *American Journal of Occupational Therapy 64*, (Suppl.), S125–S136.

American Psychiatric Association (1980) *Diagnostic and Statistical Manual of Mental Disorders* (3rd edn). Washington, DC: American Psychiatric Association.

American Psychiatric Association (1987) *Diagnostic and Statistical Manual of Mental Disorders* (3rd edn, rev.). Washington, DC: American Psychiatric Association.

American Psychiatric Association (1994) *Diagnostic and Statistical Manual of Mental Disorders* (4th edn). Washington, DC: American Psychiatric Association.

American Psychiatric Association (2000) *Diagnostic and Statistical Manual of Mental Disorders* (4th edn, text rev.). Washington, DC: American Psychiatric Association.

American Psychiatric Association (2013) *Diagnostic and Statistical Manual of Mental Disorders* (5th edn). Washington, DC: American Psychiatric Association.

American Psychological Association Task Force on Evidence-Based Practice with Children and Adolescents (2008) *Disseminating Evidence-Based Practice for Children and Adolescents: A Systems Approach to Enhancing Care.* Washington, DC: American Psychiatric Association.

Anderson, K.A., Shattuck, P.T., Cooper, B.P., Roux, A.M., and Wagner, M. (2014) "Prevalence and correlates of postsecondary residential status among young adults with an autism spectrum disorder." *Autism 18*, 562–570.

Bailey, A., Phillips, W., and Rutter, M. (1996) "Autism: Towards an integration of clinical, genetic, neuropsychological, and neurobiological perspectives." *Journal of Child Psychology and Psychiatry 37*, 89–126.

Baranek, G.T. (2002) "Efficacy of sensory and motor interventions for children with autism." *Journal of Autism and Developmental Disorders 32*, 397–422.

Barnhill, G.P. (2014) "Collaboration between Families and Schools." In L.A. Wilkinson (ed.) *Autism Spectrum Disorder in Children and Adolescents: Evidence-Based Assessment and Intervention in Schools.* Washington, DC: American Psychological Association.

Batsche, G., Elliott, J., Graden, J.L., Grimes, J., *et al.* (2005) *Response to Intervention Policy Considerations and Implementation.* Reston, VA: National Association of State Directors of Special Education.

Beery, K., Buktenica, N.A., and Beery, N.A. (2010). *Beery-Buktenica Developmental Test of Visual-Motor Integration* (6th edn). San Antonio, TX: Pearson.

Bellini, S., Peters, J.K., Benner, L., and Hopf, A. (2007) "A meta-analysis of school-based interventions for children with autism spectrum disorders." *Remedial and Special Education 28*, 153–162.

Bishop, D.V.M. (2006) *Children's Communication Checklist* (2nd edn, U.S. edn). San Antonio, TX: Pearson.

Bishop, S.L., Hus, V., Duncan, A., Huerta, M., *et al.* (2013) "Subcategories of restricted and repetitive behaviors in children with autism spectrum disorders." *Journal of Autism and Developmental Disorders 43*, 1287–1297.

Bishop, S.L., Richler, J., and Lord, C. (2006) "Association between restricted and repetitive behaviors and nonverbal IQ in children with autism spectrum disorders." *Child Neuropsychology 12*, 247–267.

Bodfish, J.W., Symons, F.J., Parker, D.E., and Lewis, M.H. (2000) "Varieties of repetitive behavior in autism: Comparisons to mental retardation." *Journal of Autism and Developmental Disorders 30*, 237–243.

Bolte, S., Dickhut, H., and Poustka, F. (1999) "Patterns of parent-reported problems indicative in autism." *Psychopathology 32*, 93–97.

Boutot, E.A. and Myles, B.S. (2011) *Autism Spectrum Disorders: Foundations, Characteristics, and Effective Strategies.* Upper Saddle River, NJ: Pearson Education.

Bowers, L., Huisingh, R., and LoGiudice, C. (2008) *Social Language Development Test: Elementary.* Austin, TX: PRO-ED.

Bowers, L., Huisingh, R., and LoGiudice, C. (2010) *Social Language Development Test: Adolescent.* Austin, TX: PRO-ED.

Boyd, B.A., Baranek, G.T., Siders, J., Poe, M.D., *et al.* (2010) "Sensory features and repetitive behaviors in children with autism and developmental delays." *Autism Research 3*, 78–87.

Boyd, B.A., McDonough, S.G., and Bodfish, J.W. (2012) "Evidence-based behavioral interventions for repetitive behaviors in autism." *Journal of Autism and Developmental Disorders 42*, 6, 1236–1248.

Brock, S.E., Jimerson, S.R., and Hansen, R.L. (2006) *Identifying, Assessing, and Treating Autism at School.* New York, NY: Springer.

Brondino, N., Fusar-Poli, L., Rocchetti, M., Provenzani, U., Barale, F., and Politi, P. (2015) "Complementary and alternative therapies for autism spectrum disorder." *Evidence-Based Complementary and Alternative Medicine 2015*, Article ID 258589, available at http://dx.doi.org/10.1155/2015/258589 (accessed July 7, 2016).

Bruininks, R.H. and Bruininks, B.D. (2005) *Bruininks-Oseretsky Test of Motor Proficiency* (2nd edn). San Antonio, TX: Pearson.

Bryson, S.E., Koegel, L.K., Koegel, R.L., Openden, D., Smith, I.M., and Nefdt, N. (2007) "Large scale dissemination and community implementation of pivotal response treatment: Program description and preliminary data." *Research and Practice for Persons with Severe Disabilities 32*, 142–153.

Bryson, S.E., Rogers, S.J., and Fombonne, E. (2003) "Autism spectrum disorders: Early detection, intervention, education, and psychopharmacological management." *Canadian Journal of Psychiatry 48*, 506–516.

Buescher, A., Cidav, Z., Knapp, M., and Mandell, D.S. (2014) "Costs of autism spectrum disorders in the United Kingdom and the United States." *JAMA Pediatrics 168*, 8, 721–728.

California Department of Developmental Services (2002) *Autistic Spectrum Disorders: Best Practice Guidelines for Screening, Diagnosis and Assessment.* Sacramento, CA: California Department of Developmental Services.

Campbell, J.M. (2005) "Diagnostic assessment of Asperger's disorder: A review of five third-party rating scales." *Journal of Autism and Developmental Disorders 35*, 25–35.

Campbell, J.M., Ruble, L.A., and Hammond, R.K. (2014) "Comprehensive Developmental Approach Assessment Model." In L.A. Wilkinson (ed.) *Autism Spectrum Disorders in Children and Adolescents: Evidence-Based Assessment and Intervention.* Washington, DC: American Psychological Association.

Carr, E.G., Horner, R.H., Turnbull, A.P., Marquis, J.G., *et al.* (1999) *Positive Behavior Support for People with Developmental Disabilities: A Research Synthesis.* Washington, DC: American Association on Mental Retardation Monograph Series.

Carrow-Woolfolk, E. (1999) *Comprehensive Assessment of Spoken Language.* Torrance, CA: Western Psychological Services.

Carrow-Woolfolk, E. (2014) *Test for Auditory Comprehension of Language* (4th edn). Austin, TX: PRO-ED.

Carter, A.S., Davis, N.O., Klin, A., and Volkmar, F.R. (2005) "Social Development in Autism." In F.R. Volkmar, R. Paul, A. Klin, and D. Cohen (eds) *Handbook of Autism and Pervasive Developmental Disorders: Vol. 1. Diagnosis, Development, Neurobiology, and Behavior.* Hoboken, NJ: Wiley.

Carter, A.S., Volkmar, F.R., Sparrow, S.S., Wang, J.J., *et al.* (1998) "The Vineland Adaptive Behavior Scales: Supplementary norms for individuals with autism." *Journal of Autism and Developmental Disorders 28,* 287–302.

Caterino, L.C. (2014) "Cognitive, Neuropsychological, Academic, and Adaptive Functioning." In L.A. Wilkinson (ed.) *Autism Spectrum Disorders in Children and Adolescents: Evidence-Based Assessment and Intervention.* Washington, DC: American Psychological Association.

Centers for Disease Control and Prevention (CDC) (2014) "Autism and Developmental Disabilities Monitoring Network Surveillance Year 2010 Principal Investigators; Prevalence of autism spectrum disorders: Autism and Developmental Disabilities Monitoring Network, 11 sites, United States, 2010." *MMWR Surveillance Summaries 63,* 2, 1–21.

Chandler, L.K. and Dahlquist, C.M. (2010) *Functional Assessment: Strategies to Prevent and Remediate Challenging Behavior in School Settings* (3rd edn). Upper Saddle River, NJ: Merrill Prentice Hall.

Chandler, S., Charman, T., Baird, G., Simonoff, E., *et al.* (2007) "Validation of the Social Communication Questionnaire in a population cohort of children with autism spectrum disorders." *Journal of the American Academy of Child and Adolescent Psychiatry 46,* 1324–1332.

Charlop-Christy, M.H., Carpenter, M.H., LeBlanc, L.A., and Kellet, K. (2002) "Using the Picture Exchange Communication System (PECS) with children with autism: Assessment of PECS acquisition, speech, social-communicative behavior, and problem behavior." *Journal of Applied Behavior Analysis 35,* 213–231.

Charman, T., Baird, G., Simonoff, E., Loucas, T., *et al.* (2007) "Efficacy of three screening instruments in the identification of autistic-spectrum disorders." *British Journal of Psychiatry 191,* 554–559.

Charman, T. and Gotham, K. (2013) "Measurement issues: Screening and diagnostic instruments for autism spectrum disorders—lessons from research and practice." *Child and Adolescent Mental Health 18,* 52–63.

Christon, L.M., Mackintosh, V.H., and Myers, B.J. (2010) "Use of complementary and alternative medicine (CAM) treatments by parents of children with autism spectrum disorders." *Research in Autism Spectrum Disorders 4,* 249–259.

Clark, C., Prior, M., and Kinsella, G, (2002) "The relationship between executive function abilities, adaptive behavior, and academic achievement in children with externalizing behavior problems." *Journal of Child Psychology and Psychiatry 43,* 785–796.

Conners, C.K. (2008) *Conners Third Edition*. North Tonawanda, NY: Multi-Health Systems.

Constantino, J.N., Davis, S.A., Todd, R.D., Schindler, M.K., *et al.* (2003) "Validation of a brief quantitative measure of autistic traits: Comparison of the Social Responsiveness Scale with the Autism Diagnostic Interview-Revised." *Journal of Autism and Developmental Disorders 33*, 427–433.

Constantino, J.N. and Gruber, C.P. (2005) *Social Responsiveness Scale*. Los Angeles, CA: Western Psychological Services.

Constantino, J.N. and Gruber, C.P. (2012) *Social Responsiveness Scale* (2nd edn). Los Angeles, CA: Western Psychological Services.

Constantino, J.N. and Todd, R.D. (2003) "Autistic traits in the general population: A twin study." *Archives of General Psychiatry 60*, 524–530.

Coonrod, E.E. and Stone, W.L. (2005) "Screening for Autism in Young Children." In F.R. Volkmar, R. Paul, A. Klin, and D. Cohen (eds) *Handbook of Autism and Pervasive Developmental Disorders: Vol. 2. Assessment, Interventions, and Policy* (3rd edn). New York, NY: Wiley.

Corsello, C., Hus, V., Pickles, A., Risi, S., *et al.* (2007) "Between a ROC and a hard place: Decision making and making decisions about using the SCQ." *Journal of Child Psychology and Psychiatry 48*, 932–940.

Cox, A., Klein, K., Charman, T., Baird, G., *et al.* (1999) "Autism spectrum disorders at 20 and 42 months of age: Stability of clinical and ADI-R diagnosis." *Journal of Child Psychology and Psychiatry 40*, 719–732.

Crane, L., Goddard, L., and Pring, L. (2009) "Sensory processing in adults with autism spectrum disorders." *Autism 13*, 215–228.

Crone, D.A., Hawken, L.S., and Horner, R.H. (2015) *Building Positive Behavior Support Systems in Schools: Functional Behavioral Assessment* (2nd edn). New York, NY: Guilford Press.

Dawkins, T., Meyer, A.T., and Van Bourgondien, M.E. (2014) "The relationship between the Childhood Autism Rating Scale-Second Edition and clinical diagnosis utilizing the DSM-5 and the DSM-IV." Paper presented at the International Meeting for Autism Research (IMFAR), Atlanta, GA. Available at https://imfar.confex.com/imfar/2014/webprogram/Paper17395.html (accessed June 23, 2016).

Dawson, G. and Osterling, J. (1997) "Early Intervention in Autism." In M. Guralnick (ed.) *The Effectiveness of Early Intervention*. Baltimore, MD: Paul H. Brookes Publishing.

Deitz, J., Kartin, D., and Kopp, K. (2007) "Review of the Bruininks-Oseretsky Test of Motor Proficiency, Second Edition (BOT-2)." *Physical and Occupational Therapy in Pediatrics 27*, 87–102.

Delis, D.C., Kaplan, E., and Kramer, J.H. (2001) *Delis-Kaplan Executive Function System*. San Antonio, TX: The Psychological Corporation.

Delis, D.C., Kramer, J.H., Kaplan, E., and Ober, B.A. (1994) *California Verbal Learning Test: Children's Version*. San Antonio, TX: Pearson.

Deprey, L. and Ozonoff, S. (2009) "Assessment of Comorbid Psychiatric Conditions in Autism Spectrum Disorders." In S. Goldstein, J.A. Naglieri, and S. Ozonoff (eds) *Assessment of Autism Spectrum Disorders*. New York, NY: Guilford Press.

DiSalvo, D.A. and Oswald, D.P. (2002) "Peer-mediated interventions to increase the social interaction of children with autism: Consideration of peer expectancies." *Focus on Autism and Other Developmental Disabilities 17*, 198–208.

Doepke, K.J., Banks, B.M., Mays, J.F., Toby, L.M., and Landau, S. (2014) "Co-occurring Emotional and Behavior Problems." In L.A. Wilkinson (ed.) *Autism Spectrum Disorders in Children and Adolescents: Evidence-Based Assessment and Intervention*. Washington, DC: American Psychological Association.

Duarte, C.S., Bordin, I.A.S., deOliveira, A., and Bird, H. (2003) "The CBCL and the identification of children with autism and related conditions in Brazil: Pilot findings." *Journal of Autism and Developmental Disorders 33*, 703–707.

Dunlap, G., Carr, E.G., Horner, R.H., Zarcone, J.R., and Schwartz, I. (2008) "Positive behavior support and applied behavior analysis: A familial alliance." *Behavior Modification 32*, 682–698.

Dunlap, G. and Fox, L. (1999) "A demonstration of behavioral support for young children with autism." *Journal of Positive Behavior Interventions 1*, 77–87.

Dunn, W. (2001) "The sensations of everyday life: Empirical, theoretical, and pragmatic considerations." *American Journal of Occupational Therapy 55*, 608–620.

Dunn, W. (2014) *Sensory Profile* (2nd edn). San Antonio, TX: Pearson.

Dunn, L. and Dunn, D. (2007) *Peabody Picture Vocabulary Test* (4th edn). Circle Pines, MN: American Guidance Service.

Ehlers, S., Gillberg, C., and Wing, L. (1999) "A screening questionnaire for Asperger syndrome and other high-functioning autism spectrum disorders in school-age children." *Journal of Autism and Developmental Disorders 29*, 129–141.

Elliott, C. (2007) *Differential Abilities Scale* (2nd edn). San Antonio, TX: Psychological Corporation.

Elliott, S.N. and Busse, R.T. (1993) "Effective Treatments with Behavioral Consultation." In J.E. Zins, T.R. Kratochwill, and S.N. Elliott (eds) *Handbook of Consultation Services for Children: Applications in Educational and Clinical Settings*. San Francisco, CA: Jossey-Bass.

Esbensen, A.J., Seltzer, M., Lam, K., and Bodfish, J.W. (2009) "Age-related differences in restricted repetitive behaviors in autism spectrum disorders." *Journal of Autism and Developmental Disorders 39*, 57–66.

Estes, A., Munson, J., Dawson, G., Koehler, E., Zhou, X., and Abbott, R. (2009) "Parenting stress and psychological functioning among mothers of preschool children with autism and developmental delay." *Autism 13*, 375–387.

Feinberg, E., Augustyn, M., Fitzgerald, E., Sandler, J., *et al.* (2014) "Improving maternal mental health after a child's diagnosis of autism spectrum disorder: Results from a randomized clinical trial." *JAMA Pediatrics 168*, 1, 40–46.

Filipek, P.A., Accardo, P.J., Ashwal, S., Baranek, G.T., *et al.* (2000) "Practice parameter: Screening and diagnosis of autism: Report of the Quality Standards Subcommittee of the American Academy of Neurology and the Child Neurology Society." *Neurology* 55, 468–479.

Filipek, P.A., Accardo, P.J., Baranek, G.T., Cook, E.H. Jr., *et al.* (1999) "The screening and diagnosis of autistic spectrum disorders." *Journal of Autism and Developmental Disorders 29*, 439–494.

Fogt, J.B., Miller, D.N., and Zirkel, P.A. (2003) "Defining autism: Professional best practices and published case law." *Journal of School Psychology 41*, 201–216.

Fombonne, E. (2003) "The prevalence of autism." *Journal of the American Medical Association 289*, 87–89.

Fombonne, E. (2005) "The changing epidemiology of autism." *Journal of Applied Research in Intellectual Disabilities 18*, 281–294.

Fournier, K.A., Hass, C.J., Naik, S.K., Lodha, N., and Cauraugh, J.H. (2010) "Motor coordination in autism spectrum disorders: A synthesis and meta-analysis." *Journal of Autism and Developmental Disorders 40*, 1227–1240.

Frost, L. and Bondy, A. (2002) *The Picture Exchange Communication System Training Manual* (2nd edn). Cherry Hill, NJ: Pyramid Educational Consultants.

Gabriels, R.L., Cuccaro, M.L., Hill, D.E., Ivers, B.J., and Goldson, E. (2005) "Repetitive behaviors in autism: Relationships with associated clinical features." *Research in Developmental Disabilities 26*, 169–181.

Ganz, J.B., Davis, J.L., Lund, E.M., Goodwyn, F.D., and Simpson, R.L. (2012) "Meta-analysis of PECS with individuals with ASD: Investigation of targeted versus non-targeted outcomes, participant characteristics, and implementation phase." *Research in Developmental Disorders 33*, 406–418.

Ghaziuddin, M. (2002) "Asperger syndrome: Associated psychiatric and medical conditions." *Focus on Autism and Other Developmental Disabilities 17*, 138–143.

Giallo, R., Wood, C.E., Jellett, R., and Porter, R. (2013) "Fatigue, wellbeing and parental self-efficacy in mothers of children with an Autism Spectrum Disorder." *Autism 17*, 465–480.

Gilliam, J.E. (2006) *Gilliam Autism Rating Scale* (2nd edn). Austin, TX: PRO-ED.

Gilliam, J.E. (2014) *Gillian Autism Rating Scale* (3rd edn). Austin TX: PRO-ED.

Gilliam, J.E. and Miller, L. (2006) *Pragmatic Language Skills Inventory*. Austin, TX: PRO-ED.

Gioia, G.A., Isquith, P.K., Guy, S.C., and Kenworthy, L. (2015) *Behavior Rating Inventory of Executive Function* (2nd edn). Lutz, FL: PAR.

Gioia, G.A., Isquith, P.K., Kenworthy, L., and Barton, R.M. (2002) "Profiles of everyday executive function in acquired and developmental disorders." *Child Neuropsychology 8*, 121–137.

Goddard, J.A., Lehr, R., and Lapadat, J.C. (2000) "Parents of children with disabilities: Telling a different story." *Canadian Journal of Counselling 34*, 273–289.

Goin-Kochel, R.P., Mackintosh, V.H., and Myers, B.J. (2006) "How many doctors does it take to make an autism spectrum diagnosis?" *Autism 10*, 439–451.

Goldstein, G., Johnson, C.R., and Minshew, N.J. (2001) "Attentional processes in autism." *Journal of Autism and Developmental Disorders 31*, 433–440.

Goldstein, S. and Naglieri, J.A. (2010) *Autism Spectrum Rating Scales*. North Tonawanda, NY: Multi-Health Systems.

Goldstein, S. and Naglieri, J. (2014) *Autism Spectrum Rating Scales (ASRS) Technical Report #2*. Toronto, ON: Multi-Health Systems.

Goldstein, S., Ozonoff, S., Cook, A., and Clark, E. (2009) "Alternative Methods, Challenging Issues, and Best Practices in the Assessment of Autism Spectrum Disorders." In S. Goldstein, J.A. Naglieri, and S. Ozonoff (eds) *Assessment of Autism Spectrum Disorders*. New York, NY: Guilford Press.

Granpeesheh, D., Tarbox, J., Dixon, D.R., Wilke, A.E., Allen, M.S., and Bradstreet, J.J. (2010) "Randomized trial of hyperbaric oxygen therapy for children with autism." *Research in Autism Spectrum Disorders 4*, 268–275.

Gray, C. (2010) *The New Social Story™ Book* (10th edn). Arlington, TX: Future Horizons.

Gray, D.E. (2002) "Ten years on: A longitudinal study of families of children with autism." *Journal of Intellectual and Developmental Disability 27*, 215–222.

Gresham, F.M. (1989) "Assessment of treatment integrity in school consultation and prereferral intervention." *School Psychology Review 18*, 37–50.

Gresham, F.M., Gansle, K.A., and Noell, G.H. (1993) "Treatment integrity in applied behavior analysis with children." *Journal of Applied Behavior Analysis 26*, 257–263.

Hale, J.B. (2008) "Response to intervention: Guidelines for parents and practitioners." Available at www.wrightslaw.com/idea/art/rti.hale.pdf (accessed June 23, 2016).

Hardan, A.Y., Gengoux, G.W., Berquist, K.L., Libove, R.A., *et al.* (2015) "A randomized controlled trial of Pivotal Response Treatment Group for parents of children with autism." *Journal of Child Psychology and Psychiatry 56*, 884–892.

Harris, S.L. and Handleman, J.S. (2000) "Age and IQ at intake as predictors of placement for young children with autism: A four- to six-year follow-up." *Journal of Autism and Developmental Disorders 30*, 137–142.

Harrison, J. and Hare, D.J. (2004) "Brief report: Assessment of sensory abnormalities in people with autism spectrum disorders." *Journal of Autism and Developmental Disorders 34*, 727–730.

Harrison, P.L. and Oakland, T. (2015) *Adaptive Behavior Assessment System* (3rd edn). San Antonio, TX: Pearson.

Hart, S.L. and Banda, D.R. (2010) "Picture Exchange Communication System with individuals with developmental disabilities: A meta-analysis of single subject studies." *Remedial and Special Education 31*, 476–488.

Hendricks, D. (2011) "Special education teachers serving students with autism: A descriptive study of the characteristics and self-reported knowledge and practices employed." *Journal of Vocational Rehabilitation 35*, 37–50.

Hill, E.L. (2004) "Evaluating the theory of executive dysfunction in autism." *Developmental Review 24*, 189–233.

Hoffman, C.D., Sweeney, D.P., Hodge, D., Lopez-Wagner, M.C., and Looney, L. (2009) "Parenting stress and closeness: Mothers of typically developing children and mothers of children with autism." *Focus on Autism and Other Developmental Disabilities 24*, 178–187.

Holmboe, K., Rijsdijk, F.V., Hallett, V., Happ, F., Plomin, R., and Ronald, A. (2014) "Strong genetic influences on the stability of autistic traits in childhood." *Journal of the American Academy of Child and Adolescent Psychiatry 53*, 221–230.

Horner, R.H., Carr, E.G., Strain, P.S., Todd, A.W., and Reed, H.K. (2002) "Problem behavior interventions for young children with autism: A research synthesis." *Journal of Autism and Developmental Disorders 32*, 5, 423–446.

Howlin, P. (1998) *Children with Autism and Asperger's Syndrome: A Guide for Practitioners and Carers.* New York, NY: Wiley.

Howlin, P. (2005) "Outcomes in Autism Spectrum Disorders." In F. R. Volkmar, R. Paul, A. Klin, and D. Cohen (eds) *Handbook of Autism and Pervasive Developmental Disorders: Vol. 1. Diagnosis, Development, Neurobiology, and Behavior* (3rd edn). Hoboken, NJ: Wiley.

Howlin, P. and Asgharian, A. (1999) "The diagnosis of autism and Asperger syndrome: Findings from a survey of 770 families." *Developmental Medicine and Child Neurology 41*, 834–839.

Huffman, L.C., Sutcliffe, T.K., Tanner, I.S.D., and Feldman, H.M. (2011) "Management of symptoms in children with autism spectrum disorders: A comprehensive review of pharmacologic and complementary-alternative medicine treatments." *Journal of Developmental and Behavioral Pediatrics 32*, 56–68.

Hyman, S.L., Stewart, P.A., Foley, J., Cain, U., *et al.* (2016) "The gluten-free/casein-free diet: A double-blind challenge trial in children with autism." *Journal of Autism and Developmental Disorders 46*, 205–220.

Individuals with Disabilities Education Improvement Act of 2004. Pub. L. No. 108-446, 108th Congress, 2nd Session. (2004).

Iovannone, R., Dunlap, G., Huber, H., and Kincaid, D. (2003) "Effective educational practices for students with autism spectrum disorders." *Focus on Autism and Other Developmental Disabilities 18*,150–165.

Ivey, J.K. (2004) "What do parents expect? A study of the likelihood and importance issues for children with autism spectrum disorders." *Focus on Autism and Other Developmental Disabilities 19*, 27–33.

Johnson, C.P., Myers, S.M., and Council on Children with Disabilities (2007) "Identification and evaluation of children with autism spectrum disorders." *Pediatrics 120*, 1183–1215.

Kabot, S. and Reeve, C. (2014) "Curriculum and Program Structure." In L. A. Wilkinson (ed.) *Autism Spectrum Disorder in Children and Adolescents: Evidence-Based Assessment and Intervention in Schools.* Washington, DC: American Psychological Association.

Kanner, L. (1943) "Autistic disturbances of affective contact." *Nervous Child 2*, 217–250.

Kao, G.S. and Thomas, H.M. (2010) "Test review: Conners 3rd Edition." *Journal of Psychoeducational Assessment 28*, 598–602.

Kasari, C., Rotheram-Fuller, E., Locke, J., and Gulsrud, A. (2012) "Making the connection: Randomized controlled trial of social skills at school for children with autism spectrum disorders." *Journal of Child Psychology and Psychiatry 53*, 4, 431–439.

Kaufman, A.S. and Kaufman, N.L. (2004a) *Kaufman Assessment Battery for Children* (2nd edn). Circle Pines, MN: AGS.

Kaufman, A.S. and Kaufman, N.L. (2004b) *Kaufman Brief Intelligence Test* (2nd edn). San Antonio, TX: Pearson.

Kaufman, A.S. and Kaufman, N.L. (2014) *Kaufman Test of Educational Achievement* (3rd edn). San Antonio, TX: Pearson.

Kern, J.K., Trevidi, M.H., Grannemann, B.D., Garver, C.R., *et al.* (2007) "Sensory correlations in autism." *Autism 11*, 123–134.

Kim, A., Szatmari, P., Bryson, S., Streiner, D., and Wilson, F. (2000) "The prevalence of anxiety and mood problems among children with autism and Asperger syndrome." *Autism 4*, 117–132.

Kleinhans, N., Akshoomoff, N., and Delis D.C. (2005) "Executive functions in autism and Asperger's disorder: Flexibility, fluency, and inhibition." *Developmental Neuropsychology 27*, 379–401.

Kleinhans, N.M., Akshoomoff, N.A., and Courchesne, E. (2003) "Executive functioning in autism and Asperger's syndrome: Results from the D-KEFS." *Journal of the International Neuropsychological Society 9*, 273.

Klin, A., Saulnier, C., Tsantsanis, K., and Volkmar, F.R. (2005) "Clinical Evaluation in Autism Spectrum Disorders: Psychological Assessment within a Transdisciplinary Framework." In F.R. Volkmar, R. Paul, A. Klin, and D. Cohen (eds) *Handbook of Autism and Pervasive Developmental Disorders: Vol. 2. Assessment, Interventions, and Policy* (3rd edn). Hoboken, NJ: Wiley.

Klinger, L.G., O'Kelley, S.E., and Mussey, J.L. (2009) "Assessment of Intellectual Functioning in Autism Spectrum Disorders." In S. Goldstein, J.A. Naglieri, and S. Ozonoff (eds) *Assessment of Autism Spectrum Disorders*. New York, NY: Guilford Press.

Klinger, M.R., Mussey, J.L., Thomas, S.P., and Powell, P.S. (2015) "Correlates of Middle Adult Outcome: A Follow-up Study of Children Diagnosed with ASD from 1970–1999." Paper presented at the International Meeting for Autism Research (IMFAR), Salt Lake City, UT. Available at https://imfar.confex.com/imfar/2015/webprogram/Paper20033.html (accessed July 7, 2016).

Koegel, L.K., Robinson, S., and Koegel, R.L. (2009) "Empirically Supported Intervention Practices for Autism Spectrum Disorders in School and Community Settings: Issues and Practices." In W. Sailor, G. Dunlap, G. Sugai, and R. Horner (eds) *Handbook of Positive Behavior Support*. New York, NY: Springer.

Koegel, R.L., Openden, D., Fredeen, R.M., and Koegel, L.K. (2006) "The Basics of Pivotal Response Treatment." In R.L. Koegel and L.K. Koegel (eds) *Pivotal Response Treatments for Autism: Communication, Social, and Academic Development*. Baltimore, MD: Paul H. Brookes.

Koegel, R.L., Schreibman, L., Loos, L.M., and Dirlich-Wilhelm, H. (1992) "Consistent stress profiles in mothers of children with autism." *Journal of Autism and Developmental Disorders 22*, 205–216.

Kopp, S. and Gillberg, C. (2011) "The Autism Spectrum Screening Questionnaire (ASSQ) Revised Extended Version (ASSQ-REV): An instrument for better capturing the autism phenotype in girls? A preliminary study involving clinical cases and community controls." *Research in Developmental Disabilities 32*, 2875–2888.

Korkman, M., Kirk, U., and Kemp, S. (2007) *NEPSY* (2nd edn). San Antonio, TX: Pearson.

Kovacs, M. (2010) *Children's Depression Inventory* (2nd edn). North Tonawanda, NY: Multi-Health Systems.

Kurth, J.A. (2015) "Educational placement of students with autism: The impact of state of residence." *Focus on Autism and Other Developmental Disabilities 30*, 249–256.

Lake, J.K., Perry, A., and Lunsky, Y. (2014) "Mental health services for individuals with high functioning autism spectrum disorder." *Autism Research and Treatment 2014*, Article ID 502420, doi:10.1155/2014/502420.

Lam, K.S.L. and M.G. Aman (2007) "The Repetitive Behavior Scale-Revised: Independent validation in individuals with autism spectrum disorders." *Journal of Autism and Developmental Disorders 37*, 5, 855–866.

Lane, K.L., Bocian, K.M., MacMillan, D.L., and Gresham, F.M. (2004) "Treatment integrity: An essential—but often forgotten—component of school-based interventions." *Preventing School Failure 48*, 36–43.

Lang, R., O'Reilly, M., Healy, O., Rispoli, M., *et al.* (2012) "Sensory integration therapy for autism spectrum disorders: A systematic review." *Research in Autism Spectrum Disorders 6*, 1004–1018.

Lange, K.W., Hauser, J., and Reissmann, A. (2015) "Gluten-free and casein-free diets in the therapy of autism." *Current Opinion in Clinical Nutrition and Metabolic Care 18*, 572–575.

Lavelle, T.A., Weinstein, M.C., Newhouse, J.P., Munir, K., Kuhlthau, K.A., and Prosser, L.A. (2014) "Economic burden of childhood autism spectrum disorders." *Pediatrics 133*, 520–529.

Lee, G.K. (2009) "Parents of children with high functioning autism: How well do they cope and adjust?" *Journal of Developmental and Physical Disabilities 21*, 93–114.

Lee, L., David, A.B., Rusyniak, J., Landa, R., and Newschaffer, C.J. (2007) "Performance of the Social Communication Questionnaire in children receiving preschool special education services." *Research in Autism Spectrum Disorders 1*, 126–128.

Lee, S., Simpson, R.L., and Shogren, K.A. (2007) "Effects and implications of self-management for students with autism: A meta-analysis." *Focus on Autism and Other Developmental Disabilities 22*, 2–13.

Leekam, S., Tandos, J., McConachie, H., Meins, E., *et al.* (2007) "Repetitive behaviours in typically developing 2-year-olds." *Journal of Child Psychology and Psychiatry 48*, 11, 1131–1138.

Leekam, S.R., Prior, M.R., and Uljarevic, M. (2011) "Restricted and repetitive behaviors in autism spectrum disorders: A review of research in the last decade." *Psychological Bulletin 137*, 562–593.

Lidstone, J., Uljarevic, M., Sullivan, J., Rodgers, J., *et al.* (2014) "Relations among restricted and repetitive behaviors, anxiety and sensory features in children with autism spectrum disorders." *Research in Autism Spectrum Disorders 8*, 82–92.

Liu, T., Hamilton, M., Davis, L., and ElGarhy, S. (2014) "Gross motor performance by children with autism spectrum disorder and typically developing children on TGMD-2." *Journal of Child and Adolescent Behavior 2*, 123.

Lord, C. and Corsello, C. (2005) "Diagnostic Instruments in Autistic Spectrum Disorders." In F.R. Volkmar, R. Paul, A. Klin, and D. Cohen (eds) *Handbook of Autism and Pervasive Developmental Disorders: Vol. 2. Assessment, Interventions, and Policy* (3rd edn). Hoboken, NJ: Wiley.

Lord, C., Pickles, A., McLennan, J., Rutter, M., *et al.* (1997) "Diagnosing autism: Analyses of data from the Autism Diagnostic Interview." *Journal of Autism and Developmental Disorders 27*, 501–517.

Lord, C., Rutter, M., DiLavore, P.C., and Risi, S. (1999) *Autism Diagnostic Observation Schedule.* Los Angeles, CA: Western Psychological Services.

Lord, C., Rutter, M., DiLavore, P.C., Risi, S., Gotham, K., and Bishop, S. (2012) *Autism Diagnostic Observation Schedule* (2nd edn). Torrance, CA: Western Psychological Services.

Loveland, K.A. and Tunali-Kotoski, B. (2005) "The School-Age Child with an Autism Spectrum Disorder." In F.R. Volkmar, R. Paul, A. Klin, and D. Cohen (eds) *Handbook of Autism and Pervasive Developmental Disorders: Vol. 1. Diagnosis, Development, Neurobiology, and Behavior* (3rd edn). New York, NY: Wiley.

MacFarlane, J.R. and Kanaya, R. (2009) "What does it mean to be autistic? Inter-state variation in special education criteria for autism services." *Journal of Child and Family Studies 18*, 662–669.

Mandlawitz, M.R. (2002) "The impact of the legal system on educational programming for young children with autism spectrum disorder." *Journal of Autism and Developmental Disorders 32*, 495–508.

Martin, N.A. and Brownell, R. (2010) *Expressive One-Word Picture Vocabulary Test* (4th edn). Novato, CA: Academic Therapy.

Mash, E.J. and Hunsley, J. (2005) "Evidence-based assessment of child and adolescent disorders: Issues and challenges." *Journal of Clinical Child and Adolescent Psychology 34*, 362–379.

Mattila, M.L., Jussila, K., Kuusikko, S., Kielinen, M., *et al.* (2009) "When does the Autism Spectrum Screening Questionnaire (ASSQ) predict autism spectrum disorders in primary school-aged children?" *European Child and Adolescent Psychiatry 18*, 499–509.

Mayes, S.D., Calhoun, S.L., Aggarwal, R., Baker, C., *et al.* (2013) "Unusual fears in children with autism." *Research in Autism Spectrum Disorders 7*, 151–158.

Mazefsky, C.A., McPartland, J.C., Gastgeb, H.Z., and Minshew, N.J. (2013) "Comparability of DSM-IV and DSM-5 ASD research samples." *Journal of Autism and Developmental Disorders 43*, 1236–1242.

Mazurek, M.O., Kanne, S.M., and Wodka, E.L. (2013) "Physical aggression in children and adolescents with autism spectrum disorders." *Research in Autism Spectrum Disorders 7*, 455–465.

Mazzone, L., Ruta, L., and Reale, L. (2012) "Psychiatric comorbidities in Asperger syndrome and high functioning autism: Diagnostic challenges." *Annals of General Psychiatry 11*, 1, 16.

Mesibov, G.B. and Shea, V. (2011) "Evidence-based practices and autism." *Autism 15*, 114–133.

Minshew, N.J., Sweeney, J.A., Bauman, M.L., and Webb, S. (2005) "Neurologic Aspects of Autism." In F.R. Volkmar, R. Paul, A. Klin, and D. Cohen (eds) *Handbook of Autism and Pervasive Developmental Disorders: Vol. 1. Diagnosis, Development, Neurobiology, and Behavior* (3rd edn). Hoboken, NJ: Wiley.

Mulloy, A., Lang, R., O'Reilly, M., Sigafoos, J., Lancioni, G., and Rispoli, M. (2010) "Gluten-free and casein-free diets in the treatment of autism spectrum disorders: A systematic review." *Research in Autism Spectrum Disorders 4*, 328–339.

Murray, M.J. (2010) "Attention-deficit/hyperactivity disorder in the context of autism spectrum disorders." *Current Psychiatry Reports 12*, 382–388.

Myers, S.M. and Johnson, C.P. (2007) "Management of children with autism spectrum disorders." *Pediatrics 120*, 1162–1182.

Nadon, G., Feldman, D.E., Dunn, W., and Gisel, E. (2011) "Association of sensory processing and eating problems in children with autism spectrum disorders." *Autism Research and Treatment*, Article ID 541926, 8 pages, doi:10.1155/2011/541926.

Naglieri, J.A. and Chambers, K.M. (2009) "Psychometric Issues and Current Scales for Assessing Autism Spectrum Disorders." In S. Goldstein, J.A. Naglieri, and S. Ozonoff (eds) *Assessment of Autism Spectrum Disorders*. New York, NY: Guilford Press.

Naglieri, J.A., Das, J.P., and Goldstein, S. (2014) *Cognitive Assessment System* (2nd edn). Austin, TX: PRO-ED.

National Autism Center (2015a) *Evidence-Based Practice and Autism in the Schools: An Educator's Guide to Providing Appropriate Interventions to Students with Autism Spectrum Disorder* (2nd edn). Randolph, MA: National Autism Center.

National Autism Center (2015b) *Findings and Conclusions: National Standards Project, Phase 2*. Randolph, MA: National Autism Center. Available at www.nationalautismcenter. org/national-standards-project/phase-2 (accessed June 24, 2016).

National Center on Response to Intervention (2010) *Essential Components of RTI: A Closer Look at Response to Intervention*. Washington, DC: U.S. Department of Education, Office of Special Education Programs, National Center on Response to Intervention.

National Professional Development Center on Autism Spectrum Disorders (2015) "Evidence-Based Practices." Available from: http://autismpdc.fpg.unc.edu/evidence-based-practices (accessed June 24, 2016).

National Research Council (2001) *Educating Children with Autism. Committee on Educational Interventions for Children with Autism*. C. Lord and J. P. McGee (eds). Division of Behavioral and Social Sciences and Education. Washington, DC: National Academy Press.

Newschaffer, C.J., Falb, M.D., and Gurney, J.G. (2005) "National autism prevalence trends from United States special education data." *Pediatrics 115*, 277–282.

No Child Left Behind Act of 2001. 20 U.S.C. 70 § 6301 et seq. (2002).

Norris, M. and Lecavalier, L. (2010) "Screening accuracy of level 2 autism spectrum disorder rating scales: A review of selected instruments." *Autism 14*, 263–284.

Odom, S.L. and Wong, C. (2015) "Connecting the dots: Supporting students with autism spectrum disorder." *American Educator 39*, 2, 12–19.

O'Neill, M. and Jones, R.S. (1997) "Sensory-perceptual abnormalities in autism: A case for more research?" *Journal of Autism and Developmental Disorders 3*, 283–293.

O'Neill, R.E., Albin, R.W., Storey, K., Horner, R.H., and Sprague, J.R. (2015) *Functional Assessment and Program Development for Problem Behavior: A Practical Handbook*. Stamford, CT: Cengage Learning.

Orsmond, G.I., Shattuck, P.T., Cooper, B.P., Sterzing, P.R., and Anderson, K.A. (2013) "Social participation among young adults with an autism spectrum disorder." *Journal of Autism and Developmental Disorders 43*, 2710–2719.

Osborne, L.A., McHugh, L., Saunders, J., and Reed, P. (2008) "The effect of parenting behaviors on subsequent child behavior problems in autistic spectrum conditions." *Research in Autism Spectrum Disorders 2*, 249–263.

Owen-DeSchryver, J.S., Carr, E.G., Cale, S.I., and Blakeley-Smith, A. (2008) "Promoting social interactions between students with autism spectrum disorders and their peers in inclusive school settings." *Focus on Autism and Other Developmental Disabilities 23*, 15–28.

Ozonoff, S. (1997) "Components of Executive Function in Autism and Other Disorders." In J. Russell (ed.) *Autism as an Executive Disorder.* New York, NY: Oxford University Press.

Ozonoff, S., Goodlin-Jones, B.L., and Solomon, M. (2007) "Autism Spectrum Disorders." In E.J. Mash and R.A. Barkley (eds) *Assessment of Childhood Disorders* (4th edn). New York, NY: Guilford Press.

Ozonoff, S., South, M., and Provencal, S. (2005) "Executive Functions." In F.R. Volkmar, A. Klin, and R. Paul (eds) *Handbook of Autism and Pervasive Developmental Disorders: Vol. 1. Diagnosis, Development, Neurobiology, and Behavior* (3rd edn). New York, NY: Wiley.

Ozdemir, S. (2008) "The effectiveness of social stories on decreasing disruptive behaviors of children with autism: Three case studies." *Journal of Autism and Developmental Disorders 38*, 1689–1696.

Ozsivadjian, A., Knott, F., and Magiati, I. (2012) "Parent and child perspectives on the nature of anxiety in children and young people with autism spectrum disorders: A focus group study." *Autism 16*, 107–121.

Pandolfi, V., Magyar, C.I., and Dill, C.A. (2010) "Constructs assessed by the GARS-2: Factor analysis of data from the standardization sample." *Journal of Autism and Developmental Disorders 40*, 1118–1130.

Parham, L., Ecker, C., Miller-Kuhanek, H., Henry, D.A., and Glennon, T.J. (2007) *Sensory Processing Measure.* Torrance, CA: Western Psychological Services.

Paul, R. (2005) "Assessing Communication in Autistic Spectrum Disorders." In F.R. Volkmar, R. Paul, A. Klin, and D. Cohen (eds) *Handbook of Autism and Pervasive Developmental Disorders: Vol. 2. Assessment, Interventions, and Policy* (3rd edn). Hoboken, NJ: Wiley.

Paul, R. and Wilson, K.P. (2009) "Assessing Speech, Language, and Communication in Autism Spectrum Disorders." In S. Goldstein, J.A. Naglieri, and S. Ozonoff (eds) *Assessment of Autism Spectrum Disorders.* New York, NY: Guilford Press.

Payakachat, N., Tilfordabab, J.M., Kovacsc, E., and Kuhlthaudede, K. (2012) "Autism spectrum disorders: A review of measures for clinical, health services and cost-effectiveness applications." *Expert Review of Pharmacoeconomics and Outcomes Research 12*, 485–503.

Pennington, B.F. and Ozonoff, S. (1996) "Executive functions and developmental psychopathologies." *Journal of Child Psychology and Psychiatry 37*, 51–87.

Pennington, M.L., Cullinan, D., and Southern, L.B. (2014) "Defining autism: Variability in state education agency definitions of and evaluations for autism spectrum disorders." *Autism Research and Treatment 2014*, Article ID 327271. Available at http://dx.doi.org/10.1155/2014/327271 (accessed June 24, 2016).

Phelps-Terasaki, D. and Phelps-Gunn, T. (2007) *Test of Pragmatic Language* (2nd edn). Austin, TX: PRO-ED.

Polyak, A., Kubina, R.M., and Girirajan, S. (2015) "Comorbidity of intellectual disability confounds ascertainment of autism: Implications for genetic diagnosis." *American Journal of Medical Genetics Part B: Neuropsychiatric Genetics 168*, 600–608.

Posserud, M., Lundervold, A.J., and Gillberg, C. (2006) "Autistic features in a total population of 7–9-year-old children assessed by the ASSQ (Autism Spectrum Screening Questionnaire)." *Journal of Child Psychology and Psychiatry 47*, 167–175.

Posserud, M., Lundervold, A.J., and Gillberg, C. (2009) "Validation of the Autism Spectrum Screening Questionnaire in a total population sample." *Journal of Autism and Developmental Disorders 39*, 126–134.

Posserud, M., Lundervold, A.J., Steijen, M.C., Verhoven, S., Stormark, K.M., and Gillberg, C. (2008) "Factor analysis of the Autism Spectrum Screening Questionnaire." *Autism 12*, 99–112.

Pottie, C.G. and Ingram, K.M. (2008) "Daily stress, coping, and well-being in parents of children with autism: A multilevel modeling approach." *Journal of Family Psychology 22*, 855–864.

Prizant, B.M. (2011) "The use and misuse of evidence-based practice: Implications for persons with ASD." *Autism Spectrum Quarterly*, Fall, 43–49.

Prizant, B.M. and Wetherby, A.M. (2005) "Critical Issues in Enhancing Communication Abilities for Persons with Autism Spectrum Disorders." In F.R. Volkmar, R. Paul, A. Klin, and D. Cohen (eds) *Handbook of Autism and Pervasive Developmental Disorders: Vol. 2. Assessment, Interventions, and Policy* (3rd edn). Hoboken, NJ: Wiley.

Rao, P.A., Beidel, D.C., and Murray, M.J. (2008) "Social skills interventions for children with Asperger's syndrome or high-functioning autism: A review and recommendations." *Journal of Autism and Developmental Disorders 38*, 353–361.

Rao, P.A. and Landa, R.J. (2014) "Association between severity of behavioral phenotype and comorbid attention deficit hyperactivity symptoms in children with autism spectrum disorders." *Autism 18*, 272–280.

Reichow, B., Salamack, S., Paul, R., Volkmar, F.R., and Klin, A. (2008) "Pragmatic assessment in autism spectrum disorders: A comparison of a standard measure with parent report." *Communication Disorders Quarterly 29*, 169–176.

Reynolds, C.R. and Kamphaus, R.W. (2015a) *Reynolds Intellectual Assessment Scales* (2nd edn). Lutz, FL: PAR.

Reynolds, C.R. and Kamphaus, R.W. (2015b) *Reynolds Intellectual Screening Test* (2nd edn). Lutz, FL: PAR.

Reynolds, C.R. and Kamphaus, R.W. (2015c) *Behavior Assessment System for Children* (3rd edn). San Antonio, TX: Pearson.

Reynolds, C.R. and Richmond, B.O. (2008) *Revised Children's Manifest Anxiety Scale* (2nd edn). Los Angeles, CA: Western Psychological Services.

Richler, J., Huerta, M., Bishop, S., and Lord, C. (2010) "Developmental trajectories of restricted and repetitive behaviors and interests in children with autism spectrum disorders." *Development and Psychopathology 22*, 55–69.

Rogers, S.J. (1998) "Empirically supported comprehensive treatments for young children with autism." *Journal of Clinical Child Psychology 27*, 167–178.

Rogers, S.J. and Vismara, L.A. (2008) "Evidence-based comprehensive treatments for early autism." *Journal of Clinical Child and Adolescent Psychology 37*, 8–38.

Roid, G.H. (2003). *Stanford-Binet Intelligence Scale* (5th edn). Itasca, IL: Riverside.

Roid, G.H., Miller, L.J., Pomplun, M., and Koch, C. (2013) *Leiter International Performance Scale* (3rd edn). Wood Dale, IL: Stoelting.

Roux, A.M., Shattuck, P.T., Rast, J.E., Rava, J.A., and Anderson, K.A. (2015) *National Autism Indicators Report: Transition into Young Adulthood*. Philadelphia, PA: Life Course Outcomes Research Program, A.J. Drexel Autism Institute, Drexel University. Available at http://drexe.lu/autismindicators (accessed June 24, 2016).

Russell, G., Ford, Steer, C., and Golding, J. (2010) "Identification of children with the same level of impairment as children on the autistic spectrum, and analysis of their service use." *Journal of Child Psychology and Psychiatry 51*, 643–651.

Russell, G., Steer, C., and Golding, J. (2011) "Social and demographic factors that influence the diagnosis of autistic spectrum disorders." *Social Psychiatry and Psychiatric Epidemiology 46*, 1283–1293.

Rutter, M., Bailey, A., and Lord, C. (2003) *Social Communication Questionnaire*. Los Angeles, CA: Western Psychological Services.

Rutter, M., Le Couteur, A., and Lord, C. (2003) *Autism Diagnostic Interview—Revised Manual*. Los Angeles, CA: Western Psychological Services.

Ryland, H.K., Hysing, M., Posserud, M.B., Gillberg, C., and Lundervold, A.J. (2012) "Autism spectrum symptoms in children with neurological disorders." *Child and Adolescent Psychiatry and Mental Health 6*, 34. Available at www.capmh.com/content/6/1/34 (accessed June 14, 2016).

Ryland, H.K., Hysing, M., Posserud, M.B., Gillberg, C., and Lundervold, A.J. (2014) "Autistic features in school age children: IQ and gender effects in a population-based cohort." *Research in Autism Spectrum Disorders 8*, 266–274.

Safran, S.P. (2008) "Why youngsters with autistic spectrum disorders remain underrepresented in special education." *Remedial and Special Education 29*, 90–95.

Sansosti, F.J., Powell-Smith, K.A., and Kincaid, D. (2004) "A research synthesis of social story interventions for children with autism spectrum disorders." *Focus on Autism and Other Developmental Disabilities 19*, 194–204.

Sattler, J.M. and Hoge, R.D. (2006) *Assessment of Children: Behavioral, Social, and Clinical Foundations* (5th edn). San Diego, CA: Sattler.

Schopler, E., Reichler, R., and Renner, B. (1988) *The Childhood Autism Rating Scale (CARS)*. Los Angeles, CA: Western Psychological Services.

Schopler, E., Van Bourgondien, M.E., Wellman, G.J., and Love, S.R. (2010) *Childhood Autism Rating Scale* (2nd edn). Los Angeles, CA: Western Psychological Services.

Schrank, F.A., McGrew, K.S., Mather, N., and Woodcock, R.W. (2014) *Woodcock-Johnson IV Tests of Cognitivech Abilities*. Rolling Meadows, IL: Riverside.

Schrank, F.A., Mather, N., and McGrew, K.S. (2014) *Woodcock-Johnson IV Tests of Achievement*. Rolling Meadows, IL: Riverside.

Section 504 of the Rehabilitation Act Legislation, 29 U.S.C. §§ 705(20) and 794.

Shattuck, P.T., Durkin, M., Maenner, M., Newschaffer, C., *et al.* (2009) "Timing of identification among children with an autism spectrum disorder: Findings from a population-based surveillance study." *Journal of the American Academy of Child and Adolescent Psychiatry 48*, 474–483.

Sheslow, D. and Adams, W. (2003) *Wide Range Assessment of Memory and Learning* (2nd edn). Lutz, FL: PAR.

Shriver, M.D., Allen, K.D., and Mathews, J.R. (1999) "Effective assessment of the shared and unique characteristics of children with autism." *School Psychology Review 28*, 538–558.

Sikora, D.M., Vora, P., Coury, D.L., and Rosenberg, D. (2012) "Attention-deficit/ hyperactivity disorder symptoms, adaptive functioning, and quality of life in children with autism spectrum disorder." *Pediatrics 130*, 91–97.

Silverman, W.K. and Hinshaw, S. (2008) "The second special issue on evidence-based psychosocial treatments for children and adolescents: A 10-year update." *Journal of Clinical Child and Adolescent Psychology 37*, 1–7.

Simpson, R.L. (2005) "Evidence-based practices and students with autism spectrum disorders." *Focus on Autism and Other Developmental Disabilities 20*, 140–149.

Skuse, D.H., Mandy, W., Steer, C., Miller, L.L., *et al.* (2009) "Social communication competence and functional adaptation in a general population of children: Preliminary evidence for sex-by-verbal IQ differential risk." *Journal of the American Academy of Child and Adolescent Psychiatry 48*, 128–137.

Smith, T. (2013) "What is evidence-based behavior analysis?" *Behavior Analyst 36*, 7–33.

Solomon, M., Miller, M., Taylor, S.L., Hinshaw, S.P., and Carter, C.S. (2012) "Autism symptoms and internalizing psychopathology in girls and boys with autism spectrum disorders." *Journal of Autism and Developmental Disorders 42*, 48–59.

Sparrow, S.S., Balla, D., and Cicchetti, D.V. (2005) *Vineland Adaptive Behavior Scales* (2nd edn). San Antonio, TX: Pearson.

Spencer, D., Marshall, J., Post, B., Kulakodlu, M., *et al.* (2013) "Psychotropic medication use and polypharmacy in children with autism spectrum disorders." *Pediatrics 132*, 833–840.

Spencer, V.G., Simpson, C.G., and Lynch, S.A. (2008) "Using social stories to increase positive behaviors for children with autism spectrum disorders." *Intervention in School and Clinic 44*, 58–61.

Stansberry-Brusnahan, L.L. and Collet-Klingenberg, L.L. (2010) "Evidence-based practices for young children with autism spectrum disorders: Guidelines and recommendations from the National Resource Council and National Professional Development Center on Autism Spectrum Disorders." *International Journal of Early Childhood Special Education 2*, 45–56.

Stevens, M.C., Fein, D.A., Dunn, M., Allen, D., *et al.* (2000) "Subgroups of children with autism by cluster analysis: A longitudinal examination." *Journal of the American Academy of Child and Adolescent Psychiatry 39*, 346–352.

Stone, W.L. and Yoder, P.J. (2001) "Predicting spoken language level in children with autism spectrum disorders." *Autism 5*, 341–361.

Stratis, E.A. and Lecavalier, L. (2013) "Restricted and repetitive behaviors and psychiatric symptoms in youth with autism spectrum disorders." *Research in Autism Spectrum Disorders 7*, 757–766.

Sugai, G., Horner, R.H., Dunlap, G., Hieneman, M., *et al.* (2000) "Applying positive behavioral support and functional behavioral assessment in schools." *Journal of Positive Behavioral Interventions 2*, 131–143.

Suhrheinrich, J., Hall, L.J., Reed, S.R., Stahmer, A.C., and Schreibman, L. (2014) "Evidence-Based Interventions in the Classroom." In L.A. Wilkinson (ed.) *Autism Spectrum Disorder in Children and Adolescents: Evidence-Based Assessment and Intervention in Schools.* Washington, DC: American Psychological Association.

Sulzer-Azaroff, B., Hoffman, A.O., Horton, C.B., Bondy, A., and Frost, L. (2009) "The Picture Exchange Communication System (PECS): What do the data say?" *Focus on Autism and Other Developmental Disabilities 24*, 89–103.

Tomanik, S., Pearson, D.A., Loveland, K.A., Lane, D.M., and Shaw, J.B. (2007) "Increasing the reliability of autism diagnoses: Examining the utility of adaptive functioning." *Journal of Autism and Developmental Disabilities 37*, 921–928.

Towbin, K.E. (2005) "Pervasive Developmental Disorder Not Otherwise Specified." In F.R. Volkmar, R. Paul, A. Klin, and D. Cohen (eds) *Handbook of Autism and Pervasive Developmental Disorders: Vol. 1: Diagnosis, Development, Neurobiology, and Behavior* (3rd edn). Hoboken, NJ: Wiley.

Travers, J.C., Krezmien, M.P., Mulcahy, C., and Tincani, M. (2014) "Racial disparity in administrative autism identification across the United States during 2000 and 2007." *The Journal of Special Education 48*, 155–166.

Twachtman-Cullen, D. (1998) "Language and Communication in HFA and AS." In E. Schopler, G.B. Mesibov, and L.J. Kunce (eds) *Asperger Syndrome or High-Functioning Autism?* New York, NY: Plenum Press.

Twachtman-Cullen, D. and Twachtman-Bassett, J. (2011) *The IEP from A to Z: How to Create Meaningful and Measurable Goals and Objectives.* San Francisco, CA: Jossey-Bass.

Twachtman-Cullen, D. and Twachtman-Bassett, J. (2014) "Language and Social Communication." In L.A. Wilkinson (ed.) *Autism Spectrum Disorder in Children and Adolescents: Evidence-Based Assessment and Intervention in Schools.* Washington, DC: American Psychological Association.

U.S. Department of Education, Office of Special Education Programs (2007) "Questions and Answers on Response to Intervention (RTI) and Early Intervening Services (EIS)." Available at http://idea.ed.gov/explore/view/p/,root,dynamic,QaCorner,8, (accessed July 26, 2016).

U.S. Department of Education, Office of Special Education and Rehabilitative Services (2014) *Thirty-sixth Annual Report to Congress on the Implementation of the Individuals with Disabilities Education Act.* Washington, DC: OSERS.

U.S. Food and Drug Administration (2014) "Beware of False or Misleading Claims for Treating Autism." Available at www.fda.gov/downloads/ForConsumers/ ConsumerUpdates/UCM394800.pdf (accessed June 24, 2016).

Vaughn, B., Duchnowski, A., Sheffield, S., and Kutash, K. (2005) *Positive Behavior Support: A Classroom-wide Approach to Successful Student Achievement and Interactions.* Tampa, FL: Department of Child and Family Studies, Louis de la Parte Florida Mental Health Institute, University of South Florida.

Virginia Department of Education, Office of Special Education and Student Services (October, 2010) "Autism Spectrum Disorders and the Transition to Adulthood." Available at www.doe.virginia.gov/special_ed/disabilities/autism/technical_asst_ documents/autism_transition.pdf (accessed June 24, 2016).

Volden, J. and Phillips, L. (2010) "Measuring pragmatic language in speakers with autism spectrum disorders: Comparing the Children's Communication Checklist-2 and the Test of Pragmatic Language." *American Journal of Speech-Language Pathology 19*, 204–212.

Volker, M.A., Dua, E.H., Lopata, L., Thomeer, M.L., *et al.* (2016) "Factor structure, internal consistency, and screening sensitivity of the GARS-2 in a developmental disabilities sample." *Autism Research and Treatment,* Volume 2016, Article ID 8243079, 12 pages. Available at http://dx.doi.org/10.1155/2016/8243079 (accessed June 24, 2016).

Volkmar, F., Siegel, M., Woodbury-Smith, M., King, B., McCracken, J., and State, M. (2014) "Practice parameter for the assessment and treatment of children and adolescents with autism spectrum disorder." *Journal of the American Academy of Child and Adolescent Psychiatry 53*, 237–257.

Wagner, S. (2006) "Educating the female student with Asperger's." In T. Attwood, T. Grandin *et al.* (eds) *Asperger's and Girls.* Arlington, TX: Future Horizons.

Wagner, S. (2014) "Continuum of Services and Individualized Education Plan Process." In L.A. Wilkinson (ed.) *Autism Spectrum Disorder in Children and Adolescents: Evidence-Based Assessment and Intervention in Schools.* Washington, DC: American Psychological Association.

Warren, Z., Veenstra-VanderWeele, J., Stone, W., Bruzek, J.L., *et al.* (2011) "Therapies for children with autism spectrum disorders." Comparative Effectiveness Review, Number 26. AHRQ Publication No. 11-EHC029-EF, Agency for Healthcare Research and Quality. Available at www.effectivehealthcare.ahrq.gov/ehc/products/106/656/CER26_Autism_Report_04-14-2011.pdf (accessed June 24, 2016).

Wechsler, D. (2008) *Wechsler Adult Intelligence Scale* (4th edn). San Antonio, TX: Pearson.

Wechsler, D. (2009) *Wechsler Individual Achievement Test* (3rd edn). San Antonio, TX: Pearson.

Wechsler, D. (2011) *Wechsler Abbreviated Scale of Intelligence* (2nd edn). San Antonio, TX: Pearson.

Wechsler, D. (2012) *Wechsler Preschool and Primary Scale of Intelligence* (4th edn). Bloomington, MN: Pearson.

Wechsler, D. (2014) *Wechsler Intelligence Scale for Children* (5th edn). San Antonio, TX: Pearson.

Weiss, J.A., Cappadocia, M.C., MacMullin, J.A., Viecili, M., and Lunsky, Y. (2012) "The impact of child problem behaviors of children with ASD on parent mental health: The mediating role of acceptance and empowerment." *Autism 16*, 261–274.

Weitlauf, A.S., McPheeters, M.L., Peters, B., Sathe, N., *et al.* (2014) "Therapies for Children with Autism Spectrum Disorder: Behavioral Interventions Update." Comparative Effectiveness Review, No. 137. (Prepared by the Vanderbilt Evidence-Based Practice Center under Contract No. 290-2012-00009-I.) AHRQ Publication No. 14-EHC036-EF, Agency for Healthcare Research and Quality; August 2014.

Wheeler, J.J., Baggett, B.A., Fox, J., and Blevins, L. (2006) "Treatment integrity: A review of intervention studies conducted with children with autism." *Focus on Autism and Other Developmental Disabilities 21*, 45–54.

White, S.W., Koening, K., and Scahill, L. (2007) "Social skills development in children with autism spectrum disorders: A review of the intervention research." *Journal of Autism and Developmental Disorders 37*, 1858–1868.

Wickstrom, K.F., Jones, K.M., LaFleur, L.H., and Witt, J.C. (1998) "An analysis of treatment integrity in school-based behavioral consultation." *School Psychology Quarterly 13*, 141–154.

Wiggins, L.D., Bakeman, R., Adamson, L.B., and Robins, D.L. (2007) "The utility of the Social Communication Questionnaire in screening for autism in children referred for early intervention." *Focus on Autism and Other Disabilities 22*, 33–38.

Wiig, E., Semel, W., and Secord, E. (2013) *Clinical Evaluation of Language Fundamentals* (5th edn). San Antonio, TX: Psychological Corporation.

Wilkinson, L.A. (2005) "Supporting the inclusion of a student with Asperger syndrome: A case study using conjoint behavioral consultation and self-management." *Educational Psychology in Practice 21*, 307–326.

Wilkinson, L.A. (2006) "Monitoring treatment integrity: An alternative to the 'consult and hope' strategy in school-based behavioural consultation." *School Psychology International 27*, 426–438.

Wilkinson, L.A. (2008a) "The gender gap in Asperger syndrome: Where are the girls?" *Teaching Exceptional Children Plus 4*, 1–10. Available at http://files.eric.ed.gov/fulltext/EJ967482.pdf (accessed June 24, 2016).

Wilkinson, L.A. (2008b) "Self-management for high-functioning children with autism spectrum disorders." *Intervention in School and Clinic 43*, 150–157.

Wilkinson, L.A. (2011) "Pragmatics." *Encyclopedia of Child Behavior and Development*, Part 16, 1138–1139.

Wilkinson, L.A. (2012) "Relationship—The fourth "R" in our schools." *Autism Spectrum Quarterly*, 8–10.

Wilkinson L.A. (2013) "School psychologists need more training in providing services to students with autism spectrum disorders (ASD)." *Autism 3*, e117, doi: 10.4172/2165-7890.1000e117.

Wilkinson, L.A. (2014a) "Introduction: Evidence-Based Practice for Autism Spectrum Disorder." In L.A. Wilkinson (ed.) *Autism Spectrum Disorder in Children and Adolescents: Evidence-Based Assessment and Intervention in Schools*. Washington, DC: American Psychological Association.

Wilkinson, L.A. (2014b) "Multitier Screening and Identification." In L.A. Wilkinson (ed.) *Autism Spectrum Disorder in Children and Adolescents: Evidence-Based Assessment and Intervention in Schools*. Washington, DC: American Psychological Association.

Williams, K., Schroeder, J.L., Carvalho, C., and Cervantes, A. (2011) "School personnel knowledge of autism: A pilot survey." *The School Psychologist 65*, 7–9.

Williams, S.K., Johnson, C., and Sukhodolsky, D.G. (2005) "The role of the school psychologist in the inclusive education of school-age children with autism spectrum disorders." *Journal of School Psychology 43*, 117–136.

Wing, L. (1981) "Asperger's syndrome: A clinical account." *Psychological Medicine 11*, 115–129.

Wing, L., Leekam, S.R., Libby, S.J., Gould, J., and Larcombe, M. (2002) "The diagnostic interview for social and communication disorders: Background, inter-rater reliability and clinical use." *Journal of Child Psychology and Psychiatry 43*, 3, 307–325.

Wing, L. and Potter, D. (2009) "The Epidemiology of Autism Spectrum Disorders: Is the Prevalence Rising?" In S. Goldstein, J.A. Naglieri, and S. Ozonoff (eds) *Assessment of Autism Spectrum Disorders*. New York, NY: Guilford Press.

Wolff, J.J., Botteron, K.N., Dager, S.R., Elison, J.T., *et al.* (2014) "Longitudinal patterns of repetitive behavior in toddlers with autism." *Journal of Child Psychology and Psychiatry 55*, 945–953.

Wong, C., Odom, S.L., Hume, K.A., Cox, A.W., *et al.* (2015) "Evidence-based practices for children, youth, and young adults with autism spectrum disorder: A comprehensive review." *Journal of Autism and Developmental Disorders 45*, 1951–1966.

Wong, C., Odom, S.L., Hume, K.A., Cox, A.W., *et al.* (2014) *Evidence-Based Practices for Children, Youth, and Young Adults with Autism Spectrum Disorder.* Chapel Hill, NC: The University of North Carolina, Frank Porter Graham Child Development Institute, Autism Evidence-Based Practice Review Group. Available at http://fpg. unc.edu/sites/fpg.unc.edu/files/resources/reports-and-policy-briefs/2014-EBP-Report. pdf (accessed June 24, 2016).

Yell, M.L., Katsiyannis, A, Drasgow, E., and Herbst, M. (2003) "Developing legally correct and educationally appropriate programs for students with autism spectrum disorders." *Focus on Autism and Other Developmental Disabilities 18*, 182–191.

Young, E.C., Diehl, J.J., Morris, D., Hyman, S.L., and Bennetto, L. (2005) "The use of two language tests to identify pragmatic language problems in children with autism spectrum disorders." *Language, Speech, and Hearing Services in Schools 36*, 62–72.

Zamora, I., Harley, E.K., Green, S.A., Smith, K., and Kipke, M.D. (2014) "How sex of children with autism spectrum disorders and access to treatment services relates to parental stress." *Autism Research and Treatment*, Article ID 721418, doi:10.1155/2014/721418.

Zirkel, P. (2011) "Autism litigation under the IDEA: A new meaning of 'disproportionality'?" *Journal of Special Education Leadership 24*, 92–103.

Zirkel, P. (2014) "Legal Issues Under IDEA." In L.A. Wilkinson (ed.) *Autism Spectrum Disorder in Children and Adolescents: Evidence-Based Assessment and Intervention in Schools.* Washington, DC: American Psychological Association.

Zuckerman, K.E., Mattox, K., Donelan, K., Batbayar, O., Baghaee, A., and Bethell, C. (2013) "Pediatrician identification of Latino children at risk for autism spectrum disorder." *Pediatrics 132*, 445–453.

INDEX